Money-Smart Secrets for the Self-Employed

Linda Stern

RANDOM
HOUSE

Money-Smart Secrets for the Self-Employed

Copyright © 1997 by Linda Stern

Published in the United States by Random House, Inc., New York and simultaneously in Canada by Random House of Canada, Limited.

Library of Congress Cataloging-in-Publication Data
Stern, Linda.
   Money-smart secrets for the self-employed / Linda Stern.
     p.   cm.
   Includes index.
   ISBN 0-679-77711-3 (pbk.)
   1. New business enterprises-United States—Finance. 2. Small business-United States-Finance. 3. Home-based businesses-United States-Finance. 4. Self-employed-United States.
5. Entrepreneurship-United States. I. Title.
HG4027.6.S74 1997
658.15-dc20
                        96-41483
                        CIP

Typeset and printed in the United States of America

Publisher	Charles Levine
Development Editor	Jennifer Dowling
Production Editor	Joseph Vella
Editorial Assistant	Megan Schade
Cover Design	Electrik Graffiti
Interior Design	VersaTech Associates, San Diego, California
Page Composition	Sybil Ihrig, VersaTech Associates
Proofreader	Sally Leal

First Edition
0 9 8 7 6 5 4
July 1999
ISBN: 0-679-77711-3

New York Toronto London Sydney Auckland

Dedication

For Ken
who is always on my side
even though he knows all of my secrets, financial and otherwise

And for Ben and Laura
Without whom I never would have had the pleasures of self-employment

Contents
at a Glance

Contents

Contents

Contents

6 Riding a Roller-Coaster Income Without Falling Off 125

7 You Have to Spend Money to Make Money 137

8 Money, Money, Who's Got the Money? 167

Contents

Contents

13 Unlucky Chapter 13: How Not to Run Your Business 283

14 The Annual Checkup 293

Acknowledgments

It takes a village to write a book, too. And whom to thank first? Perhaps *Home Office Computing* Editorial Director Bernadette Grey, who gave me my first assignment at the magazine and continues to be a professional inspiration and a friend. And Nick Sullivan, whose professionalism, energy, determination, and willingness to put himself on the line really made this book happen. There are many editors who deserve my gratitude for engendering ideas, giving me lots of space to fill in the magazine, and making me look good, especially David Hallerman and Gail Gabriel.

Then there's the Random House family, who dedicated time, energy, expense, and expertise to make sure that this book became the best it could be. Tracy Smith brought this title in and then disappeared into another Random House division before I had the chance to work with her. Charles Levine, publisher of the Reference & Information Publishing Division, is a truly dedicated professional whose high standards and warmth make him a delight to deal with. Thanks also go to Managing Editor Jennifer Dowling, expert Copy Editor Janice Borzendowski, Production Editor Joe Vella, and production pro Sybil Ihrig at VersaTech Associates.

Of course, a journalist is nothing without her sources, and in my years of writing about money and small business I've had the good fortune to work with so many experts, it would take the rest of the section and the first two chapters to name them all. Some who stand out are Ted Barna at

Acknowledgments

Kwasha Lipton, Robert McKinley at Ram Research, Steve Green and Dan Musisco at the American Institute of CPAs, Tom Ochsenschlager of Grant Thornton, David Drucker, Harold Evensky, Gerri Detweiler, Fred Steingold, Norman Boone, Susan Dawson, Mark Eisenson, Stuart Kesler, and many wise folks at Ernst & Young and Arthur Andersen. I've tried to give credit where it is due to many others throughout the book.

A special thank-you is owed to Paul and Sarah Edwards, the work-at-home mavens, for setting the highest professional standards with their own books and articles, and for their many years of collegial support and counsel. And to Kimberly Stanséll, whose research helped add color and texture to my writing.

My special gratitude is reserved for my fellow villagers—the *Home Office Computing* readers whose favorable feedback kept me in the magazine month after month and year after year. They have shared their personal stories again and again and have made me understand that even when I'm home alone in my basement with my computer, I'm not alone.

Introduction

The day I quit my steady newspaper job, everything changed. My finances got wacky. The first thing I noticed was that I stopped getting paychecks, and sometimes went a month or more without receiving any checks at all. But my expenses went down, too. I stopped buying $40 blouses and $60 shoes at lunch time to amuse myself. I stopped spending $6 a day, every day, on those lunches.

In fact, my expenses went down dramatically. The panty hose, the gas, parking and train fare disappeared, as did the impromptu dinners out because I was too tired to shop, cook, and clean. I also discovered that our family tax bill went down, too: Since I (at least initially) wasn't making much, the IRS didn't want much out of me either. So the net loss I suffered in walking away from work was smaller than I thought it would be.

Then I realized that more than my salary was missing: I no longer had life insurance. Or a retirement plan. And I couldn't very well build a great freelance writing career without spending some money, could I? Like on a computer, postage, paper, phone calls and much, much more. Not to mention childcare, since there were two children playing a key role in my go-solo decision.

And so I became a financial fanatic. With my family budget in mind, I absorbed everything I could about the finances of self-employment. I learned to budget on two fronts, and shift money for financial and tax advantage from my personal life to my business life and back again. I learned to save money on the things that didn't matter, and commit sums to those that did. I learned to overcome my self-effacing wimp nature to negotiate with editors who would have me earn less than I needed to write *and* eat. I learned to say no to work that wouldn't pay, and to invest money in work that would.

I learned the cruelest lesson of all, and yes, it hit one April: That gross is a far cry from net. There's a hidden cost to self-employment, and it comes in the form of higher Social Security and Medicare taxes, lost benefits, and a tax system that doesn't always treat the small business owner with the same rules as the big boys get to play by.

But I learned something else. This is really fun! What started, for me, as a temporary respite from a busy newsroom turned into a life-long commitment to self-employment.

Let me tell you what happened next: My husband, observing how much fun I was having, quit his job, too, to follow his own path as a self-employed advertising copywriter. So much for that steady paycheck that had given me the courage to go it alone!

Our finances got crazy for a second time. Out went the health insurance. In came the second computer, the second and third phone line. Out went any safety net whatsoever. (To the extent that an advertising agency job could be considered a safety net; I guess we weren't giving up all that much.)

Again we learned to adjust our finances. We learned to charge rates that wouldn't just pay for fax paper, but would pay for the health insurance, retirement, and vacation benefits we were giving up from our jobs. (After all, why be self-employed if you can't take vacations?) We learned to charge rates high enough to afford the soccer-shoes-station-wagon-orthodonture bills of our chosen (at least for the time being) suburban child-rearing lifestyle.

We learned, after one year in which almost half of every penny we earned went to Uncle Sam, how to avoid tax traps, minimize after-tax spending and maximize the money we legally pulled out of our businesses. We learned about the loopholes that allow self-employed people to write off at least some of their pleasures.

We learned how and when to turn work down, how to invoice so we could get paid fast, and when it was worth paying somebody else to do it all for us.

We learned how to live on a wacky budget: Which bills to pay first and which to sit on for a while, until the next check came in. How to move some clients (but not all of them) to monthly retainers. How to pay bills when we had the cash, and how to use credit cards productively when we didn't. And we learned how to take care of ourselves. We learned how to set money aside for the day when we want to do something different. And how to shop for benefits.

I, personally, discovered that I was a geek at heart who would rather play with a spreadsheet than a soccer ball. I learned how to project income, keep track of family expenses, keep great tax records and pay bills by computer. I explored every new piece of financial software. There was something about seeing our net worth build on a computer screen that made me even better about managing our money. And I learned how to use those computer tools to make solid financial decisions fast.

Of course, I haven't just made a hobby of personal finance, I've made a career of it too. It turns out that money ranks right up there with sex as a subject that readers and editors can't get enough of. And so the more I wrote about money, the more I wrote about money.

I started writing for *Home Office Computing* magazine in 1989, because all of the people in it were like me. Self-employed people who loved their work, but also put a very high value on their personal and family lives. In eight years of writing for *Home Office Computing*, I have talked to hundreds of entrepreneurs who have put their own spins on the same financial journey. I have learned their secrets: How they make ends meet, and do far better. How they build their businesses and enrich themselves, spend, save, and travel while they build the lives they want to live.

And I had one other advantage. Not only did I get to interview real people like myself, I got to talk to all of the experts, too. If I needed to set up a retirement account, I wouldn't be stuck asking my local banker, I could write an article about it. And in doing so, interview any retirement expert I wanted. I talked to pros at banks, brokerages, the IRS, the nation's biggest accounting firms, and the smaller specialty consultants who know so much more than the rest of us about their fields. And I learned their secrets, too: The loopholes that let you save 100 percent of your income tax free for retirement; or build a tuition fund on the business. The tricks that will keep you flying below IRS radar. The right things to say when you are trying to borrow money, raise your rates, or negotiate your best deal on some new equipment.

It's been years that I've been gathering this data, seeing what worked and what didn't, and thinking, "shouldn't this be a book?" Now it is, and I'm happy to turn it over to you. May you profit from it and prosper, so that your money can be the tool it's supposed to be, instead of the driving force in your life's decisions.

And please, tell me your secrets. Write and let me know the financial tricks of your trade—how you scrimped, saved, and spent your way into that new be-your-own-boss American Dream. I'd like to hear it all, and who knows? You might end up in print yourself, though if you prefer, your secret will be safe with me.

Linda Stern 72160.1546@compuserve.com

1

© Phil Foster 1997

"You can have all those rewards
and still make more than you would
in that old salaried position."

Prosperity Without Paychecks

Or: How to Crack Your Monthly Nut without Turning into One

These are the financial milestones on the road to entrepreneurial success:

- ❏ The first exhilarating day you don't go into someone else's office.
- ❏ The first paycheck you don't get.
- ❏ The first client check you *do* get.
- ❏ The day you discover "gross" and "net."

After that, you've got it made.

Here is the most well-kept secret of the self-employed: Working for yourself is the most fun you can have, and get paid for it.

It doesn't even matter if, like many in the '90s, you find yourself pushed involuntarily into working for yourself. You're going to like it (maybe you already do). You'll like it (maybe you already do) because it's the only way you really get to define your job and the work that you produce. You can add your own flair to your products or services, see ideas that would get stomped in the workplace flourish under your own direction, and be the master of your professional destiny. You can, as most work-for-yourself zealots usually point out, write your own schedule, so you can work hard and play hard and still take time, mid-afternoon, to smell the roses.

chapter

1

You can have all those rewards and still make more than you would in that old salaried position.

But along with this wonderful world of possibilities is one other package that gets dumped in your lap: absolute, total responsibility for your own financial health, now and in the future. You have to make it happen, and you have to keep it happening.

In a sense, this is a blessing. Too many workers today are learning too late the bitter lesson that companies are not parents, and they are not going to take care of you. We self-employed pick up on that early. We're not going to throw away thirty years on a company that dumps us in the end without health insurance or an adequate retirement income—unless it's our own, and we've made our own financial mistakes.

When you are solely responsible for your financial health, there's much you have to do. You have to:

- ❏ Figure out how much to charge, and how to get it.
- ❏ Find sources of cash to build your business, and to pull your family out of tight spots.
- ❏ Stay in control of costs, both personal and business costs.
- ❏ Negotiate a complicated and threatening income tax system that can deliver the biggest breaks, and the biggest burdens, to people who work for themselves.
- ❏ Manage cash flow that's likely to dance to a different rhythm from the bills that lockstep their way into your mailbox.
- ❏ Afford and buy your own safety net of personal and professional insurance.
- ❏ Plan and save for your own retirement.
- ❏ Keep records even the IRS will love.
- ❏ Decide where and how you really want your money spent.

You won't do this all at once, and you won't do it perfectly, especially the first time through. You'll learn with experience and through the financial tips that experts, friends, and colleagues offer. But first, you need all of the facts for decision-making and the tools for interpreting them. This book will give you many of the facts. For the tools, look to your computer.

USING YOUR COMPUTER
TO HELP MAKE FINANCIAL DECISIONS

If you still don't have a computer, put this book down right now and go get one! Windows and Macintosh have made them easy to use; truly great software have made them impossible to ignore, and market forces have made them affordable. Any money that you spend on a computer system will come back to you many times over, and many of the calculations and tips carried in this book are computer-based.

Where are you going to shop? There's probably a small computer store within a couple of miles of your home, or a computer consultant listed in the yellow pages who can help you figure out what to buy. You can save money by reading the computer magazines to make your own decisions and then buying from a computer superstore like Best Buy, CompUSA or MicroAge. Or you can order your system by mail order from one of the national firms which advertise in all of the computer magazines.

You can charge and earn and budget and spend and get taxed without computers: thousands of years of human history prove that. But computers and the financial programs they run add a new dimension to financial planning. They make it much easier and much smarter. With a few keystrokes, you can see the probable outcome of your financial decisions. You can learn about a budget from the inside out, watching numbers on the screen change rapidly in response to one little savings measure or bank deposit. You can "guesstimate" your retirement, figure your taxes, and decide precisely how much to charge for your goods and services. And you can do all of this easily and simply, even if (especially if, perhaps) you got D's in math and never did memorize those multiplication tables.

The programs do it all for you. There are two different computerized approaches to financial planning: specialized task programs, and a basic spreadsheet. This book explores both of them.

SECRET: *Don't make yourself crazy: It's only money. Look upon all of your buying, saving, spending, and planning decisions as a great experiment. You will learn something from every financial decision you make, and sometimes all you will get out of it is the insight to do it better the next time around. That's okay, because the only people who never make money mistakes have a bigger problem; they are chronic liars.*

Remember, unlike muscle tone, financial fitness usually improves with age.

Specialized Programs

Invest in a Checkbook Program

No matter what you need to do, there's a computer program set up to do it for you. Later on, we'll see programs set up to enable you to invoice, meet a payroll, plan retirement, and more.

But a solid personal finance program should be on your basic software shelf. Programs like market leader Quicken or Managing Your Money will track every family penny. They will show you how much you are earning on investments, and they will teach you the truth about family net worth—that a debt paid is as good as (sometimes better) than a sum saved.

There are whole books (not this one) written about how to manage family finances in Quicken and similar programs; and especially if your income will be variable as you build a business, it's a good idea to use one of these products to track family money. But for most financial planning decisions, learn to love a spreadsheet.

SECRET: *For Macintosh (and potential) owners only: Don't be scared by all of the hype that says you can't crunch numbers unless you're in a Windows or DOS environment. Everything that appears in this book can be accomplished easily on a Mac. I know, because I used one; that's how this book was written.*

Learning to Love Your Spreadsheet

There's no financial or business decision you can make that you couldn't make better if you knew, or could reasonably project, the outcome. And that's what your computer spreadsheet can do for you, in a flash.

A spreadsheet, for those who have never seen one, is like a giant calculator that remembers every number and what you want to do with it. It's a grid system of columns and rows, into which you put formulas. Most spreadsheet programs today don't require you to know the formulas, either. You can just use pull-down menus that say add, or average, or multiply, and thy will be done.

The beauty of a spreadsheet is this: Once the formulas are in place, you can change the numbers any way you want. So if you want to see how much you'll make this year, and February comes in higher than expected, you can change one number on your spreadsheet and immediately see a different year-end result.

Of course, a spreadsheet eats a calculation like that for breakfast. You can learn—and this book will demonstrate—how to use spreadsheets for the following tasks:

- ❏ Track your home equity.
- ❏ Predict your earnings.
- ❏ Decide how much you need to make this year.
- ❏ Set prices.
- ❏ Record your expenses for tax purposes.
- ❏ Do your taxes.
- ❏ Figure your estimated taxes.
- ❏ Do break-even analysis.
- ❏ Predict your cash flow.
- ❏ Compare car or computer leases.
- ❏ Track employee hours.
- ❏ Set hourly rates.
- ❏ Do mid-year tax planning.
- ❏ Analyze loans and likely payments.

It's likely that there are many more spreadsheet plans you could invent on your own. Once you get comfortable using them, for example, you can plan the PTA budget or a family vacation in a flash.

To get started using spreadsheets, first check your hard drive: You may already have a spreadsheet. All of the integrated Works programs have full-featured spreadsheet programs on them. All of the ones in this book were originally created in Microsoft Works for the Mac. Other stand-alone spreadsheet brand names are Quattro Pro, Lotus, and Excel.

To learn the commands of your spreadsheet program, spend a little bit of time playing with it, and (sorry) reading the manual. Or just keep the manual by your side when you format your first spreadsheet. There's one coming up in just a few pages!

Before You Quit, Get Fit

Tempting as it might be to march into the boss's office singing a Johnny Paycheck song right this minute, you're better off planning your transitional budget before you start your self-employment. David Drucker, a financial planner who started a partnership in 1984, credits his own spreadsheet planning sessions with saving his sanity and financial stability. "I've had lean times and I've been worried sometimes, but I never had to borrow any money to make ends meet. I attribute that to good planning in the beginning." The Computer Solution on page 10 demonstrates Drucker's method of planning a transitional budget on a spreadsheet.

Of course, you'll need more than a solid budget to finance your transition to self-employment: You'll need some actual cash. Drucker tells clients looking to leave jobs to fix themselves a cushion. Pay off all of your credit cards, tighten your expenses as much as possible, and try to get a jump on business expenses before you leave the salary. You can, for example, set up your home office and pay for a first marketing effort while you are still at your job. Then think about lining up a transitional client.

SECRET: *Don't be surprised if your boss becomes your first client. It's usually hard to line this up in advance, but keep some honey in your voice when you quit, and be prepared to attract some sweet offers. Instead of saying "I'm outta here!" try "I love working on these projects, and I'm going to miss you, but I need to do this for myself." In more cases than not, the company is sorry to lose you, worried about replacing you, and asks if you can continue to fulfill some of your duties during a transitional period.*

If you've thought through your transition, don't be afraid to put some of your own savings on the line. Scott and Diane Nelson were hotel workers in Altamonte Springs, Florida when they fell in love and started saving money for a wedding and a house down payment. Then the entrepreneurial urge hit, just as the only airport-shuttle business in the busy Orlando region went on the market. "I promised Diane that if she let me take the $10,000 we had stashed away for a down payment and put it down on a van and some business cards and insurance, we would buy a house three times as big in three years," Scott remembers.

She did, he did, and they have, with a down payment that was $23,000 three years later, saved from money earned by their Gold Key Transportation company.

Money in the bank, a short-term loan from relatives or a home equity line can provide the cash you need to make it during the early months. Just make sure, before you start drawing down your nest egg, that you've planned the leanest, meanest budget possible to get you started.

Once you've set up your personal transitional budget, you're ready to set up your company so the money will flow from it as readily as you need it to. That's what you'll learn in the next chapter.

And Now, Prepare to Budget

There's probably not a money book on the shelves that doesn't start with this dry bit of advice: Record everything you spend until you know what your spending patterns are. Then you can make a budget.

It would be nice if this book could be different, but it's not, because you really can't come up with a spending plan until you have a spending history, though you really don't have to write every newspaper and chewing gum purchase into a little spiral book. You can move ahead only if you have a pretty good idea of where your money goes. If you are preparing to leave a job for full-time self-employment, you'll need to know how much money you'll have to produce in the early months of your business to make it all work. Even if you already are self-employed, getting that detailed history will help you plan better for your future. But before you begin that budget, take a few minutes to think about how being self-employed differs from the paycheck life.

What You Gain When You Leave a Job

Losing or leaving a job isn't all about giving up money. You give up expenses, too. Like commuting, success dressing, and—at least initially—income and payroll taxes that you don't have to pay on money you're not earning.

You also give up some second-tier expenses you may not think are job-related. There's the money you spend making yourself feel better because you are tired, overworked, or just crabby about being in the wrong job. There's the money you spend on child care or home care because you don't have the time to do it all yourself. Then there's the money you dole

COMPUTER SOLUTION:
FIGURING INCOME REPLACEMENT

When you are preparing to leave a job to start a business, crunch your budget to see how much you absolutely must pull out of your business to get through the first year. For all the reasons mentioned, this doesn't mean that if you are quitting a $40,000 job, you need to bring in $40,000.

In this example, Mark and Sarah are figuring out how much they'll need if Mark quits his job as a commercial artist. They each make $38,500 a year. When he quits, some costs will go up and some will go down. This spreadsheet tracks those costs and helped Mark and Sarah figure out their first year finances. They set up two budget columns, one for their two job lifestyle and the second for their "Mark quits" plan. Basically, the only formulas are this: The spreadsheet adds the incomes in line 6, totals the expenses in line 24 and subtracts line 24 from line 6 to reach the net income in line 26. The number that shows up in cell C26 is the number that Mark would have to bring in to keep the family eating for the first year.

There's one more number. Mark and Sarah weren't sure how to guesstimate their future income tax burden. So this is how they did it: They looked up last year's tax return and saw that they paid a total of $10,500 in taxes on $77,000 in income. So they divided their income into their taxes and discovered their average tax rate is 13.6 percent. They used that figure in Cell C21 to estimate how much tax they would pay on future reduced income. In reality, the tax would probably be even lower than this, since a greater percentage of their income would be taxed at a lower rate, but for planning purposes, this average tax rate method is close enough.

And now, look at the numbers. Mark and Sarah added more money for the health insurance, life insurance, and food and utilities they expect him to consume working at home. They cut back on their estimates for child care, restaurant meals, vacations, and that catch-all miscellaneous category that everyone has. (You could label A22 Black Hole instead of Miscellaneous, if you'd like.)

Like all of the other spreadsheets in this book, this one appears twice—once with formulas, so you can set it up on your own computer, and once with sample numbers filled in.

FIGURING INCOME REPLACEMENT: Formula View *(continued)*

	A	B	C
1		With the Job	With the Business
2			
3	**Income**		
4	Sarah's salary	$38,500.00	$38,500.00
5	Mark's salary	$38,500.00	$0.00
6	**Total Income**	=SUM(B4:B5)	=SUM(C4:C5)
7			
8	**Expenses**		
9	Mortgage	$15,000.00	$15,000.00
10	Utilities	$4,300.00	$5,300.00
11	Food	$5,500.00	$6,500.00
12	Restaurant meals	$2,100.00	$1,100.00
13	Auto expenses	$6,000.00	$6,000.00
14	Commuting costs	$2,010.00	$1,005.00
15	Health insurance	$1,200.00	$4,000.00
16	Life insurance	$0.00	$250.00
17	Home insurance	$350.00	$400.00
18	Child care	$7,800.00	$5,400.00
19	Clothing	$4,375.00	$1,500.00
20	Vacation	$5,000.00	$1,200.00
21	Income taxes	=B6*.136	=C6*.136
22	Miscellaneous	$5,750.00	$925.00
23	Savings	$7,115.00	$0.00
24	**Total Expenses**	=SUM(B9:B23)	=SUM(C9:C23)
25			
26	**Net**	=B6–B24	=C6–C24
27			
28			

FIGURING INCOME REPLACEMENT: Data View (*continued*)

	A	B	C
		With the Job	With the Business
1			
2			
3	**Income**		
4	Sarah's salary	$38,500.00	$38,500.00
5	Mark's salary	$38,500.00	$0.00
6	**Total Income**	**$77,000.00**	**$38,500.00**
7			
8	**Expenses**		
9	Mortgage	$15,000.00	$15,000.00
10	Utilities	$4,300.00	$5,300.00
11	Food	$5,500.00	$6,500.00
12	Restaurant meals	$2,100.00	$1,100.00
13	Auto expenses	$6,000.00	$6,000.00
14	Commuting costs	$2,010.00	$1,005.00
15	Health insurance	$1,200.00	$4,000.00
16	Life insurance	$0.00	$250.00
17	Home insurance	$350.00	$400.00
18	Child care	$7,800.00	$5,400.00
19	Clothing	$4,375.00	$1,500.00
20	Vacation	$5,000.00	$1,200.00
21	Income taxes	$10,500.00	$5,236.00
22	Miscellaneous	$5,750.00	$925.00
23	Savings	$7,115.00	$0.00
24	**Total Expenses**	**$77,000.00**	**$53,816.00**
25			
26	**Net**	**$0.00**	**($15,316.00)**
27			
28			

FIGURING INCOME REPLACEMENT (*continued*)

Mark and Sarah discover that they can make it through year one if Mark nets just $15,316 and not the $38,500 it feels like he's giving up. They can cut that back even further by giving up a vacation altogether or putting a real effort into eating cheap (self-employment might be worth a year of beans, rice, and always filling budget popcorn.)

The Business Budget

Of course, there's something missing in that budget, right? Where is the money Mark will spend to build his business? It's not there. Maybe, it's not there because Mark accounted for it separately. Maybe the couple already has savings that Mark will use to build his business. Maybe he already invested all the big bucks in equipment, stationery, and art supplies that he needs to get started. Maybe his parents have given him a generous gift.

But to properly figure out how much he needs to make to turn that $15,316 over to the family, he has to pull up another spreadsheet (shown on the next two pages) to determine how much he'll have to gross. The quickest way to do that is to construct a simple profit and loss statement, but to do it upside down. Instead of the usual income on top and expenses on the bottom, Mark reverses it. At the top, he puts the net needed, and then he adds up all of his expected expenses. Note that he does quick guesstimates of some of his expenses by figuring how much he'll spend weekly or monthly, and then letting the spreadsheet do the multiplying for him (Cells B7, B10 and B12.) And note that Mark remembers to guesstimate his self-employment tax by multiplying his net business income by .13 in Cell B14.

Finally, he adds his expenses to his net and comes up with the gross amount—aftertaxes—he would have to make to keep his business running and feed his family for a year. That figure is $29,177. If Mark raids his savings account or finds start-up capital another way, he would only have to earn $22,177 to keep it all running.

FIGURING INCOME REPLACEMENT: Formula View *(continued)*

	A	B
1	Mark's Business	
2		
3	**Net Needed**	**$15,316.00**
4		
5	Expected expenses	
6	Start-up investment	$7,000.00
7	Monthly phone fees	**=70*12**
8	Internet account	$120.00
9	Subscriptions	$420.00
10	Postage, shipping	**=85*12**
11	Supplies	$250.00
12	Local travel	**=65*12**
13	Legal, accounting help	$240.00
14	Self-employment tax	**=B3*.13**
15	Client entertainment	$1,200.00
16	**Total Expenses**	**=SUM(B6:B15)**
17		
18	**Gross Needed**	**=B3+B16**

The Bare Bones Budget

The secret to successfully starting and keeping a business rolling is the ability to live on less, both professionally and personally. Mark and Sarah cut back substantially on their lifestyle to afford the business, and they probably could cut back more. As the years progress and they prosper, they can again take vacations, eat dinners out, and afford other luxuries.

Mark, too, can scrape through a first year without spending himself silly, but as his business grows, so will his business expenses. On the simplest level, the more work he does, the more supplies he will run through. He

---

FIGURING INCOME REPLACEMENT: Data View *(continued)*

	A	B
1	Mark's Business	
2		
3	**Net Needed**	**$15,316.00**
4		
5	Expected expenses	
6	Start-up investment	$7,000.00
7	Monthly phone fees	$840.00
8	Internet account	$120.00
9	Subscriptions	$420.00
10	Postage, shipping	$1,020.00
11	Supplies	$250.00
12	Local travel	$780.00
13	Legal, accounting help	$240.00
14	Self-employment tax	$1,991.00
15	Client entertainment	$1,200.00
16	**Total Expenses**	**$13,861.00**
17		
18	**Gross Needed**	**$29,177.00**

will eventually have to save to buy newer equipment, travel to trade shows, and more.

But by starting on a shoestring, Mark and Sarah have proven to themselves that they can make Mark's self-employment dream come true. You can too.

out buying Girl Scout cookies from your co-workers' kids, and the money you spend on your own to make you better at the job you do.

SECRET: *This is not a book about how you can get rich working while the baby sleeps. If you intend to be productive and make money on your own, child care expenses don't completely disappear until your kids are around twelve or thirteen. And even then, it gets called summer camp for a few more years. When you work for yourself, however, you have a little more leeway to manage child care costs and schedules.*

So the bottom line on quitting is this: You aren't giving up as much as you think you are, in terms of dollars.

And what you're gaining is flexibility. In a paycheck job, you have no flexibility. You get exactly the same amount of dollars week in and week out. You can shop smart and stretch it a bit, but you can't really shift your money around to fit your priorities. You can't manage the contributions you make to your retirement plan or time your tax payments: Chances are, these items are set at the beginning of the year and come out of your paycheck in like amounts, week in and week out, regardless of what's going on in your family money life.

You are also gaining a better risk: Sure, in a job, that paycheck will be there every Friday, no matter what. But it's not going to get surprisingly bigger any time soon either. And you always have the risk that the paychecks will stop forever. Conversely, you don't have much upside risk, other than the (far from obligatory, in the late '90s) 3 percent to 4 percent cost-of-living adjustments you'll wait a year for.

When you work for yourself, some of your expenses are lower, and more important, you win the flexibility to manage those expenses on your own terms. And while the downside risks can be substantial, there's a pretty big upside risk, too: You could end up making a lot of money working for yourself.

What You Lose: The Hidden Costs of Self-Employment

All that joy and flexibility has a price tag, of course. It's in that gray area between gross and net: The checks your business pulls in do not represent the money you get to keep. There are a few hidden costs to self-employment that you need to know about early.

Perhaps the biggest one is self-employment tax. The self-employment tax is the money you pay the government for your Social Security and Medicare taxes. If you are an employee of a company, you pay 6.2 percent of your salary (for salaries up to $65,400; then it stops) in Social Security and another 1.45 percent of your salary in Medicare taxes. Your employer pays the same amount for you.

When you work for yourself, you pay both halves, for a total of 15.3 percent of your income. You get to write off some of that in a way that pulls your effective tax down to about 12 percent or 13 percent, but that's still high enough. Think about adding 12 or 13 percent to your current tax rate.

There are other costs as well. Do you need the services of a good library to do your job? A subscription to *The Wall Street Journal*? A computer, modem, and fax machine? The good news about self-employment is these all become legitimate tax deductions. But the bad news is that you have to buy them for yourself first. There's no company infrastructure to tap into.

Finally, don't forget these hidden costs of self-employment: Like no retirement plan, health insurance, dental coverage, life insurance, or fifteen days paid vacation. As you'll learn later in the book, you need to charge enough money to build those benefits back into your life.

YOU MUST REMEMBER THIS: THE LESSONS OF CHAPTER 1

- Your computer is the tool that will make all of your planning possible.
- When you leave your job, you'll lose benefits but you'll lose expenses, too.
- Good planning will save you from future failures.
- You will be able to afford this!

2

© David Wink 1997

"*You need a money system. A plan that gives structure to your business and to your financial life.*"

Setting Up a
Cash Flow System
That Really Flows

"**You** have to have a system. Get organized and put everything in its place. And have a clean, quiet, well-lit spot to study in." These were my father's oft-repeated words when I was about fourteen, and not very organized.

Dad was right. I'm still not so sure about the clean desk part, but you definitely need a system—especially if you are working for yourself. And even more especially if you are working at home.

You need a money system. A plan that gives structure to your business and to your financial life. A routine that separates personal money from business money, and allows easy access to cash. A plan that gets you paid when you need the money. And a structure that establishes your business as a legal entity.

If you are just setting up a business, you need to establish these systems; if you are already in business, you may need a tune up. Here are some decisions you will have to make:

❏ What form will your business take? There are legal and tax implications for all of the possibilities.

❏ How will you get paid? Will you just pull money out of the business when you need it, or establish a regular salary and live within it?

❏ Where will you keep your money?

❏ What kinds of bank accounts will you need and use?

❏ What personal financial systems should you have in place to ease the financial stress of self-employment?

These decisions will affect your financial health and wealth for a long time, so take the time to set up your system carefully. But don't make yourself crazy about it: Nothing is irreversible. As a matter of fact, marketplace conditions and tax laws change so frequently that you should make these decisions over and over. As your business grows and tax laws change, the systems that worked for you initially may no longer be right.

Task 1: Choose a Business Form

Should you Inc. yourself? There are many attorneys and accountants who would answer with a quick yes, but wait a minute ... not so fast! Every business form has its advantages and disadvantages, and for every break you pick up, you may be adding costly layers of complexity. In some cases, you can lose breaks and pick up complexity anyway. Here's a brief survey of the forms you should consider, but first think about what all business forms have in common, they:

❏ Allow you to deduct all of your business expenses from your business income before it becomes taxable.

❏ Allow you to hire employees and offer them a wide range of benefits, including health insurance and retirement benefits.

❏ Allow you to set up a retirement plan for yourself.

And, one way or the other, all allow you to be sued.

SECRET: *If you are a one-person company, it is pretty hard to distance yourself completely from personal liability. Even if you incorporate, a move that theoretically indemnifies you as an owner of a company, you can still be sued as a director or an employee. I'm not an attorney, and you should talk to one to get the straight story on liability, but don't assume that a form called a Limited Liability Company can protect you from all legal judgments. There are companies that specialize in protecting your assets from legal judgments, but most of them are in the Netherlands Antilles or Zurich, which is where they'll want your money to be, too.*

The Best Business Form for You

Although business entities all have financial implications that can affect your bottom line, this decision is not primarily a financial decision; it's a legal one. So consult an attorney who specializes in business liability and business taxes to find out which form really would work best for you. Because this is primarily a book about money, not the law, the lists here focus on the financial pros and cons of the different business entities.

Sole Proprietorship

Absolutely the easiest form of business to establish, the sole proprietorship is like a negative checkoff. If you don't set up any other form of business, but you are actually in business, you already are a sole proprietor. As a sole prop, your business finances flow directly into your personal finances. You are personally responsible for the company's debts, and reap all of the profits. Your business income, expenses, and annual profit are reported on a Schedule C tax form, which is part of your personal 1040 form. So all of your profits are taxed at your personal tax rate.

The bulk of this book is aimed at the sole proprietor, which is the most common form of small business ownership, and where most of us start out. What's the good news and the bad news?

❏ This is the only business entity that can take the home office deduction, allowing you to write off a portion of your mortgage and utilities in the company.

❏ It's the cleanest, simplest way to start a business.

❏ Your health insurance deduction is limited to 40 percent of your health insurance premiums, and that deduction comes off of your personal tax form and not your business form.

❏ The IRS is watching! Audit rates for sole proprietorships are higher than for any other business entity. The tax collectors recognize that the flow-through of money from business to your personal tax form leaves a lot of room for finagling. Corporations can fudge figures, too, but they usually have accountants who sign off on the numbers.

❏ If you hire an employee, and he or she does something so wrong that it causes someone to sue your company and win, you can lose everything.

Partnerships

If you have a partner, you can't be a sole proprietor, right? The next easiest arrangement is a partnership. Partnerships allow you to work with your strengths. When you have a partner, you can bounce your ideas off another person. You can join forces with someone who is a good salesman if you're a hide at home and create type, or with a bookkeeper if you're good at people skills but not as numbers oriented as you should be.

SECRET: *You don't have to be in the same place to be partners. Essential Data, a communications mail order business, is run out of the homes of partners Bruce McKeag, who lives in San Jose, and Mike Dousman, in Sacramento. Every night they share files by modem so they can keep up with each other's activities.*

Even the best partnerships can go awry. Before formally setting up a partnership, make sure both (or all, you can have more than two) of the partners have the same goals and philosophies for the business you're building. Even when partners work well together and share a common vision, partnerships are likely to end eventually, when one partner is ready to move out of the business before the other.

So even though an oral agreement is legal, you should have a document that spells out the roles and responsibilities of each partner. Decide at the very beginning how to handle the business if one partner wants out, or dies. Usually, this is handled by a buyout agreement that gives either partner first dibs on the other's share. You can have as many partners as you like in a legal partnership, as long as you aren't in the business of producing soup (too many cooks, etc.).

The financial pros and cons?

- ❑ Tax-wise, you are treated as a sole proprietor, except that there is one more layer of forms to file. The partnership tells the IRS how much money it earned, but every individual partner reports that income on his or her own personal tax return.

- ❑ Health insurance deduction has the same limitations.

- ❑ No home office deduction is allowed.

- ❑ Forget liability protection. Not only can you lose your house for something you do or your employee does, now you have a partner to worry about, too!

- ❑ Establishing a partnership may not put more or less money in your hands, but it may make you hassle more over the money you have. Major problems can develop when partners have very different ideas about how money should be spent or saved. If partners contribute inequitably, but draw money equally out of the business over long periods of time, the partnership is probably doomed.

SECRET: *Don't rush into a partnership agreement if you are work-ingwith your spouse. The benefits can be far better if one spouse owns the company and the other spouse becomes the employee. See Chapter 9.*

S Corporations

Subchapter S corporations seem sort of quasi. They are like sole propri-etorships, in that income and losses are passed through personal taxes, and most employee benefits for owners are limited. They offer limited personal liability and one way to minimize taxes (you can minimize your salary and reward yourself with dividends instead, a strategy that will save self-employment [Social Security and Medicare] taxes), though the dividends are still subject to income taxes. But you can't go overboard. The IRS takes a dim view of people who take artificially low salaries and reward themselves generously with dividends and perquisites. For exam-ple, Marcia took no salary at all and pulled everything out of her S corpo-ration as dividends. She discovered she couldn't feed her retirement account, deduct her health insurance premiums or use the child care credit because she had no salary to show for her work.

The pros and cons?

❏ Your personal property remains at less risk of liability in case of suits.

❏ You can take some income as dividends and reduce your self-employment taxes.

❏ You can cut these taxes even more by making your kids share-holders and paying dividends to them at their low tax bracket.

❏ But there is no home office deduction, and health insurance deduction has same limitations as sole proprietor.

Limited Liability Company

This is the new kid on the corporate block. Limited liability companies (LLCs) are state-sanctioned entities, legal in almost every state and the District of Columbia. They have the pass-through tax structure of all of the entities discussed so far, but they offer greater indemnification against lawsuits. Because every state has its own concept of exactly what a lim-ited liability company is, it's important to get yours set up by a lawyer. And that won't be cheap: California reportedly charges upwards of $800 just to register and license a limited liability company. Those financial pros and cons?

- ❏ Benefits, income, and taxes are structured similarly to S corporations or partnerships, with a couple of key exceptions: An owner's basis in an LLC is increased by his or her share of the company's debt. And since losses may be deducted up to the amount of basis, that means that an LLC may afford you better tax treatment for business losses. That said, who sets up a legitimate business specifically for the way it will treat all their losses?

- ❏ You can't avoid the self-employment tax by taking dividends instead of salary, as you can in an S corp.

- ❏ Limited liability companies are so new they are not well understood or established. You may spend more in legal fees setting up and maintaining an LLC than it's worth.

Real C Corporations

This is the organization preferred by seriously large companies like General Motors, but you may find that it helps you, too. When you are fully incorporated as a C corp, you become an employee of the company as well as the owner. That means you can get full health coverage, life insurance, and other fringe benefits. A "C" corp is a separate taxable entity, so you have to file a separate corporate return. And you have to issue stock, pay a fair amount of money to accountants and lawyers, and endure a few tiers of complicated paperwork.

The financial facts?

- ❏ Corporate tax rates are often lower than individual tax rates at the same levels of income. So if you intend to leave a lot of money in your company at year's end (to invest in new equipment, advertising, growth, etc.), you can save money by having that cash taxed at the corporate rate rather than the personal rate. How different are the rates? Well, if you are a corporation, you have to make more than $10 million before you are taxed at 35 percent, but the personal 36 percent bracket starts at around $124,650 if you are single and $151,750 if you are married. But once you pull it out for personal use, you have to pay personal tax on it, too, so you would be subject to double taxation on the money.

- ❏ You can get every fringe benefit that is legal in a company setting, even if you are the big boss.

- ❏ Big break: You can leave money in your corporation, have it taxed at the lower corporate rate, and then lend it to yourself. If it's less than $10,000, you don't even have to pay interest on it. But you do have to sign a proper promissory note and pledge collateral.

This is a good way to take money out of the business with a minimum of taxes.

SECRET: *I rethink this question about once every year, at tax time. I look at my writing business, which is a sole proprietorship, and think about incorporating. I spend a lot of time (and usually money) figuring out my taxes every which way, and never come out ahead as a corporation. But I have heard too many attorneys and accountants praise the benefits of incorporation to take that answer as a given, so next year I'm likely to go through the same exercise.*

If all of these considerations make you dizzy, take a glance at this handy crib sheet. It will tell you at a glance if your chosen entity fits your financial priorities.

If you are concerned about ...	Your best business entity choices are ...
Keeping it simple	Sole proprietorship, partnership
Retaining a lot of money in the business	C corp
Writing off large losses	S corp
Protecting yourself from lawsuits	C or S corp; limited liability corp
Working with a partner, and allocating income disproportionately	Partnership or LLC, (not an S corp, where disproportionate allocations aren't allowed)
Raising money	C corp, if you see yourself "going public"
Protecting your home office deduction	Sole proprietorship
Writing off your health insurance	C corp; or hire your spouse (see Chapter 10)
Shelter some earnings from self-employment tax	S corp
Saving money on CPAs and lawyers	Sole proprietor, partnership
Lowering bottom line taxes	There are so many variables and considerations, you really have to crunch every number and see where you come out best.

Getting Legal

Once you've chosen your business entity, you have to make it legal. Partners and sole proprietors can do that in the privacy of their own homes, simply by filing the appropriate tax forms when they file their income tax returns. But corporations must file the right papers with the right state authorities and typically hire attorneys to do so, at $500 or more a pop.

SECRET: You don't have to hire expensive help. You can incorporate yourself. The Company Corp, available online (corp@incorporate.com) will walk you through the right papers for around $50. For $70, you can buy Incorporation software from Unabridged Software (800-248-7630.) That puts all the right forms on your hard drive so you can fill 'em and file 'em yourself.

Meeting state requirements is another story. Gale Publishing offers a directory of state business licensing requirements, but it runs 1,140 pages. It wouldn't hurt to invest in one of those "how to start a business in (your state here)" books that appear in the business section of almost every bookstore.

SECRET: While you are setting up everything right, get an employer identification number (EIN) from the IRS, even before you need one. You'll use this number in establishing and reporting on your retirement accounts, and to pay payroll taxes on any employees you might eventually have. To get an EIN, file form SS-4 with the IRS.

Task 2: Make Some Basic Accounting Decisions

In the next chapter, we'll get to the details of financial record keeping for your business and your family. But while you are establishing your basic business system, you need to make a couple of decisions about how you will account for your business.

Decide What Your Business Year Will Be

For most entrepreneurs, this isn't much of a decision; all of those flow-through forms almost always require that you adopt the calendar year as your fiscal year. If you are a C corporation, however, you may prefer setting up a different fiscal year. Why? If your business is seasonal, you might choose to end your fiscal year during a slow period, so you have time to prepare your taxes. And so that the profits you pick up during your busy time can sit in your account for a while before you send them to the IRS!

Decide to Use Either the Cash or Accrual Method of Accounting

Cash is way easier; it's a simple system in which you declare income when you receive it and expenses when you pay for them. In accrual accounting, you must declare the income and the expenses when they are "fixed." So, if you invoice a client for $2,000 in December 1997, and he pays you in January 1998, your 1997 income would be different under the two accounting systems. Under the accrual system you would have to declare that income in 1997; under the cash system, it would be deferred until 1998. And what if your client is a deadbeat who never pays you? Under cash accounting, it never happened. Under accrual accounting, you can write off income that is never going to show up. So you would declare it in 1997 and reclaim it on your 1998 taxes.

What if you bought a computer system in 1997 and the computer supplier sent you a bill that you didn't pay until 1998? (You'd be very lucky, because most computer sellers want their money immediately!) You'd also have different tax consequences under the two systems. Cash accounting users would not be able to deduct the computer expenses until 1998. Accrual users could write off the computer when they signed the purchase order. (Note that if you buy something at year-end on a credit card and don't pay the bill until the final year, that still counts as having spent the money when you handed over your piece of plastic. You can accelerate a year-end expense even if you don't have the cash for it by putting it on a card.)

For a small business owner, cash accounting gives you much more control of your money flows for tax purposes—but you aren't always allowed to use it. If you are in a business that stocks inventories, you must use the accrual method, at least for evaluating the inventory. You can use both in the same business, if life isn't complicated enough for you.

A word of caution: Consider carefully before you pick an accounting method. The IRS frowns on businesses that go back and forth, suspecting that they are doing so to lose taxable income in the cracks between methods. So unless your business changes in a fundamental way (you start or stop acquiring inventories, for example,) you have to ask the tax agency's position to switch. And how do you say "Mother may I?" to the IRS? File Form 3115, and hope that you qualify for an exemption from the $500 application fee that goes with it.

Figure Out How You Want to Be Paid

There are two fundamental ways of getting paid by your business: You can take out money when you need it and it's there, or you can establish a regular paycheck for yourself. There's a big difference!

The Take-It-As-It-Comes Approach

There's no fuss, no muss to this approach. When your big client checks come in, you pull money out of the business to pay your mortgage, orthodontist, and credit card bill. You take grandma and the kids out to dinner or spring for a new suit. When the big check doesn't come in, forget the suit, go to grandma's for dinner, make the orthodontist wait, pay a minimum on the charge, and get nervous about the mortgage.

The advantage to this approach is its discipline: If the money isn't there, you don't spend it. It's also an easier method to adopt, because you don't need to worry about capitalizing your business to give you a paycheck when there's not enough money coming in. And it allows for a more integrated approach to work and life planning—you see the whole picture.

SECRET: *If you are a sole proprietor, there are a million different reasons why you will be writing checks to yourself from yourself. You sign them and endorse them. And deposit them from business to household accounts, or vice versa. It feels weird the first few times you do it, but get used to it.*

There's a danger here, too—of course. Unless you are smart about saving money and living on less than you have during the flush times, you can get into serious budgetary troubles by not holding enough during flush times to carry you through down times. And by steadily emptying your business of cash, you may fail to leave enough in for the business to grow.

If you are going to use this method of getting paid, have some backup systems in order: a spouse with a paycheck, overdraft protection on your family checking account, a couple of credit cards you can use in a crunch, and money in the bank.

The Regular Paycheck

How do you get a regular paycheck when you are just starting in business? It can get kind of absurd. First, you have to take personal cash, either from a bank account or a loan, and use it to capitalize the business. Put it in a business account, so that your business has a cushion of cash upon which to operate. Then, figure out an appropriate salary for yourself, and pay yourself by check on a regular schedule.

Make those checks as small as possible. To figure out how much your business should pay you, figure out the bare bones minimum that you need to live on. Look at how much you can realistically expect your business to earn. And come up with a figure that is as close to the former as you can stand.

What's the point of this paycheck approach? It does help your family budget. Maybe there isn't a lot of money coming in, but you always know how much and when it will be there. It also serves as a disciplining agent: You don't take more than you need so you have cash left to accumulate for business purposes, or to take out and save for a rainy day.

But there's a big danger here, too. What if not enough money is coming in and you just keep issuing yourself paychecks? If your business really isn't supporting you, the paycheck trick isn't going to help for long; instead, you'll just be digging a deeper and deeper hole.

Task 3: Get a Bank Account—or Two, or Three!

So you have your business name and your business plan and your first client. Where are you going to deposit that first check? Chances are, you're going to open a brand spanking new business checking account, and that's good. But take a moment before you do to consider this: You may not need a separate business checking account, and you may not want one.

SECRET: *When it comes to business and family finances, it's true, as the song goes, that you gotta keep 'em separated. But there is no law or requirement that you must keep separate checking accounts if you are a sole proprietor. What you need to keep separate are your financial records. So if you can keep good records of your business income and expenses, it doesn't really matter to the IRS which account the money is flowing through. In fact, it's a good guess that more fraud occurs when personal expenses are run through business accounts than when money is commingled in personal accounts.*

The Myth of the Separate Checking Account

Why wouldn't you want a separate business checking account? Consider these possibilities:

- ❏ You always run business and personal errands together, and don't want to carry around two checkbooks.
- ❏ You don't like the extra fees associated with a business checking account.

❑ You don't want to spend the time it takes to reconcile two bank accounts.

❑ You can't afford the extra days the bank holds your deposits before it credits them to a business checking account.

❑ Life is a little more complicated when you have to go to the bank, deposit your money in one account, wait a few days, transfer it from that account to your personal checking account, and then pay bills. You may not want the extra step, or the headaches, of always trying to figure how much cash to leave in each account.

Those are all good reasons not to, but there are ways to work around most of them. And there is a lot to recommend a business checking account:

❑ You can keep really clean financial records for your business.

❑ You don't have the problem of tracking the same expenses twice, which is what you do when you pay for them out of your family checkbook, then record them elsewhere as a business expense.

❑ It does look more professional.

❑ If you operate your business under a name different from your given name, you don't have a choice anyway: You must have a business account at the bank to deposit and cash your checks.

Douglas Perreault, a Florida CPA, tells his clients to maintain separate checking accounts so that if their businesses are audited, they can limit the scope of the IRS's examination. He suggests that once your personal checkbook is open before an auditor, that gives them a license to go fishing.

 SECRET: *There are a few other alternatives to the expenses of a business checking account. If your business is in your personal name (like my business is called Linda S. Stern) then you can just open a separate personal checking account that is solely for your business. If you are going to be making a lot of deposits to your account—say you sell a low-priced product, but don't have many expenses, you can also consider opening a business savings account linked to a personal checking account instead of just a business checking account. The fees will be lower and the interest higher.*

What Accounts? Where?

The bottom line is you don't have to feel guilty and it's not illegal if you don't have a separate business checking account, but in the long run, you probably are better off with one. Ideally, you should have:

❏ A business checking account, which you will use to deposit all income and pay all expenses of your business. Whenever you start to have more cash built up than you need, you can transfer it to …

❏ A business savings account that will earn interest and keep fees on your checking account down. Keep the minimum required in your savings account to avoid fees on your checking account. And send excess to …

❏ A money market mutual fund—in your business name or your personal name—that you will use as your emergency fund. Ideally, this will not be at your bank, but at a mutual fund family or brokerage, where rates will be higher. If you are disciplined, you can use the same account to accumulate money for your estimated tax payments and upcoming big business expenses. But if you suspect you'll double-spend the same dollars, set up separate accounts for those must-have set-asides.

❏ A business credit card so you can shop and entertain conveniently, and track these business expenses separately from your family expenses. Does this mean you need an American Express Gold Card? Absolutely not, unless you travel in some pretty superficial status-conscious circles. Any MasterCard or Visa will do nicely.

SECRET: *A nice alternative to the business checking account is one of the new full-featured money market mutual funds that allow unlimited checking. United Services Government Securities Savings (800-873-8637) offers unlimited checking, higher interest, and no bank fees. E-Fund (800-533-3863), charges an annual fee of $35, but gives you a debit card so you can use your local ATM to access cash.*

Other Things to Ask Your Banker

The constant mergers and ever-higher fees make the banking industry feel less competitive even if it really isn't. But you should still get your bank to work for you. The convenience of bank-by-mail and the coming-of-age of online banking means you are no longer limited to the bank on the corner, though that convenience is still worth something. Find the bank that will give you the best mix of the following services at the best price:

❏ Free or low-cost checking.

❏ Overdraft protection on your business checking account.

❏ Saturday hours.

❏ Online connectivity, so you can download your statements in a form compatible with the checkbook management or accounting program you are using.

❏ ATM access to your business accounts.

❏ "Sweep" features that will allow you to move unused cash from checking into a savings account that earns interest, and "sweep" it back into checking when you need it.

SECRET: Most banks really stick it to business account holders by charging insane amounts for business checks. Avoid this altogether by mail ordering your checks. You can get little carry-around checks from Current (800-426-0822) or Checks in the Mail (800-733-4443.) And order the computer checks that work with your accounting software. You'll save money and time!

SECRET: Consider a lock box. This is a special service that banks offer businesses, like mail order businesses, that have lots of checks coming in every day. The check gets mailed directly to a post box to which your bank has access. Every day, the bankers open the mail, take out all the checks, and deposit them to your account. This saves time, and if you really have a heavy cash flow—thousands and thousands every week—it can earn you money in interest, too—of course, for a fee.

SECRET: Buy each bank account separately. The old idea that you had to keep all of your accounts at one bank so the banker would like you if you needed to borrow money really is just an old idea. The new idea is commoditize every bank service you want (checking account, money market fund, etc.) and get it where the price and services are right. If you ever find yourself looking for a business loan, then you can consolidate your accounts and use them as a bargaining chip—deliver them to the banker who gives you the best loan.

Task 4: Set Up Some Safeguards

It's always something, right? The more you plan, the less likely you are to face catastrophe, but as bumper stickers remind, stuff happens. Maybe your business will be slower to start than you think; or your prized client won't pay on time; or you'll have to take time off of work for your sister's wedding; your cat's surgery; or jury duty. The more thorough you've been in setting up your emergency resources, the better you'll be able to sleep at night. You'll have the ability to stay in business through troubled times.

That All-Important Emergency Fund

You already know you need an emergency fund. What you may not already know is that if you are self-employed, you may need a bigger emergency fund than your cushy-job-holding neighbor. You need to sock away enough cash to keep your family eating and your business running during a crisis. And if you are self-employed, you may not have some of those other safety nets, like unemployment insurance, severance pay, and employer-paid disability insurance.

There's good news, here, too. In today's economy, other money is available that you can tap to reduce your need for a liquid emergency fund. Professional advisers say you may not need the kind of cushion your parents had, because if times are tough, you can tap your credit cards, your home equity, or your spouse's salary.

How much should you keep in an emergency fund so that it can bail out you, your business, and your family in times of trouble? Here's a simple formula. Adjust it to fit your own situation.

> Emergency fund = six months keep-the-business-going budget
>
> + six months lean mean family budget
>
> + sleep tight factor
>
> − sure-thing receivables
>
> − spouse's 6 month contribution
>
> − other emergency resources

Use the money market mutual fund you selected for your emergency fund. And make sure you don't double-count your dollars. If you are using the same account to accumulate estimated taxes and save for your next computer, don't count those deposits toward your emergency fund.

Get a Good Credit Card, or Take Two, They're Small

Here's a rash generalization that probably will work for you: Don't bother with all of the rebate cards on the market today. Find a basic credit card that offers cash back for every penny you charge; the going rate is 1 percent. Then use that card for everything you would normally charge. You can buy an airline ticket faster that way than you can juggling too many cards with too many bonuses.

As a self-employed person, you might find yourself more dependent on credit than the next person, because your cash may come in irregularly and you might need to use credit cards to float you until the next check comes in. But:

❏ Try your very hardest to pay off balances every month. If you do, make sure you have a no-fee credit card and don't worry about the interest rate.

❏ If you end up carrying big balances, go for the lowest rate card you can find, even if you have to swallow an annual fee to do it. And reform!

An easy way to find a good card is to contact Ram Research (301-695-4660.) This company sells very inexpensive lists of low rate and no-fee cards.

Other Safeguards

If you haven't quit your job yet (or even if you have) try to have these personal financial practices in place before you cut the cord. If you're already self-employed, make your way down this checklist as fast as possible.

❏ Get overdraft protection on your personal checking account. Make sure your personal checks look really different from your business checks, so you don't mix up and accidentally use the wrong checks.

❏ Line up a home equity line of credit if you own your home; you don't ever have to tap it, just make sure it's there.

❏ Pay off your credit cards so that you have no debts other than your home, and possibly a car.

❏ Have enough full and frank discussions with your immediate family so that everyone understands money will be a little irregular for a while.

Task 5: Setting Up That Cash Flow System

The real secrets of cash flow management, of collecting money quickly and then squeezing it until it cries, are in Chapters 5, 6, 7, and 8. But first, you have to establish a cash flow system. Once you have your business entity established, your bank accounts opened, your systems in place, and your if-all-else-fails backups available, this isn't too hard.

Establish a routine of banking and bill paying that fits comfortably in your schedule. But keep these pointers in mind:

❏ Go to the bank often, so you can quickly deposit every check you receive. This is true for three reasons. Maybe your bank holds them for a week before it credits them to your account. Maybe they get credited immediately, and post interest. Maybe the check you got in the mail is good today, but will bounce tomorrow. For all of those reasons, the faster that money gets to the bank, the better.

❏ Establish a rhythm for paying business bills. Twice a month is often enough to keep most of your suppliers happy.

❏ After your business bills are paid, transfer money from your business to your personal accounts, and pay family bills twice a month. This gives you enough time to accumulate the cash you need to pay most bills without having to constantly be writing checks and switching money between both accounts.

❏ After every bill-paying session, if you have more than a small cushion left in your checking accounts, write a check to your money market emergency fund.

❏ Strongly consider setting up automatic deposit plans for your retirement and other savings accounts. When your investment company pulls cash automatically out of your checking account, you barely miss it. But it will accumulate. More about this in Chapter 12, where we really plan for retirement.

❏ Keep stellar records of your business spending and pretty good ones of your personal finances, too.

And now that you're systems are in place, you're ready to start keeping the books! The next chapter explores a variety of bookkeeping systems in detail.

YOU MUST REMEMBER THIS: THE LESSONS OF CHAPTER 2

- Your first act as a business owner is to decide what legal form your business should take; each has its own legal and tax implications.

- Even before you have money, establish some bank accounts that will let your money flow as it should.

- Everyone has emergencies. Plan ahead of time for yours.

3

© Michael Moran 1997

*"Without adequate documentation,
you'll lose valued tax deductions
or even the legitimacy of
your business itself."*

Rudimentary Recordkeeping

"**K**eeping the books" is such a quaint phrase. Who actually has ledgers these days? Instead, you're likely to have anything from a shoebox to a software package serving as your accounting system. But, whatever shape it's in, it could be the most important part of your business. Without adequate documentation, you'll lose valued tax deductions or even the legitimacy of your business itself. You could forget to send bills, lose track of the ones you've sent, and miss opportunities to charge clients for your expenses.

Without good records, you can't really run a business at all. At first, it will be just money slipping through the cracks. But you won't be able to make business decisions later because you won't remember the last decision. Most of us think of keeping records to please Uncle Sam, but your recordkeeping system should do a lot more than just help you fill out your tax return.

Depending upon the form and structure of your business, following are some of the items a good recordkeeping system should provide.

❏ **All the tax data you need, and justification in case of audit.** Make sure every program you use tracks your expenses by tax category.

❏ **Regular profit-and-loss statements.** At a minimum, you should be able to quickly add up all of your income, subtract all of your expenses, and discover what's left.

❏ **A balance sheet.** This tells you what your business owns and owes. For a one person service business, expect both parts to be small. But if you find yourself with a negative balance sheet, look carefully to make sure you aren't overextending yourself on debt that your business can't cover.

❏ **A cash budget.** How much money came in and went out this month? What do you expect next month? Will you make enough in sales this year to pay for a new copier and a part-time assistant? A good set of accounting records will tell you.

❏ **The data that drives decisions.** If you provide more than one kind of product or service, or handle more than one kind of customer, try to find a system that lets you code them. Then you can make long-range plans that let you target those parts of the business that are most profitable. Otherwise, you can end up spinning your wheels for clients who aren't paying enough to cover the axle grease, while your more profitable clients are being overlooked.

❏ **An impartial reality check.** Are you spending your business into the ground, but feeling good because of all the new stuff around you? Or feeling insecure despite happy profits? Look at numbers that won't lie. A good accounting program might tell you, "Yes, October was a bad month last year, too." Or "Don't even think about that new modem until you pay these bills."

❏ **A way to track pass-through costs.** Do you bill your clients for long distance calls, travel, or other expenses? Not if you don't know what they are!

❏ **Accounts receivable.** If you invoice for your services, you'll want a program that will print invoices, track what's owed you, and age the invoices.

❏ **Payroll.** Yuck! This is really complicated, but not with the latest software programs. They'll automate federal, state, and local taxes; accrue vacation pay; crunch medical benefits; and more.

❏ **Inventory tracking.** A good program will tell you what you have left, when you need to order more, the name and address of the supplier, and how much you paid for it last time.

❑ **Time tracking.** If you bill by the hour, you need to keep track of those hours.

❑ **Ratio analysis.** To really take your company's temperature, you will need to know these kinds of numbers: your debt level, your total receivables, your monthly cash flow, and the like.

❑ **What-if games.** What if you dropped this problem client? What if you stopped developing your own pictures and sent them all out? What if you hired an assistant to help you catch up at the office? A good accounting system will let you play around with alternatives.

❑ **A level of comfort.** When you pick a recordkeeping system that fits your computing and accounting style, you'll feel better about keeping it up.

Keep Track of Taxes

Believe it or not, most one-person businesses lose out on deductions because they forget to write them down. Avoid that by having a clear idea ahead of time about which items are deductible in your business and by saving every piece of paper that justifies an expense. Run to the grocery for some bread and buy business envelopes while you are there? Don't forget to save the receipt!

Consider that your tax recordkeeping has two parts: the computer program (or paper ledger; but that's doubtful) where you will enter a record of all of your expenses, and the paper trail. Make sure that every receipt has a home and a number.

*S*ECRET: *Here's the quickest, lowest-tech, lowest-maintenance way to keep your tax records. Every year, buy an accordion folder with alphabetized sections. Label each section with a category of business tax deduction, such as advertising, dues and publications, freight. Whenever you get a receipt or canceled check that relates to a business expense, throw it in the right section. Even if you do nothing more than this, you'll be organized for your February visit to your tax preparer. If you enter your expenses in a computer program, use the number on the canceled check or receipt as the identification number of the transaction.*

Before you set up your recordkeeping system, check Chapter 4 to make sure you are aware of all of the deductions coming to you. Then look at the IRS's Schedule C, Profit or Loss from Business (reproduced in Chapter 4), to see how you should be organizing those expenses. Create a recordkeeping system that reflects those items. For example, you'll want to track postage (currently considered an "other expense") as separate from your office expenses or supplies.

SECRET: *Every year the IRS reduces the line items it lists on Schedule C. For example, freight and publications are two categories of expenses that used to get their own lines but now get lumped, unlisted, in "other expenses." Is this because the IRS is hoping you'll forget to write them off? No one's talking. Remember that just because the IRS doesn't list a business expense on the form doesn't mean you can't take it.*

Other Records

Besides keeping track of category totals, there are other records to keep that will help you validate your deductions. Keep an auto mileage log in your car, to record every business trip's purpose, destination, and mileage. For business meals and entertainment, keep a record of the date, amount, place, the name and relationship of the person you dined with, and the business purpose of the meeting. Write them on your charge slip if you'd like. When you combine business and pleasure on a business trip/family vacation, keep a daily log of the times you spend working and the time spent on personal activities.

Select a Computerized Recordkeeping System

If you're reading this book, there's a good chance you want your records on computer. You can keep a set of business books on paper—just like Bob Cratchit! For a bare bones, but reliable approach, set up a column for every category of expense and income. Then use each line to record one transaction. But it's not likely you'll want to stick with paper and pencil once you preview the wide variety of software that's available for tracking your business finances. Most have gone beyond basics to offer fairly sophisticated accounting procedures at a nominal cost.

When you are picking your financial software, try to get demos, particularly if you are looking at an expensive program. Interview colleagues in your field to find out which programs work for them. Ask your accountant what he or she recommends. And be prepared to dump a program you've already bought if you decide that it's not a good fit. Better to do that than waste years cramming your figures into a program you don't like.

And before you set up your computerized accounting program, there's one more item to take care of: Make sure that you have a reliable and foolproof backup system. Don't risk losing a year of accounting data to a hard drive crash. Many professional accounting programs prompt you to do automatic backups before you quit the program; you can buy free-standing backup software, or you can just be religious about copying and protecting files on your own.

Now, here's an overview of the main approaches you can take to getting an accounting program. You may grow from one to another as your business grows. For a summary of these methods, check out the chart on page 55.

SECRET: *Sometimes it pays to pick an accounting system just because it "talks" to your accountant. Sara and Adam Viener started using Quicken to track the finances in their bulletin board system because their accountant uses it. He offered them a discount on his services if they could give him records on disk. Even without the discount, you can save money entering data into a program your accountant or tax preparer already uses. You won't have to spend time or money translating your records.*

Write Your Own Spreadsheet

If you already have Lotus, Excel, or even an integrated Works program on your computer, you can track expenses without buying a new program. The sidebar starting on page 45 shows you how to set up a spreadsheet to track your expenses and income for tax purposes.

There's beauty in using your own spreadsheet: You can play what-if games to your heart's content, set up the categories exactly to reflect your business, and get to it fast. But compared to today's financial management programs, you give up a lot, too, doing your own. A spreadsheet can't easily print out an invoice or balance your checkbook, for instance.

But even if you decide to use an off-the-shelf accounting program, you may decide to use a spreadsheet to supplement it in the ways described throughout this book. A spreadsheet will enable you to analyze numbers that come from another program.

Use a Personal Finance Program

Think Quicken, the market leader, or Microsoft Money, gaining popularity. These programs are simple; you can quickly customize them to reflect the categories of business. They'll print out a profit-and-loss statement (though they'll call it an income and expense report) and a balance sheet (though it will be called a net worth statement.) They won't, however, track inventory, print invoices, or easily let you track individual jobs or clients, and you can forget payrolls.

But for a small sole proprietorship, either of these might be all the program you need. Quicken will allow you to split transactions, reconcile your checking account in moments, print detailed reports of activities in every expense category, and more. By the time you read this, it is likely to also allow you to dial up your bank by modem, download transactions, and be done for the day.

Try Small Business Bookkeeping Software

The next baby step up gets you a program, like QuickBooks, that is almost as easy to work as a personal finance program, but gives you more business support. These programs will do invoices, track clients, and generate the kinds of categories you are likely to have in a business.

These programs do of course take a little longer to learn, because they include more business accounting terms and fewer personal finance ones. But setup remains comparatively simple, and it's hard to conceive of a report they won't print out for you.

Move Up to Full-Fledged Accounting

QuickBooks Pro, M.Y.O.B. with Payroll, and Peachtree Accounting go even further. These programs can track time, or work with free-standing time-tracking software; support cash or accrual accounting; keep inventories; enable job/project tracking; and allow you to maintain different departmental budgets.

*S**ECRET:** I am moving up this chain myself. For the first few years of my freelance writing business, I used a simple spreadsheet that I had created to track expenses. As I got busier, and realized that a checkbook program would do more for me, I moved up to Managing Your Money. Once I grew a small payroll, I bumped up to small business accounting software. Now I use Quickbooks Pro; it does everything I need except clean my desk!*

COMPUTER SOLUTION:
A SIMPLE SCHEDULE C SPREADSHEET

The spreadsheet shown on the following pages provides a quick and relatively easy way of tracking expenses for a Schedule C tax return. You can set up this spreadsheet in a couple of hours at most, and see at a glance where you are spending your money and how your bottom line looks.

To set it up, create three general columns on the left for the date, details, and tracking number of your income and expense transactions. Then create a different column for each Schedule C income and expense line item that pertains to your business. For example, If you sell items in your business, include a Cost of Goods Sold column; with a service business you probably don't have to. Other Schedule C deductible expenses include advertising, supplies, entertainment, and the like.

It's easy to add extra wrinkles. Add up your total mileage in cell F4, and use cell F5 to multiply it by .315 for the mileage deduction on your car. Add up all of your entertainment expenses in cell R3, and then multiply them by .5 in cell R4, to get the total entertainment deduction.

Set every column to add automatically at the top (line 4 of the spreadsheet.) Then in the upper left-hand column, you can summarize the spreadsheet. In cell C1, total expenses from all of the columns. In cell C2, subtract those expenses from your receipts (cell D4) and you'll have a running tally of your net profit. You can use that figure to estimate your taxes.

A SIMPLE SCHEDULE C SPREADSHEET: Formula View (continued)

	A	B	C	D	E	F	G	H	I	J
		Total	=SUM(E4:U4)	GROSS	ADVER-		PARKING	COMMIS-	EMPLOYEE	
1		Expenses		RECEIPTS	TISING	MILEAGE	/TOLLS	SIONS/FEES	BENEFITS	FREIGHT
2		Net Profit	=D4–CI							
3						5546				
4	NO.	DATE	NOTES	=SUM(D5: D305)	=SUM(E5: E305)	=F3*.315	=SUM(G5: G305)	=SUM(H5: H305)	=SUM(I5: I305)	=SUM(J J305
5	10	1/0/00	Phone bill							
6	40331	1/0/00	Smith payment	$1,600.00						
7	6	1/0/00	Computer ship							$17.0
8	43	1/0/00	UPS							$17.0
9	2904	1/0/00	Trademark search							
10	81	1/0/00	Copying							
11	49	1/0/00	Postage							$34.0
12	9	1/0/00	FedEX							$20.0
13	16	1/0/00	Cable TV							
14	17	1/0/00	Jones payment	$3,000.00						
15	25	1/0/00	Books, mags.							
16	32	1/0/00	Copying							
17	33	1/0/00	ASJA meeting							
18	35	1/0/00	Books							
19	32198	1/0/00	Direct mail list		$800.00					
20	28	1/0/00	Wastebasket							
21	14411	1/0/00	Bergman payment	$5,000.00						
22	2388	1/0/00	Wesson payment	$3,000.00						
23	32	1/0/00	Agent lunch				$8.00			
24										
25		1/0/00	Annual mileage			$5,546.00				
26										
27										

K	L	M	N	O	P	Q	R	S	T	U
GER-CES	OFFICE EXPENSES	MACHIN-ERY/RENT	REPAIRS	SUPPLIES	TAXES	TRAVEL	ENTER-TAIN	UTILITIES/PHONES	OTHER EXPENSES	OTHER EXPENSES
							=R3*.5			
M(K5: K305)	=SUM(L5: L305)	=SUM(M5: M305)	=SUM(N5: N305)	=SUM(O5: O305)	=SUM(P5: P305)	=SUM(Q5: Q305)	=SUM(R5: R305)	=SUM(S5: S305)	=SUM(T5: T305)	=SUM(U5: U305)
								$147.00		
$5.00										
								$26.00		
										$57.00
$5.00										
									$45.00	
										$119.00
	$8.00									
						$75.00				

A SIMPLE SCHEDULE C SPREADSHEET: Data View (*continued*)

	A	B	C	D	E	F	G	H	I	
1		Total Expenses	$2,944.47	GROSS RECEIPTS	ADVER-TISING	MILEAGE	PARKING /TOLLS	COMMIS-SIONS/FEES	EMPLOYEE BENEFITS	FR
2		Net Profit	$9,656.00							
3						5546				
4	NO.	DATE	NOTES	$12,600.00	$800.00	$1,746.99	$8.00	$0.00	$0.00	
5	10	1/0/00	Phone bill							
6	40331	1/0/00	Smith payment	$1,600.00						
7	6	1/0/00	Computer ship							
8	43	1/0/00	UPS							
9	2904	1/0/00	Trademark search							
10	81	1/0/00	Copying							
11	49	1/0/00	Postage							
12	9	1/0/00	FedEX							
13	16	1/0/00	Cable TV							
14	17	1/0/00	Jones payment	$3,000.00						
15	25	1/0/00	Books, mags.							
16	32	1/0/00	Copying							
17	33	1/0/00	ASJA meeting							
18	35	1/0/00	Books							
19	32198	1/0/00	Direct mail list		$800.00					
20	28	1/0/00	Wastebasket							
21	14411	1/0/00	Bergman payment	$5,000.00						
22	2388	1/0/00	Wesson payment	$3,000.00						
23	32	1/0/00	Agent lunch				$8.00			
24										
25		1/0/00	Annual mileage			$5,546.00				
26										
27										

K SER-VICES	L OFFICE EXPENSES	M MACHIN-ERY/RENT	N REPAIRS	O SUPP-LIES	P TAXES	Q TRAVEL	R ENTER-TAIN	S UTILITIES/ PHONES	T OTHER EXPENSES	U OTHER EXPENSES
							$75.00			
$10.00	$8.00	$0.00	$0.00	$0.00	$0.00	$0.00	$37.50	$173.00	$45.00	$57.00
								$147.00		
$5.00										
								$26.00		
										$57.00
$5.00										
									$45.00	
										$119.00
	$8.00									
						$75.00				

COMPUTER SOLUTION:
A WALK THROUGH SOME ACCOUNTING WINDOWS

You've got to love a program that goes all the way from answering "Help! What's a fiscal year?" to demonstrating effortless invoicing, estimating, and payroll deducting without ever making you look at a debit or credit. QuickBooks Pro from Intuit is such a program, and a good example of state-of-the-art small business accounting software. A second, only marginally more dense program, is M.Y.O.B., by Bestware.

Both programs offer excellent examples of why we all have computers on our desks in the first place. For close to $100 each, they offer the kind of accounting complexity that cost upwards of $500 less than five years ago. And they wrap it in a seamless package that enables you to carefully account for every penny of your firm's activities with a minimum of debiting and crediting.

Starting up QuickBooks is as easy as it gets. You scroll through a friendly interview that asks you questions you can answer about your business, even if you've never done accounting. Here is the Interview screen:

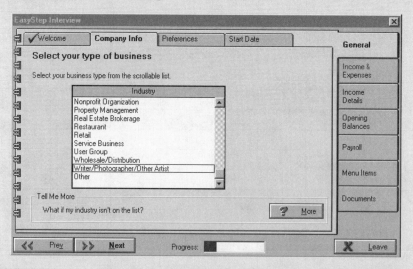

Tell the program what kind of business you have, and it automatically loads the kinds of expenses you'll keep track of. Tell it what kind of tax

A WALK THROUGH SOME ACCOUNTING WINDOWS (*continued*)

return you file (such as a sole proprietorship form) and it will automatically track your expenses in a format that can be copied directly into your tax forms. Should you get confused along the way, QuickBooks explains all. That's when the "Help! What's a fiscal year?" button comes into play.

QuickBooks also offers industry-specific help throughout the program. Enter that you are a writer, for example, and it tells you that writers usually use cash accounting, rarely need to keep inventories, and typically file sole proprietor returns.

As noted, M.Y.O.B. is slightly more complicated to set up. Key in your basics—accounting period, name, address, and the like—and it, too, prompts you for a business type and then loads the correct categories of income and expense. Then you're in the heart of the program, setting up your accounts and expenses on your own. The interface is simple.

If you're the "ignore the manual" type, you can get along nicely with either program. Following is a Help screen from M.Y.O.B.:

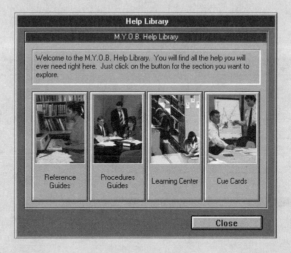

Both do payroll in a snap, though QuickBooks requires you to add your own local tax information, while M.Y.O.B. has county taxes included in its database.

A WALK THROUGH SOME ACCOUNTING WINDOWS *(continued)*

Both programs use the same basic system. You enter all of the people and companies you deal with, by name, address, account number, or any other way you'd like to track them. They are categorized as employees, vendors, or customers. When you sell a good or service, you enter an invoice that records the type of income you are entering. For example, if you make your money selling widgets and consulting about widgets, the invoice lets you track your consulting income and your widget-selling income separately. Once the money comes in, you enter it as a deposit to your checking or bank account and as a payoff for the invoice. In this way, the programs track all of your money in two ways: where you are putting it and what you earned it for.

The invoicing portions of the programs enable you to track receivables. Every morning you can go to your computer and learn that Stuart Slowpay still owes you $4,235, and just how late it is. You can print out reports showing exactly how much of different kinds of work you've done for each or all of your clients; how much money is coming in, and where it's going when it goes out.

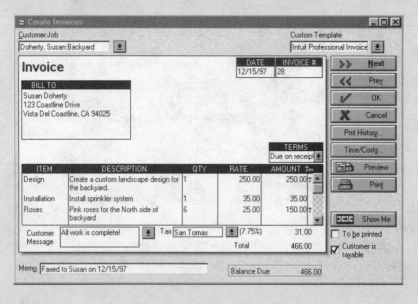

A WALK THROUGH SOME ACCOUNTING WINDOWS *(continued)*

Both QuickBooks (left) and M.Y.O.B. (above) make inventory tracking possible so that is integrated with sales. Sell too many widgets, and both programs prompt you to order or make more in a hurry.

QuickBooks goes further than M.Y.O.B. in the time-tracking category. M.Y.O.B. imports data from TimeSlips, a popular time-tracking program, but QuickBooks does time-tracking for you. Intuit is pushing it as the integrated one-box software system for small businesses.

Both programs offer a bonus in the contact management arena. Once you've entered all of your customers and vendors in the programs, they will serve as fairly comprehensive contact programs, linking with letters, envelopes, and labels, and letting you record notes about your contacts without going to a separate program.

Be forewarned, though, neither of these programs is without a learning curve. Expect to spend a few hours or days getting up to speed on either one; or hire a consultant to set it all up for you. But that's a minimal investment for a recordkeeping system that Bob Cratchit would have traded Tiny Tim for!

When professional bookkeepers hunt for accounting software, they know what they want. Some of the features they demand are ones you should, too, though not every business has every requirement. Here's a quick checklist:

❏ Will the program support cash accounting? It's what most small businesses use.

❏ Can you customize invoices?

❏ Can you keep past accounting periods "open?" That means you can go back and record late activity.

❏ Can you correct errors? Some programs are so strict in the way they build an audit trail that you can never change a figure already entered. Not good for an amateur bookkeeper!

❏ Will the program save as you go? Will it back up automatically, or at least prompt you to back up?

❏ Can you upgrade? What if you start out simple, with no inventory, employees, or time-tracking, and then decide you want to grow? Do you need to reinvent your accounting system, or can you build onto the program you already have?

❏ Interface. Do you like the way the program looks? Is it easy enough for you to work with?

❏ Will the program age invoices? Will it do it on whatever schedule you want?

❏ Are its tax tables up to date? If you are going to have a regular payroll, how much will it cost you to keep your tax tables timely?

❏ Will your accounting software fill out the forms you want and need, like 1099s, W-2s, and more?

❏ Do you need to buy forms? Where will you get them? Most programs these days come with a catalog of associated forms, like checks, invoices, and more. Some also allow you to design your own forms, so you can print on plain paper and avoid the extra expense.

❏ Does it let you track individual projects or jobs?

Buy a Specialized Program

Open any trade magazine and you can find an accounting program designed specially for your line of work. Attorneys can find programs that bill hours, manage escrow accounts, and handle expense pass-throughs

Choosing Your Accounting System: What's Best for You?			
System	**Method**	**Pros**	**Cons**
Your own spreadsheet	Customize it to total income, sort expenses by category, and subtract from income.	Simple to keep up. Doesn't require new software. Can be customized.	Unless you are adept at massaging data, it may not give you the reports you'd get from an accounting program.
Personal finance (a.k.a. checkbook) program	Software like Quicken or Microsoft Money can be customized with business categories.	Enough reports to please most small businesses; you may already be using the software for your personal finances	No invoicing. No inventory control.
Small business bookkeeping	Programs like QuickBooks are written to fulfill the accounting needs of small businesses without the accounting jargon.	May look like checkbook programs but produce more comprehensive business reports and invoices; allow individual project tracking.	Usually weak inventory control and no payroll included.
Small business accounting	You'll need to know some accounting to keep up with programs like Peachtree Accounting, M.Y.O.B., and QuickBooks Pro.	These will age receivables, manage inventory control, and more in a format your CPA will be happy to see.	Expect to invest some time (or consultant money) to get the program set up. Learn debits and credits.
Specialized accounting package	Off-the-shelf software geared to ad agencies, law firms, gift shops, and more; these are written for a specific industry.	A program that understands your business can help you set up your records in a way that really fits, and may even give you guidance about how to organize finances.	Most are expensive, and not very adaptable. Unless your company is a textbook case, you may end up trying to fit square pegs into round holes.
Hire a bookkeeper	A professional who will do it all for you: make sense of your paper jungle and deliver informative and pertinent reports when you want them.	You know your finances are being handled by an expert, and you can spend your time running your business instead of accounting for it.	Unless you closely oversee the bookkeeper, you may never learn the financial basics; this costs more than doing it yourself; data may come in at a lag.
Customized software	Hire a computer specialist with an accounting background to customize a system, and you can get every piece of pertinent data as well as a system that runs exactly the way you want it to.	This solution will fit you better than any off-the-rack program, and can offer any feature you need. It can combine your address book, supply ordering, and appointment calendar with your finances.	This top-of-the-line solution will cost more than any of the others; it may leave you overly dependent on the consultant who sets it up for you.

like a charm. Advertising agencies have a program that marks up printing costs, allocates creative budgets, and more.

These programs cost more but have a clear advantage. They are already set up for the way you work. They may even give you some insights into how your colleagues and competitors work. The down side is, they really tie you in, too. If you run your company a little bit differently, you might have to spend a lot of time working around the program just to accommodate your preferences.

Buy Customized Software

If you're really picky, you can always hire a consultant to write a database program that does your accounting for you. This is an especially good solution if you run a retail business or have several employees keying in data for you; the programmer can make it fail-safe, so no one can mess up your records by entering a sale or payments.

Brigitte Pipkin, a beauty shop operator, invested $10,000 in a system like this a few years ago. She thinks it was well worth it. For her money, she got a point-of-sale system that tracks products sold, inventory, individual customer spending behavior, and stylist activity. It eats questions like this for breakfast: How many bottles of her new shampoo line has she sold since Tuesday? How much should she send in for her next quarterly payroll taxes? Are the reminder cards she sent out before Christmas working? How much does she usually earn in February?

Clearly, the high-priced, full-featured, or customized program is usually not necessary for a small, home-based business. But boy, can it do a lot for a bigger business.

Basic Bookkeeping Choices

Your bookkeeping system can be as simple as a bunch of entries in a spiral notebook (not recommended!) or as complicated as a multi-thousand dollar custom-made database system. Each has its advantages and disadvantages.

The good and bad news is that you can expect to change your bookkeeping system regularly as your business and need for detailed information grows. So if you don't pick the right system, don't fret—just switch to another.

In selecting your approach, try to find systems that will grow with you, or that at least will accept data from systems that are lower on the food chain.

Setting Up a System and a Schedule

If you stick with a program of entering your expenses weekly, it will take only a few minutes of your time. But, let it slide, and you can end up spending entire Saturdays with little receipts, trying to reconstruct how you spent that $4.25 three months ago.

*S*ECRET: *If you really, truly, hate to deal with financial recordkeeping, hire someone else to do it for you. Better than not getting it done at all, or done badly. You can pay a bookkeeper $15 or $20 an hour to sort out all of your receipts, balance your checkbook, keep up your receivables, and hand you all the reports you'd ever want to read.*

Keep a Business Journal

If you want to go beyond bookkeeping, keep a daily business journal. This not only can help you validate expenses for tax purposes, it can help you manage your business. At the end of the year, for example, if you are reviewing your books and see that April was a rough month, you can go back to April in your journal. It will remind you of the client from hell you had almost wiped out of your memory; the money you wasted on three sets of laser checks while you fiddled with different accounting programs; or the two weeks you spent in non-billable ruminations about your future. A business journal serves the same purpose as a personal diary: It helps you learn from past mistakes.

What Do You Do with All of the Paperwork?

The accordion folder solution mentioned earlier in this chapter is optimum for keeping business receipts straight. But you'll probably want to save written reports about your business finances, too. Many entrepreneurs like to keep financial statements in a three-ring binder; it allows them to compare years of history in a few minutes, without taking up too much file cabinet or hard drive space.

There are some papers you should save forever, even if you have to keep them in storage away from your office. Among them:

- ❏ Records pertaining to employees, even if they've quit or been fired. You never know when they could call you out of the blue, looking for their retirement funds or suing you for some unknown reason.

- ❏ Tax returns. Even if you never refer to them again (and you will) it's a fun history to have of your financial life. Always keep a copy of your annual federal and state tax returns.

❏ Annual retirement fund statements. You might choose to keep these in a notebook, instead of a file drawer.

❏ Original plan documents related to your retirement accounts.

❏ Business insurance policies that are in force.

❏ Active warranties on all that expensive computer and telephone equipment.

❏ Active contracts: Loan agreements, employment agreements, supplier terms, leases, and the like.

❏ Annual financial reports. A year-end summary of profits and losses, assets and liabilities will be a valuable future tool for serious planning and even reminiscing.

Finally, Tossing with Temerity

Don't confuse recordkeeping with never throwing out a piece of paper. Even business owners can eventually toss something, if for no other reason than to make room for the next pile of papers. Following are some records you can easily throw away.

❏ Your monthly or quarterly retirement account statements, once they've been supplanted by a year-end statement.

❏ Backup materials that support your tax deductions, seven years after filing. Until then, an audit is possible. Keep a copy of your annual tax return forever, just in case. (And don't throw away records pertaining to the improvements you've made to your home. You'll need them when you eventually sell your house.

❏ The old insurance policy documents that have been supplanted by your new policy. (A surprising number of people never throw away an insurance company paper.)

❏ Monthly financial reports, after five years. Perhaps you will want to summarize these on a spreadsheet, so you can always have a record of what Januarys past and present were like for your business. Perhaps your software does this. At some point, you won't want reams and reams of monthly reports.

❏ Software manuals for programs you gave up on—or replaced—long ago.

❏ User instructions for equipment you have upgraded or replaced.

The Five Hour Family Financial Cleanup

Everyone knows you can't really get down to business until your personal matters are squared away. It's an especially good time to get your personal paperwork cleaned up if you are making way for a new home office. Here's a five-hour crash course that will leave your personal financial records unbelievably organized.

15 minutes

Search desks, cabinets, drawers, shelves, and other hiding papers for all wayward papers. Just dump them in a box, as big as it takes.

20 minutes

Label a stack of file folders; and remember the organizer's secret for perfect filing: every category has a space-saving hanging folder and one manila (or colored) folder inside it. Use these labels:

- ❏ **Bank accounts:** A separate file for each account. You'll keep monthly statements for a year, and then annual statements.
- ❏ **Car:** For receipts for repair work, insurance, and loan information.
- ❏ **Credit cards:** Save all the fine print that comes with your cards. Save receipts until you can check them against your monthly statement. Throw out every monthly statement when a new one comes in, unless it has deductible charges on it. Then, keep it with your tax records.
- ❏ **Health:** A copy of your health insurance policy along with blank insurance forms. Keep, indefinitely, immunization records and other treatment records still important to your care.
- ❏ **Home:** Appraisals, homeowners association information, and copies of official documents. Save all receipts that document permanent home improvements you've made.
- ❏ **Income Tax—Current:** Anything pertaining to this year's taxes including child care records, charitable receipts, and the like. (Of course, you'll keep your business tax records with your business files.) Label one 9 x 12 inch envelope for this year's taxes. On the front, list all of the papers you'll need to complete the taxes, such as statements from your bank accounts. During tax season, as the appropriate forms come in the mail, cross them off your list and put them in the envelope.

❏ **Income Tax—Previous:** One copy of every year's return up to last year's.

❏ **Life Insurance:** Your policy, as well as your agent's name, address, and phone number.

❏ **Investments:** Separate files for separate brokerage or mutual fund accounts, for retirement funds, and other investments.

❏ **Loans:** Separate folders for student loans, mortgages, home equity loans. Include amortization schedules and loan agreements.

❏ **Major purchases and valuables:** Receipts and active warranties for all of the major appliances and valuables in your home.

❏ **Retirement:** Your current Social Security estimates (do this once every three or four years), your IRAs, rollovers, and current retirement plans.

❏ **Safe-deposit box:** Additional copies of the documents that are in your actual safe deposit box, as well as the keys to the box and the box number and bank name.

2 minutes

Label a file folder To Be Copied and leave it on your desk, floor, or wherever you are working.

10 minutes

Set up personal bill paying box in a plastic mesh or wire box, about the size of a shoebox. Include envelopes, pens, postage stamps, a calculator, address labels, paper clips, and a small calendar. Keep mortgage and car loan payment books in this box. As new bills come in, put them here. When it's time to pay them, this box and a flat surface will be all you need.

2 hours and 30 minutes

It's time to file. Put the appropriate records in the correct file folders, as explained. Put tax-related items in the tax envelope, and check them off as you put them in. Put all unpaid bills in the bill box. Put all original copies of important documents, including insurance policies, stock, bond, and bank certificates, will, car title, adoption papers, divorce decrees, and passport in the To Be Copied folder.

15 minutes

Compile a master list of all of your bank accounts, with the account numbers and name, address, and phone number of the bank, the type of account, signers and location of the passbook or certificate. Put the list in the Bank Accounts file.

25 minutes

List all of your credit cards, including account numbers, issuing institutions, and phone numbers to call in case of loss or theft. Keep in the Credit Cards file.

30 minutes

Take the To Be Copied folder to a copy shop and make copies of everything in it.

20 minutes

On the way back, stop at the bank and rent a safe deposit box if you don't already have one. Put all of the original documents into the box.

8 minutes

Go home and file the copies in the Safe Deposit Box file.

2 minutes

Call the Social Security Administration at 800-234-5772 for a postcard to request your Personal Earnings and Benefit Estimate Statement. When you receive the card, fill it out and send it in. When your report comes, check it against your past tax returns to make sure the government has an accurate record of your earnings, and file it in your Retirement folder. You should update that report every three years; once a mistake has been on the books longer than that, it's much tougher to clean up.

3 minutes

Take out the trash. No need to save everything! Toss: canceled checks for everyday nondeductible expenses as food, cash, and dry cleaning; old medical bills once they and the insurance claims have been paid and you're sure you won't be deducting them on your taxes; monthly brokerage and bank statements that have been superseded by annual statements, credit card bills; old utility bills and rent receipts (if you're not using them to deduct home office expenses); and expired warranties and directions you will never use for products you no longer own.

The Payoff: Tax Simplification

A good set of financial records will do a lot for you, not the least of which is simplifying your tax preparations and justifying your write-offs. In the next chapter, you'll learn the ins and outs of taking business deductions. Make the most of them!

YOU MUST REMEMBER THIS: THE LESSONS OF CHAPTER 3

- You don't just need to spend money and earn money, you need to track it!

- There's a computer-based bookkeeping system for you.

- You'll probably outgrow it in a few years anyway, and have to switch systems.

- With good records you'll run your business better, collect faster, save more and really cut your taxes.

© Bob Eckstein 1997

"The first tax hurdle many entrepreneurs have to face is proving they are indeed running a business, and not just claiming a costly hobby."

The Big Green Tax Machine

Legal ways to put the house, the car, the Caribbean and the cleaning on the business

There are two common views of the tax status of the sole proprietor. Those who subscribe to the "what a scam!" view see a home-based business as an empty shell that houses enough sweet and meaty deductions to render life essentially tax-free. Scam proponents believe that you can set up a business, run your life out of it, and deduct everything from a trip west for your cousin's wedding to your kid's braces to your latest hot car. They are wrong.

The second view, at the other end of the spectrum, is the "cross to bear" view of self-employment taxes. You have to pay both parts of the Social Security tax yourself. Your income is taxed at high personal rates. You're a target for the IRS. You're a shlump who doesn't even get to write off legitimate benefits like insurance that any self-respecting employee would get. The cross believers see all 40,500 pages of the tax law, regulations, and rulings as a personal burden so weighty it might crush their fledgling business to death at any moment. Happily, they are wrong, too.

The truth lies in the middle. When you work for yourself, you get many great write-offs, including some that can be used to bolster your lifestyle. But you do have to pay hefty Social Security and Medicare taxes. The trick to post-tax prosperity is figuring out how to maximize deductions and minimize taxes while staying on the right side of the audit-bait line.

One Degree of Separation: That Arm's Length

A sign of personal success is when you can fully integrate your professional and business life. But that's not a sign of taxpayer success. Even if your life's work and play are inseparable, your expenses can't be. It's critical that you keep your business and personal expenses separate in your records, as described in Chapter 3. Otherwise, you can mix up and lose valid deductions, or even jeopardize the legality of your business.

Most sole proprietors file a Schedule C form with their personal tax returns. This form lists your business income and expenses, and ends with a single number that is your net business income. That number gets pasted into your main personal 1040 tax form, and personal deductions are taken against it. Since there is also a 15.3 percent self-employment tax, which pays for Social Security and Medicare, levied against your Schedule C net income up to $65,400, there is one key rule of personal/business tax management that applies: A deduction is worth more if you take it in your business than if you take it on your 1040. Do your best to keep any expenses that could go either way as business expenses—and check out the front page of Schedule C, which appears on page 67.

What's a Deduction Worth?

Like most Americans, Jennifer is in the 28 percent federal tax bracket. And typical, too, is her combined state/local income tax rate of 6 percent. Her self-employment tax is 15.3 percent of her business income, but half of that is deductible from her 1040. Her self-employment tax is further reduced because it is applied only to 92.93 percent of her bottom line, making her effective self-employment tax rate roughly 12 percent. Add it all up and her marginal tax rate on business income is 28 + 6 + 11.8, or 46 percent!

That means whenever she spends money on a deductible item, she's only really spending about half in after-tax dollars. Therefore, a $39 software program costs her $21 after taxes; a $200 fax machine, $108; a $5,000 trip to New York to interview ad agencies, $2,700. Put another way, Jennifer saves $2,410 in taxes by remembering to deduct the software program, the fax machine, and the New York trip.

FEDERAL SCHEDULE C

SCHEDULE C (Form 1040)	**Profit or Loss From Business**	OMB No. 1545-0074

(Sole Proprietorship)

► Partnerships, joint ventures, etc., must file Form 1065.

Department of the Treasury Internal Revenue Service (10) ► **Attach to Form 1040 or Form 1041.** ► **See Instructions for Schedule C (Form 1040).**

19 96

Attachment Sequence No. **09**

Name of proprietor

Social security number (SSN)

A	Principal business or profession, including product or service (see page C-1)	**B Enter principal business code** (see page C-6) ►
C	Business name. If no separate business name, leave blank.	**D Employer ID number (EIN), if any**

E Business address (including suite or room no.) ► ....
   City, town or post office, state, and ZIP code

F Accounting method: **(1)** ☐ Cash **(2)** ☐ Accrual **(3)** ☐ Other (specify) ► ....

G Did you "materially participate" in the operation of this business during 1996? If "No," see page C-2 for limit on losses. ☐ Yes ☐ No

H If you started or acquired this business during 1996, check here . . . . ► ☐

Part I Income

1	Gross receipts or sales. **Caution:** If this income was reported to you on Form W-2 and the "Statutory employee" box on that form was checked, see page C-2 and check here . . . . ► ☐	1	
2	Returns and allowances	2	
3	Subtract line 2 from line 1	3	
4	Cost of goods sold (from line 42 on page 2)	4	
5	**Gross profit.** Subtract line 4 from line 3	5	
6	Other income, including Federal and state gasoline or fuel tax credit or refund (see page C-2) . . .	6	
7	**Gross income.** Add lines 5 and 6 . . . . ►	7	

Part II Expenses. Enter expenses for business use of your home **only** on line 30.

8	Advertising	8		19	Pension and profit-sharing plans	19	
9	Bad debts from sales or services (see page C-3) . .	9		20	Rent or lease (see page C-4):		
				a	Vehicles, machinery, and equipment .	20a	
10	Car and truck expenses (see page C-3)	10		b	Other business property . .	20b	
11	Commissions and fees . .	11		21	Repairs and maintenance . .	21	
12	Depletion	12		22	Supplies (not included in Part III) .	22	
				23	Taxes and licenses	23	
13	Depreciation and section 179 expense deduction (not included in Part III) (see page C-3) .	13		24	Travel, meals, and entertainment:		
				a	Travel	24a	
14	Employee benefit programs (other than on line 19) . .	14		b	Meals and entertainment .		
15	Insurance (other than health) .	15		c	Enter 50% of line 24b subject to limitations (see page C-4) .		
16	Interest:						
a	Mortgage (paid to banks, etc.) .	16a		d	Subtract line 24c from line 24b .	24d	
b	Other	16b		25	Utilities	25	
17	Legal and professional services	17		26	Wages (less employment credits) .	26	
18	Office expense	18		27	Other expenses (from line 48 on page 2)	27	

28	**Total expenses** before expenses for business use of home. Add lines 8 through 27 in columns . ►	28	
29	Tentative profit (loss). Subtract line 28 from line 7	29	
30	Expenses for business use of your home. Attach **Form 8829**	30	
31	**Net profit or (loss).** Subtract line 30 from line 29.		
	• If a profit, enter on **Form 1040, line 12,** and ALSO on **Schedule SE, line 2** (statutory employees, see page C-5). Estates and trusts, enter on Form 1041, line 3.	31	
	• If a loss, you MUST go on to line 32.		
32	If you have a loss, check the box that describes your investment in this activity (see page C-5).		
	• If you checked 32a, enter the loss on **Form 1040, line 12,** and ALSO on **Schedule SE, line 2** (statutory employees, see page C-5). Estates and trusts, enter on Form 1041, line 3.	**32a** ☐ All investment is at risk.	
	• If you checked 32b, you MUST attach **Form 6198.**	**32b** ☐ Some investment is not at risk.	

For Paperwork Reduction Act Notice, see Form 1040 instructions. Cat. No. 11334P Schedule C (Form 1040) 1996

Value of Business/Personal Deductions						
If your marginal income tax rate is...	15%	28%	31% (income up to $65,400)	31% (income over $65,400)	36%	39.6%
And your combined state/ local income tax rate is . . .	6%	6%	6%	6%	6%	6%
Your personal tax rate is . . .	21%	34%	37%	37%	42%	46%
A $1,000 deductible personal expenses, after taxes, costs	$790	$660	$630	$630	$580	$540
Your marginal business tax rate is . . .	34%	46%	49%	39%	44%	48%
The same expense, deducted from your business, after taxes, costs	$660	$540	$510	$610	$560	$520

SECRET: *You always will save more in taxes by making an expense deductible against your business, but the true worth of a business deduction is a complex calculation that could give even a spreadsheet a headache. First, here's an overly simple chart that shows roughly how much a business and a personal deduction are worth in tax savings at various brackets. After you enjoy the ease with which this chart allows you to guesstimate your tax picture, note the qualifiers that follow it. It's a handy guide, but don't bring it to an IRS audit with you!*

Note that the higher tax brackets can be easier on your wallet than the lower tax brackets. So that 31 percent bracket is the worst or the best deal of all, because the 12.4 percent that is the Social Security portion of your self-employment tax drops out after you've reached $62,700 in income. So at the higher brackets, the self-employment tax isn't as much of a hit. It amounts to only the 2.9 percent Medicare tax, which doesn't phase out at any income level. And at the higher brackets, the deduction you get when half of your self-employment tax is subtracted from personal taxable income is worth more. This all gets especially rocky in the 31 percent tax bracket. It's a few thousand dollars into that bracket when the Social Security tax gets dropped. So if you barely squeeze up into the 31 percent bracket, your marginal business tax rate is likely to be the worst anyone pays.

Enough caveats! You can see that there is no tax bracket at which a personal deduction is worth more than a business deduction. Nevertheless, you may choose to beef up your personal income for nontax reasons—so you can maximize retirement savings or look good to a bank loan officer. But at any bracket, the more business deductions you can swing, the lower your taxes will be.

Of course, in many expense categories, you don't have the choice of deducting it as a business or personal deduction. Either it's a business expense, or you can't deduct it at all. This chapter lays out what you need to know to claim every possible deduction and do it right. Get the big green tax machine working for you, instead of against you.

Get Help

If you are reading this book, chances are you are a do-it-yourself type who may even enjoy preparing your own tax return. But even for you, it will pay to hire a pro to give you pointers.

To find the right tax professional for you, find one whose business is about the same size as yours. That's where you'll stand the best chance of finding a tax preparer with solid expertise and the time to give you the attention you need and deserve. Seek a tax preparer who handles other businesses that are like yours. If you are having your taxes prepared, only a CPA, an enrolled agent, or a tax attorney can represent you before the IRS or in tax court.

Avoid preparers who never get audited (too cautious), always get audited (too dangerous), promise refunds (a telltale sign of the preparer who'll pledge anything and deliver headaches and penalties) or are overly dependent on pencils and papers in an era of truly amazing tax-preparation software. And avoid any preparer who claims to know the whole tax code. Remember those 40,500 pages? Nobody knows it all!

A good tax professional can show you where you are light on deductions or where you might be sticking your neck out too far. He or she probably will save you more in taxes than his or her fee.

SECRET: *You'll improve your tax picture if you reverse your tax preparation practices for one year. If you are used to doing your own taxes, hire a professional to review them. If you usually hire them out, do a rough draft yourself, so you can see exactly how your tax picture comes together.*

Guesstimating Estimated Taxes

It's a fact of self-employed life that you'll have to pay estimated taxes on your income. These are due four times a year. For tax year 1998, they must be mailed by April 15, June 15, September 15, and January 15, 1999.

Estimated tax payments substitute for the taxes an employer would otherwise withhold. You can reduce them if you have an employed spouse, by having your spouse have as much as possible withheld from his or her paychecks.

But paying the estimated taxes is no big deal, if you know the rules, and if you're disciplined enough to remember to save the money. You'll have to file a brief Form 1040ES with your payment to the IRS four times a year. And if you have a state income tax, you'll have to do the same thing on the state level.

These are the rules of estimated taxes: By January 15, 1999, you will need to have paid the following to escape penalties:

❑ Ninety percent of your federal tax liability for 1998. Or 100 percent of the federal taxes you paid for 1997. If you earned over $150,000 last year, are married, and you filed jointly (or $75,000 singly), then this figure is 110 percent of last year's income.

SECRET: *If you expect to make more this year than last, just go with that 100 percent of last year's rule. It saves lots of number crunching, and keeps more money in your bank account working for you. Make sure you are saving enough to pay the extra tax on extra income when it comes due next April.*

You also have to weigh your estimated tax payments reasonably, by the income you're receiving. If you are going with the 100 percent of last year's taxes method, divide by four and pay 25 percent in each quarter.

If your income is really erratic, pay in proportion to the income you receive every quarter. The IRS can penalize you if you make buckets of money in the early part of the year, but make the bulk of your estimated taxes toward the end of the year.

If you are filing a Schedule C for your business as part of a joint tax return, the estimated taxes should be paid in the first name on the joint return. So if Fred's name and Social Security number come first on your return, but Betty runs the business, the estimated taxes on the business should be filed under Fred's name and Social Security number, not Betty's. That's because the IRS keeps all filing relative to a single tax return under that one Social Security number. This is important: The IRS once lost $5,000 of mine that way.

COMPUTER SOLUTION:
AN ESTIMATED TAXES SPREADSHEET

You can get a quick fix on your estimated tax situation, and keep an eye on your taxes all year, by setting up the spreadsheet that appears on the following pages. This will keep a running tally of your net income and federal tax liability all year. To set it up, copy the formulas given here. Where I've estimated figures (under income, expenses, deductions, last year's taxes and other taxes withheld), do your best to estimate your own figures.

If you do this quarterly, you can either guesstimate what your annual business income and expenses will be, or take the last quarter's results and extrapolate them to a full year.

For the total taxes, use the tax tables given, which are for 1996, or get a copy of the 1997 schedule from the IRS.

AN ESTIMATED TAXES SPREADSHEET: Formula View (continued)

	A	B
1	**An Estimated Taxes Spreadsheet**	
2		
3	Business Income	39000
4	Business Expenses	9000
5	**Net Business Income**	**=B3–B4**
6		
7	Other family income	27000
8	**Total net family income**	**=B5+B7**
9		
10	Deductions	9500
11	Exemptions	4
12	*2550	=B11*2550
13	Credits	340
14	**Total subtractions**	**=Sum(B10,B12,B13)**
15		
16	**Net taxable income**	**=B8–B14**
17		
18	Total taxes (from table)	=B16*.15
19	SE tax	=B5*.12
20	**Total taxes**	**=B18+B19**
21		
22	You must pay at least	=B20
23	Or	
24	100 percent of last year's taxes	9550
25	**The smaller one:**	**=Min(B22,B24)**
26	Other taxes withheld	4235
27		
28	**Minimum estimated tax payments for the year:**	**=B25–B26**
29	**Quarterly due:**	**=B28/4**
30		

AN ESTIMATED TAXES SPREADSHEET: Data View (continued)

	A	B
1	An Estimated Taxes Spreadsheet	
2		/
3	Business Income	$39,000.00
4	Business Expenses	$9,000.00
5	**Net Business Income**	**$30,000.00**
6		
7	Other family income	$27,000.00
8	**Total net family income**	**$57,000.00**
9		
10	Deductions	$9,500.00
11	Exemptions	4
12	*2550	$10,200.00
13	Credits	$340.00
14	**Total subtractions**	**$20,040.00**
15		
16	**Net taxable income**	**$36,960.00**
17		
18	Total taxes (from table)	$5,544.00
19	SE tax	$3,600.00
20	**Total taxes**	**$9,144.00**
21		
22	You must pay at least	$9,144.00
23	Or	
24	100 percent of last year's taxes	$9,550.00
25	**The smaller one:**	**$9,144.00**
26	Other taxes withheld	$4,235.00
27		
28	**Minimum estimated tax payments for the year:**	**$4,909.00**
29	**Quarterly due:**	**$1,227.00**
30		

Business or Hobby? You're Not Having Too Much Fun, Are You?

Don't think, just because you love what you do, that it isn't a business. Consider the case of Jim Lockwood, a life-long western movie enthusiast. Lockwood's leather reproduction business, Legends in Leather, requires him to travel to western conventions, mingle with his childhood idols, collect western books, videos, and artifacts, and play dress up on a regular basis. "It's like living a childhood dream," says Lockwood.

Nevertheless, it's also like running a business. Lockwood puts in eight-hour days, earns a profit, and takes every legal deduction that's coming to him, including the spurs and cowboy hats. That's because he's careful to run Legends on a business-like basis.

The first tax hurdle many entrepreneurs have to face is proving they are indeed running a business, and not just claiming a costly hobby. If you have a business, you can take tax losses in bad years and write off equipment in a hurry. If you are making some money on what's essentially a hobby, you can't take any losses and may find your entire tax return challenged.

If your hobby is starting to eat up your life, it might be worth turning it into a business. Here's how Josh did it. Josh was a photographer just for fun. Over the years, he invested thousands of dollars in equipment, and started making money around the edges. Last year he made $3,000 shooting weddings and family portraits for his friends. This year he wants to get a new computer and Adobe Photoshop, which is software capable of manipulating images onscreen. And he wants to buy a new, large format camera.

More important, he wants to quit his evening job at the bookstore, where he earned $28,000 last year, and be a professional photographer. He expects to spend $12,000 before he is done buying his equipment, promoting his business, and getting a pager. About $8,000 of his expenses will be equipment, the rest would be regular business expenses, like travel, supplies, and phone bills.

If Josh were to continue calling his photography a hobby, he would declare the $3,000 as "other income" on the front page of his 1040 form. And he would deduct $3,000 worth of his expenses as hobby-related. But that deduction would be valid as a miscellaneous deduction on his 1040 only to the extent it exceeded 2 percent of his adjusted gross income. In Josh's case, that would give him a deduction of $2,360. His net taxable income would be $640, and he would have lost $9,000 in deductions.

chapter

4

Business or Hobby? You're Not Having Too Much Fun, Are You?

Now let's say Josh decides he is in business. He doesn't even have to quit his other job. His $3,000 goes on a Schedule C, as do most of his expenses. He can deduct up to $3,200 in equipment expenses the first year by depreciating his equipment and save the remaining $4,800 to deduct in following years. And he can deduct the additional $4,000 in regular business expenses too. His net business income would be a negative (–$5,800), which would reduce his taxable bookstore earnings.

His total federal tax as a hobby: $2,998.00

As a business: $2,032.00

Net savings: $966.00

If at all possible, be a business.

How? The key to being a legitimate business in the eyes of the IRS is in having a profit motive, not in making a profit. To prove that he is a business, Josh must keep careful records and demonstrate that he has marketed himself as a professional photographer, acted in a businesslike manner, and tried to make money at it. If he is submitting photos to publications, he should even save his sheaf of rejection letters: They are proof he is marketing himself as a business.

The IRS understands that people often spend more than they earn in the early years of building a business. But for obvious reasons, the Feds frown on side businesses that generate large losses along with psychic rewards for taxpayers, especially when those taxpayers have other sizable sources of income and the side businesses are things like horse breeding, sailboat renting, and antique dealing.

SECRET: *There's a safe harbor. If your business has been profitable in three out of the last five years, you don't have to prove you are a business. The IRS has to prove you aren't. But they can if you aren't legit. Don't take $40,000 in losses for two years and claim a $125 profit in the third and think you are home free.*

Historically, the courts have been lenient in this area. A famous case from the 1970s still provides the basis for tax law in the hobby versus business decision. Gloria Churchman was an artist who had been painting, sculpting, and exhibiting for twenty years without ever making a profit. She traveled nationwide to meet gallery owners, lectured about art, set up her own gallery, printed posters and books, and happily wrote off all of those expenses, often several thousand dollars a year. She even sold a few paintings and posters, reporting no income for 1970 and 1971, and income of $250 for 1972.

But Churchman kept trying to make money, and she kept meticulous records. And in 1977, the U.S. Tax Court was persuaded. "It is certainly conceivable in our view that she may someday sell enough of her paintings to enable her to recoup the losses, which have meanwhile been sustained in her intervening years," the court held, citing Churchman's high-energy marketing of her work and her qualifications as a locally recognized art lecturer.

Prove It!

To determine whether an individual activity is a legitimate business or not, the IRS uses these nine points to evaluate the seriousness of your intent:

1. Whether you carry on the activity in a business-like manner.
2. Whether the time and effort you spend on the activity indicate you intend to make it profitable.
3. Whether you are depending on income from the activity for your livelihood.
4. Whether your losses from the activity are due to circumstances beyond your control or are normal in the start-up phase of your type of business.
5. Whether you change your methods of operation in an attempt to improve the profitability of the activity.
6. Whether the activity makes a profit in some years, and how much.
7. Whether you, or your advisers, have the knowledge needed to carry on the activity as a successful business.
8. Whether you were previously successful in making a profit in similar activities.
9. Whether you can expect to make a future profit from the appreciation of the assets used in the activity.

You don't have to meet all nine points to prove you are a business. It's more a loosely defined smell test. Keep records of all of your expenses, and of your failures, too. A sheaf of rejection letters can prove a would-be writer really is marketing himself or herself as a business.

*S*ECRET: *Many tax professionals believe the IRS has a secret tenth point: the degree of satisfaction you take in your work. In other words, if you are having too much fun, maybe your work is a hobby and not a business. Maryland tax advisor Susan Dawson specializes in artists and writers, and frequently has to explain the serious component of her clients' work to IRS auditors. She puts herself in their place: What if you had to spend forty hours a week in a little cubicle, nitpicking returns of people who play with paint. Who wouldn't be a little resentful of Josh, who writes off more trips than the IRS agent has time to take?*

The Home Office Hurdle: Worth Jumping!

When you take the home office deduction, are you waving a red flag in the eyes of the Internal Revenue Service examiners? And if you are, what does that mean?

For years, tax sages have warned that claiming a home office increases your chances of being audited, and the IRS has done its part to justify that paranoia. The courts have tightened eligibility, so even if you have a home office for your business, you may not be able to deduct it.

But if you can, you should. Forget your fear of the red flag. In fact, the IRS has found more fertile targets for hidden tax dollars. And the number of home office workers has swelled to the point where it's no longer like fishing in a barrel for the IRS. The barrel has been washed away by a tsunami of as many as 20 million home-based businesses. Most of them are legitimate and a waste of the tax auditor's time.

There are, however, some apocryphal stories about the thoroughness of home office auditors that are almost funny. One making the rounds tells of an auditor who found personal mail in the wastebasket of a home office and disallowed the office because it wasn't used "exclusively" for business. In fact, some friendly auditors even allow de minimis personal use. But we're talking really minimis: like having to walk through your office to get to another room in your house.

*S*ECRET: *The IRS examiner almost never comes to your home office as a first step. Chances are he or she will write a letter, asking for photos if the question is the exclusivity of your home office. You have plenty of time to move that sofa bed before they come calling.*

A HOME BASIS/HOME OFFICE SPREADSHEET

Keep track of every penny you put into your home, whether you take the home office deduction or not. If you take the home office deduction, you'll need these numbers to figure your write-off. If you don't, you'll still need to know how much you've spent on your home so you can reduce your taxes when you eventually sell it.

Your *home basis* is the total amount spent on the permanent structure that is your home and land. It includes the amount you paid for the home and improvements such as additions, new heaters, renovations, and some permanent landscaping. It doesn't include temporary fix-ups, like a paint job, a summer garden, or curtains you can take with you.

When you sell your home, you will have to figure your taxable capital gain by subtracting your home basis from your selling price. The higher your basis is, the lower your taxes will be down the road and the lower your taxes will be now, if you are depreciating a portion of your home for a home office.

The next spreadsheet tracks your home basis for your final sale and does the calculations necessary for your home office deduction. You can copy the formulas, and find the fixed numbers from your own life. Note that I've pasted example values in column C all the way down, just to show you how the spreadsheet works. Save your receipts, with numbers corresponding to the ones listed in column D, and you'll always be able to justify your home investment to the IRS.

Note the following:

- You have to subtract the land value of your property to figure the home office deduction.

- Cell B4: Derive the land percentage of your home basis by checking your real estate tax assessment form. Divide your land value by your total assessed value to get the percentage.

- Cell B7: Divide the square footage of your home office by the square footage of your house to get this percentage.

- Cell B8: Use IRS instructions with form 4562, Depreciation and Amortization, to find the right depreciation percentage for your situation

- Cell A16: Remember to subtract depreciation deductions you've already taken from your basis total.

HOME BASIS/HOME OFFICE SPREADSHEET: Formula View (continued)

	A	B	C	D
1	A Home Basis Spreadsheet			
2				
3	Total Basis	=Sum(C12:C101)		
4	Land Percentage	.28		
5	Land Reduction	=B3*B4		
6	Net Building Basis	=B3–B5		
7	Prorated Home Office Portion	=B6*.18		
8	Depreciate by Table			
9				
10	Home Basis Activity	Date	Cost	Record No.
11				
12	Initial Purchase	04/01/94	125000	1
13	New Fence	04/27/95	1100	457
14	Kitchen Redo	06/15/95	17000	332335
15	Replace roof	07/15/95	3000	24
16	Less 1995 depreciation	04/15/96	(1225)	37
17	Replace back door	05/15/96	325	2256

HOME BASIS/HOME OFFICE SPREADSHEET: Data View (*continued*)

	A	B	C	D
1	A Home Basis Spreadsheet			
2				
3	Total Basis	$145,200.00		
4	Land Percentage	0.28		
5	Land Reduction	$40,656.00		
6	Net Building Basis	$104,544.00		
7	Prorated Home Office Portion	$18,817.92		
8	Depreciate by Table			
9				
10	Home Basis Activity	Date	Cost	Record No.
11				
12	Initial Purchase	04/01/94	$125,000.00	1
13	New Fence	04/27/95	$1,100.00	457
14	Kitchen Redo	06/15/95	$17,000.00	332335
15	Replace roof	07/15/95	$3,000.00	24
16	Less 1995 depreciation	04/15/96	($1,225.00)	37
17	Replace back door	05/15/96	$325.00	2256

Proving It

Qualifying for the home office deduction became more difficult in 1993, when the Supreme Court disqualified the home office deductions claimed by Nader Soliman, a Gaithersburg, Maryland, anesthesiologist. Soliman's home office was used exclusively for his business, and it was the only place he had to set up appointments, bill patients, and keep records. But the nature of Soliman's work meant that it had to be performed away from the office. He couldn't very well anesthetize someone at home who was going to operated on at a hospital ten miles away, could he?

The court upheld the IRS's narrow view that Soliman's "principal" place of business was not his home office; it was the hospital operating rooms where he plied his trade.

Soliman was out of luck, and with him are all of the carpenters, photographers, computer consultants, and others who do what they do in the field, instead of in the office. As this book goes to press, there is legislation in Congress that would override the Soliman decision, but it hasn't passed yet.

To legitimize your qualifications for the home office deduction, you need to keep your office (which can be a room, more than one room, or a clearly defined part of a room) clear of all family or personal use.

*S*ECRET: *If you take work home from a salaried position and do it in your home office, that puts the kibosh on your home office deduction. Doug Perreault, a Florida CPA, has gone so far as to tell clients to keep their computer on a rolling cart to pull it out to do nonbusiness stuff and bring it back in for business uses. That works, but then you can't deduct your whole computer. A better answer is to get a second computer for the personal use.*

If you fail to qualify because you do a lot of work in the field, you can try to bring more work home, reorganize your business to spend more time there, or make your home office the official place where you meet with your clients and colleagues.

*S*ECRET: *Late last year, Congress eased up slightly on the home office deduction for people who use their home offices to store inventories. Now home-based workers who don't otherwise qualify for the deduction—like photographers who do the bulk of their work away from the office—can still deduct the space they use for slides and negatives. Those people who spend many hours on the road selling can deduct the space used to stash their wares. This change is effective for 1996 tax returns.*

ENTREPRENEUR'S ANGST: ARE YOU A TARGET?

Oh, probably. The IRS figured out a long time ago that people with businesses, especially side businesses, and especially cash side businesses, could hide income, take wildly inflated deductions, and cheat on their taxes far more easily than the average Joe or Jane Paycheck. That's why self-employed taxpayers have a higher chance of being audited than do people without businesses.

If you file a Schedule C, your chances of getting audited are as high as one in twenty-five, depending upon your income. Only one of every 125 non-schedule C taxpayers go under the scope. What's more, the IRS has gotten smarter in two different ways. It has started a market segment specialization project, which focuses on fraud-heavy businesses and attempts to learn everything it can about them. And it has a new "economic reality" focus that aims at hidden income instead of phony deductions. So beware: if your tax forms show you earn $23,000 a year, but you live in Beverly Hills, drive a Lexus, and have a second house on Maui; the IRS will be on your case.

Auditors are getting smarter about using inductive reasoning to guess how much you really make based on the lifestyle you live. And they can learn plenty about your lifestyle by examining bank returns, vehicle registration records, and real estate tax information.

 *S*ECRET: *You can trip yourself up by showing a pittance in income but large amounts for lifestyle write-offs like the home mortgage deduction or real estate taxes. If you get a significant amount in non-taxable income—gifts, an inheritance, or a loan payback—document it with your tax return to avoid those raised eyebrows and intensive questions.*

Once the IRS decides to administer an economic reality audit, be careful. Most tax advisors recommend that the taxpayer just not go at all. The tax advisor is in a better position to say "I don't know" to the lifestyle questions, which can go like this:

- What is the largest amount of cash you had at any time in 1994?
- What's your educational background?
- How many cars do you have? What is your monthly payment?

ENTREPRENEUR'S ANGST (*continued*)

- Where is your safe deposit box?
- What kind of home improvements did you make this year?
- Did you lend any money in 1994, or receive loan repayments?

Even if you are Mr. or Ms. Honesty, this is a lot to remember and reconstruct two or three years after the fact. Do what you can when you file your return to make sure it isn't an eyebrow-raiser, but not to the point of ignoring legitimate deductions.

As for those Market Segment Specialization Project auditors, they know a lot about you if you run or are in one of the following businesses which the IRS has identified as abuse-laden:

- Architecture firm
- Law firm
- Auto body and repair shop
- Beauty and barber shop
- Bed and breakfast establishments
- Entertainment industry
- Farming
- Fishing
- Food vending
- Gasoline retailing
- Mortuary and cemetery
- Restaurant
- Taxi cab driving
- Trucking

The IRS is on to many of the tricks of these trades. Beauticians will be asked to show appointment books, for example, and the IRS may interview other stylists in your area to ask about average tips. Bed and breakfast owners who spend all year traveling on antiquing and "research" junkets can find their write-offs limited.

ENTREPRENEUR'S ANGST (*continued*)

The good news about the Market Segment Specialization Project is that it's no secret. The IRS has published a series of audit guides for its examiners. You can get a copy of the guide for your business and learn what they're looking for by contacting the IRS.

The bottom line on entrepreneurial audits is this: Your chances of getting audited are higher, but that doesn't make your tax return any less legitimate. Document all of your expenses, note any abnormalities about your situation, and don't worry. If you do get picked for audit, you'll have the paperwork to prove your position.

How Much Money Are We Talking About?

If you claim the home office deduction, it can cut your annual income tax bill by $1,000 or more, because it enables you to deduct from your business income a portion of your rent or your mortgage, your heating, cooling, electric and water bills, and a portion of your home's actual cost.

Once you claim a home office, you can deduct money you spend to spruce it up—paint, wallpaper, carpets, and lamps. You can even depreciate home improvements that are business-related, if for instance you built cabinetry along one wall to hold your brochures and supplies.

And declaring a home office can also get you lots of additional automobile mileage write-offs. Commuting costs from your home to your office are not deductible. But the costs of driving from your home office to your client's business are.

SECRET: *If you're rebuilding your office, use stand-alone products instead of built-ins whenever possible, suggests Doug Perreault. A freestanding cabinet can be written off in one year, as long as you stay under the $17,500 write-off limit, or depreciated over seven years. A built-in cabinet will have to be depreciated over forty years, because it will be considered real estate.*

SECRET: *Be creative! Jeff (fake name, real story) wrote off many of the renovation costs of his 100-year-old Victorian home, by moving his home office regularly. He would move his office into one room, fix it up, paint it, decorate it, write off expenses, and then move his office into the next room.*

Home Office Deduction Checklist

If you are claiming a home office, get the most out of it. Make sure you take every one of these deductions that fits:

- ❏ Fix-up costs to get a new office ready, like plastering and painting.
- ❏ Decorating costs like wallpaper and carpets, curtains, and lamps.
- ❏ Your rent, if you rent.
- ❏ For homeowners, a prorated portion of your mortgage interest.
- ❏ Depreciation on your house.
- ❏ A prorated portion of your gas, electric, and water bills.
- ❏ A prorated portion of your homeowner's insurance.
- ❏ A prorated portion of your condo fees.
- ❏ A prorated portion of your real estate taxes.
- ❏ A prorated portion of some of your home maintenance costs, like roof repair or a new heating system that benefit your home office.

SECRET: *Some of the home office deductions may be deductible elsewhere on your tax forms anyway—you can take real estate taxes and mortgage interest off of your 1040 form. But, remember that 46 percent figure! A $3,000 write-off on your 1040 will save you $1,020. But in your business, it will save you $1,380.*

But Wait!

There's one catch that might make you less interested in taking the home office deduction. Current law requires that if you are claiming a home office deduction and you sell your house, you have to "recapture" all of the home office depreciation you've claimed and pay taxes on it. You can't just roll it over into the value of your next house or offset it with the capital gains exclusion that older homeowners get.

But you still might find the write-off worthwhile. It allows you to retain use of the money for quite a while before you have to face those taxes. And the tax rate on that recaptured depreciation is capped at 25 percent. This is a particularly complex part of tax law, so if you're approaching the sale of your house, talk to a tax pro. There are some circumstances where you may not have to recapture any depreciation you took before May 7, 1997, when the tax law went into effect.

COMPUTER SOLUTION:
THAT TERRIFIC TAX SOFTWARE

You can afford to ignore a lot of the work in this chapter if you are willing to work with the tax software on the market today. Intuit is the market leader with its Turbo Tax and MacInTax Products. Others are CA-Simply Tax and Kiplinger's Tax Cut. You can buy any one for under $40, and it will take almost all of the work out of taxes.

All of these programs will calculate your home office deduction, remind you of write-offs you might have forgotten, figure depreciation, tell you how much to pay in estimated taxes, and, of course, fill out and even file your forms for you. Turbo Tax and MacInTax come on CD-ROMs that also offer substantive personal and business tax advice. I am hooked on MacInTax myself.

 SECRET: *It's worth using one of these programs all year, even if you pay someone else to do your taxes. You can easily change a figure and play what-if games with your tax picture.*

Its important to understand the tax aspects of your business life so you can structure your income and expenses to minimize your taxes. But before taxes, comes income. In the next chapter, you'll learn how to maximize yours. The following screens are from Kiplinger's TaxCut.

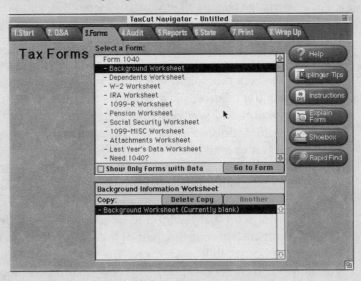

THAT TERRIFIC TAX SOFTWARE *(continued)*

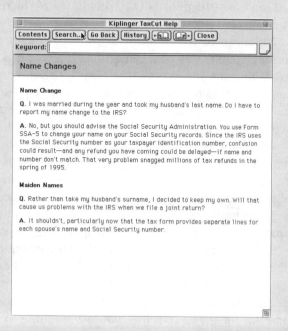

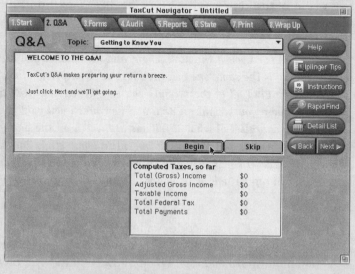

Equipment

Clearly, the computer, copier, cabinet, and clock you use in your business are legitimate expenses that should be deducted against your business earnings. But how do you do it?

Welcome to the wonderful world of depreciation! The concept of depreciation is this: You can deduct the cost of a piece of equipment, but over the years you actually are able to use the equipment, not all at once. Tax law writers have classified equipment by the number of years of useful life it has. There are three-, five-, seven-, and nine-year classes. They actually believe a computer will last five years, for example.

When you depreciate equipment, you have to use the IRS formulas for determining how fast you write them off, which depends on the kind of equipment, when you started using it for business, and what percentage of it you use for business. There are many good tax books that explain depreciation; and even better, all of the major tax preparation software programs will do it for you. So I'll spare you the details here.

Except to note the following: The kind of equipment that is fun to use, like video cameras, computers, and cellular phones, tend to be listed by the IRS as deserving of special scrutiny. If you want to depreciate these items, you have to make sure you use them more than 50 percent of the time for business, and that you will continue to use them more than 50 percent of the time for business for the years the IRS thinks that equipment should have a useful life.

*S*ECRET: *Even if the desk, chair, and file cabinet you are using for business today is the same one you used last week for personal use, you still can write them off. Find all of the receipts you can. When you can't find a receipt, document where you bought an item and how much you paid for it. Then get a reasonable appraisal of what the items are worth on the day you convert them to business use. If you're turning an entire home study into a business office, it might be worth just bringing in an estate appraiser to add it all up for you. Then you can write it off as you would any other equipment you were buying.*

That Lovely Section 179

There's a piece of tax code, called Section 179, that allows small businesses to treat depreciable equipment as a current expense, up to an annual limit of $18,000 for 1997. It allows you to write off that much equipment in the year that you buy it instead of calculating its depreciable and deductible percentages. Thanks to this provision, you probably won't even have to worry about all of that depreciation stuff, especially if you are in a service business that buys only a limited amount of equipment every year. Thanks to this provision, you can save thousands of dollars in taxes and almost as many pieces of paper. Remember that 46 percent? Use Section 179 and you'll only pay $3,240 for that $6,000 computer set up.

There's more good news. Just before it left town last year, Congress upped the amounts you can deduct under Section 179. Here's the new phased in limits:

- ❏ For tax year 1996, you can deduct up to $17,500
- ❏ For 1997, the limit is $18,000
- ❏ For 1998, the limit is $18,500
- ❏ For 1999, the limit is $19,000
- ❏ For 2000, the limit is $19,500
- ❏ For 2001 and 2002, the limit is $24,000
- ❏ For 2003, the limit is $25,000

But remember this: The 179 deduction covers the entire tax return. So if you have one Schedule C business and your spouse has another, that $18, 000 limit has to cover both of you. Your 179 deduction is limited, too, by the amount of money you make. You can't take more off in 179 than you're putting in in gross revenues.

SECRET: *Invest in a second computer. Keep one clean and all business, which is important for your deduction, but is also for the security of your business data, your own professionalism, and piece of mind. Use the second computer for the personal or family purposes, and know that it is available as a back-up computer should your business machine get sick.*

The Car

I know someone—heck, we all probably know someone like this—who gets a spiffy new car every two years. He shuttles his kids around in it, takes family vacations in it, and winks if I ask about the expense. "Heck, I just get the business to buy it," he says.

Is this possible? Yes. Legal? Maybe, depending on the way it's set up. Here's how you can set it up to get the most for your mileage.

It's All Business!

It's very easy, especially if you work out of a home office, to justify many of your car trips as having a business purpose.

- ❏ If you drive around to visit all of your clients, or even if you do work at their offices, it's deductible.
- ❏ If you run to the grocery to buy milk, bread, eggs, and a new box of envelopes for your company, it's a business trip.
- ❏ If you take a family vacation, and stop a few times on the way to visit prospects, the mileage is most likely deductible.

Claim every mile that you can for your company.

Keep a Mileage Log

The simplest way to justify your auto expenses is to keep a mileage log. At the beginning of the year, put a fresh little notebook or clipboard on your dashboard and write your car's current mileage on page one. Then every time you go anywhere that you can construe a business purpose, record the starting and ending miles, the total miles driven, and the business purpose of the trip.

SECRET: *Keeping a mileage log in your car makes deducting mileage easier, but it isn't mandatory. The IRS has also accepted reconstructed records based on calendars or other records. But it is more work. And don't fret if you've been lazy about your log. The IRS allows you to extrapolate a month or two of typical driving into a twelve-month deduction.*

At the end of the year, write the year's closing mileage at the bottom of the entries and put the book with the rest of your tax records. Figure out your total miles and your business miles and calculate the percent of total miles that you drive for business.

Once you have that number, you can chose from two methods of deducting your expenses.

Either Take the Mileage Deduction . . .

The most straightforward, easiest way to deduct the business use of your car is to take a mileage allowance. For tax year 1998, the IRS allows a .325 per-mile deduction. Add up all of the miles in your log, multiply by 0.325, and that's your mileage deduction.

There are a few conditions under which you can't take a mileage allowance and must instead figure actual expenses for your automobile deduction. You can't take mileage if you lease the car, or if more than one car is used in your business at the same time.

If you take the mileage allowance, you still can deduct the external costs of driving, like tolls and parking fees. And you can deduct the business portion of the interest you pay on your car loan as well as the business portion of the sales taxes you pay on a new car. Prorate the business portion by the percentage of business miles you drive.

. . . Or Deduct Actual Expenses

If you're willing to do a bit more work, you can probably get a larger deduction by figuring your actual auto expenses instead. Actual expenses—which include the cost of the car and everything you spend on it—tend to come out higher, unless you have a car that's very inexpensive to run.

Deducting actual expenses is, however, much more complicated than taking the allowance. You have to maintain painstaking records of all the money you spend on your car—gasoline, tires, insurance, tune-ups, and the like. This can be made easier if you pay for all car-related expenses with a separate business credit card or checking account. And you have to learn to depreciate your car, using a complicated series of calculations that we'll get to in a minute.

When you deduct actual expenses, the amount you may deduct is prorated on the basis of your business use of the vehicle. If you use a car 60 percent for your business and 40 percent for yourself, based on mileage, you may deduct 60 percent of your actual expenses.

The more business mileage you have, the less valuable certain fixed costs become. Whether you travel a little or a lot, your depreciation and insurance won't change. Say, for example, that your prorated business share of your insurance is $700—at .325 a mile, it would take 2,154 miles of business driving to best that.

If you're willing to keep all the records and do all the math, you might want to figure your deductions both ways and decide which way to go. But choose carefully: It's twice as complicated and costly (and in some cases illegal) to switch methods once you've started using one.

SECRET: *The less you drive, the more worthwhile it is to take actual expenses. A prorated portion of your insurance, tags, and car's underlying value is likely to beat the .325-a-mile plan. If you're more inclined to keep an old car forever, like some book authors we know, you might find it more worthwhile to take mileage.*

Auto Depreciation and the Luxury Limit

If you are taking the actual costs, the key to the biggest auto deductions is the money you spend to buy the car. Tax laws allow you to write off the car's value over time, as wear and tear makes it worth less. If you use it mostly for business, you may be allowed to accelerate depreciation—write off the car more quickly than its value actually declines. In other cases, you can take only a straight-line method of depreciations, in which you divide your basis in the car (roughly, the amount you paid for it) by the number of years in its useful life and deduct that amount every year for the life of the car.

Sometimes, you'll find it worth taking a Section 179 deduction, a move that allows businesses to deduct the full cost of their equipment (up to $18,000) in the year that it is bought and first used in business.

You can determine which depreciation method to use on the basis of your business-use percentage. If you use your car less than 50 percent for business, you must use the straight-line depreciation. If you use the car 50 percent or more in business, you can opt for an accelerated depreciation.

All of the depreciation methods are constrained by the luxury car cap, which limits eligible deductions. This provision was originally written by Congress to eliminate taxpayer underwriting of luxury automobiles, but as auto prices have gone up, the IRS's concept of luxury has gone down.

Assuming that you use your car 100 percent for your business and choose to depreciate it, you can never take more in a year than the following preset amounts, which are adjusted each year for inflation: You can't deduct more than $3,060 in the first year of use. In the second year your limit is $4,900 and in the third year, $2,950. In each of the next two years, you can deduct $1,775.

These figures are for cars used 100 percent in business. If there is partial business use, the luxury car limits must be prorated by the same percentage. So in the first year of depreciating a car that you use 60 percent for business, you can't take more than $1,836 ($3,060 x .6), no matter how costly a car it is.

The Trips

And, finally, for that tax advice you've been waiting for: How can you go to the Bahamas on the business?

Trips are tricky. You are allowed to have fun on a business trip, just not too much fun. Think of it like this: If you went to Florida for a week to take the kids to Disney World and see your mother, and stopped off on the way to take a client to lunch, you'd be able to deduct the lunch, or 50 percent of it anyway. If you went to Florida for a convention and took your mother to lunch, you can deduct the trip, and 50 percent of your lunch, but not your mother's. If you went to a convention at Disney World, and your family explored the Magic Kingdom while you worked, you could write off the cost of a single hotel room, your own airline ticket (or the car trip for everyone), all of your costs, but none of your family's. And if you went to the Magic Kingdom after your day's meeting was done, you might run into Jiminy Cricket, who would tell you to always let your conscience be your guide.

*S*ECRET: *Tax laws treat international travel differently because it's, well, different. The rules are designed to prevent you from using your business as an excuse to deduct a continental vacation, but they actually allow a fair amount of leeway on international trips. To qualify for a full deduction on your travel costs, you must limit your personal time on an international trip to less than 25 percent of your time abroad, and you must stay fewer than eight days. You can deduct your total airfare without prorating it.*

Once a trip is deductible, it's really deductible. That means, while you are on the road, you can deduct the following, so save the receipts:

- ❏ Meals: Only 50 percent of meals are deductible on the road, just as only 50 percent of business meals are deductible.
- ❏ Taxis, buses, and car rentals
- ❏ Shipping
- ❏ Lodging
- ❏ Dry cleaning and laundry
- ❏ Phone calls
- ❏ Tips
- ❏ Incidentals, like newspapers and computer rental fees

*S*ECRET: *There's a legal way to avoid saving all your meal receipts. If you can really prove you went to Chicago for four days by showing travel tickets, you can use the IRS's own meal allowance figures for how much money you probably spent eating there. This approach only works if you are the type to skip meals and eat cheap; the levels are low when compared with typical expense account dinners. For example, the IRS daily meal allowance for Chicago is $38. As with any other meal deduction, you're only allowed to take half of that. And once you've decided to use the standard allowance, you've got to stick with it all year. You can't use both methods in the same year.*

The Many Miscellaneous Money Savers

Don't let fear of an audit cheat you out of the many deductions you'll have coming to you. Here are some more to remember.

The Retirement Account

One of the biggest breaks of self-employment are the tax-deferred retirement accounts available to you. Remember to deduct them at tax time. All the details on this topic are covered in Chapter 15.

Ya Gotta Eat, Right? And Other Yummy Deductions

Go out to lunch once a month with a colleague. Share tips, advice, and insight about the market. You take him or her one month, he or she can take you the next. That's legitimate and deductible, up to the 50 percent limit that applies to meals.

Have a party for all of your clients. Even if it's at your house and you cook the food. That's deductible, too.

Spend a lot of time doing market research on the Internet? Deductible!

Remember, there's a business purpose for so much of what you do and so much of what you can do. Most entrepreneurs err by missing deductions, not by taking too many. We forget to keep receipts, or worry that an item will raise a red flag.

*S*ECRET: *You really don't have to keep a slip of paper for every cab ride you take. The IRS now accepts miscellaneous deductions like meals, cab rides, newspapers, and the like under $75 without a receipt. You should still document each expense and its business purpose in your checkbook, accounting program, calendar, or recordbook, however.*

The "Deductions Galore" sidebar lists many of the deductions you might overlook. But it's not exhaustive, so go for the gusto and remember the golden rule: When in doubt, deduct.

Don't Worry, Be Profitable

Don't be discouraged by all of the tax trappings of this chapter. Once you've worked through them once, you won't have to revisit many of them again. And you can always hire a pro to steer you through the whole mess.

But try hard to understand the concepts of how your business will be taxed. Then you can structure your income and expenses to minimize those taxes.

DEDUCTIONS GALORE!

Don't lose a single deduction. Here are some of the items you can be taking off your business:

- **All those supplies.** Your work and personal life may be integrated, but your stapler and tape dispenser shouldn't be.
- **Meals.** Business meals are 50 percent deductible, on the theory that you have to eat anyway.
- **Your home office.** Don't let a red flag rumor deny you this lucrative deduction.
- **Office furnishings.** If you originally bought your desk and lamp for personal use, but "converted it to business use," find that old receipt! It's depreciable.
- **The pretty stuff.** Posters, rugs, curtains, clocks, and ashtrays, (yech!) and so on.
- **The useful stuff.** Shelves, extension cords, surge suppressers, the office radio.
- **Cleaning fees.** Hire someone to come in and clean your office every week or two. If the person cleans your whole house, prorate the part that is spent on your home office.
- **Computer equipment.** Extra phone service. You can't write off basic phone service if you share a personal and business line. But you can write off the business related extras—call waiting, voice mail, conference calls, and the like.
- **Online charges.** You use the Internet and America Online to network, chat with colleagues, market your skills, and keep in touch. That's a business expense!
- **Interest.** Did you run up your MasterCard buying all of that computer equipment? If it takes a while to pay off, remember that business interest is deductible even if consumer interest isn't.
- **Gifts for clients and colleagues.** Once a year, do you buy a basket of fruit for your best customers? Up to $25 per recipient is deductible.

DEDUCTIONS GALORE! *(continued)*

- **Your good impression.** Do you give speeches or make television appearances for your business? You can deduct payments made to a video trainer, who might tell you what to wear and how to act.

- **Uniforms.** Only if they are really uniforms that you wouldn't wear in real life. That blue shirt the video trainer told you to buy may seem like a uniform, but it isn't.

- **Maintenance.** If you have your fax machine and computer serviced annually, that's deductible. So are replacement toner cartridges.

- **Dues.** Congress did away with the deduction for social clubs, but memberships in professional organizations are still very much a business expense.

- **Conferences.** Make an annual pilgrimage to your professional society's meeting in Florida in February. Definitely deductible!

- **Child care.** Don't make the mistake of thinking you can work while the baby sleeps. And don't forget that you're eligible for the child care credit, even if you work at home.

- **The smarts.** Take a computer course to help you in your business, or continuing education courses so your license remains legit?

- **Health insurance.** Take 45 percent of your health insurance off of your 1040, or hire your spouse and deduct 100 percent from your business. (See Chapter 11.) Note that before it left town in 1997, Congress raised the health insurance write-off for entrepreneurs for the second time in two years. Here's the new schedule by which that deduction will accelerate: This year and in 1999, take 45 percent; in 2000 and 2001 take 50 percent; in 2002 take 60 percent; in 2003 through 2005, take 80 percent; in 2006 take 90 percent; and finally, in 2007, you can start deducting 100 percent of your health insurance premiums off of your 1040 form.

- **The library.** There's no business that isn't made better by having professional reference works around. You can deduct your library of books and CDs as if they are business equipment.

- **Subscriptions.** Whatever you read to keep abreast of your business you can deduct.

DEDUCTIONS GALORE! *(continued)*

- **Cable TV.** Are you a financial advisor who needs to check the stock market regularly and see what the talking heads are saying on CNBC? A musician who spends more time glued to MTV than you should? A writer who monitors CNN compulsively? If you use the cable stations for your business, it's a deduction.

- **Getting there.** If your office is at home, every trip you make away from the office for any business purpose is deductible, whether you travel by car, limo, taxi, or bus. If you go to the grocery to buy a new notebook, and pick up a week's worth of groceries while you're there, call it a business trip.

- **Advertising.** This doesn't mean you have to buy thirty seconds of TV time during the Super Bowl. A business notice in your son's yearbook, an ad in your church directory, shirts for your daughter's softball team all count.

- **Insurance.** Did you bump up your homeowner's policy to cover your business equipment? Deductible!

- **Tax preparation fees.** Do you hire someone to do your personal tax return? Does he or she spend most of the time working up your Schedule C? Be sure to have that itemized when you are billed and deduct the business-related part as a business expense.

- **Overdraft fees, and other bank expenses.** If your income really fluctuates, you might want to sign up for overdraft protection and similar bank services, knowing the annual charges will reduce your taxes.

And remember that taxes don't come first—income does. The next chapter explores the best techniques for maximizing that income. May you be so successful that you are always paying taxes!

YOU MUST REMEMBER THIS: LESSONS FROM CHAPTER 4

- A business deduction is worth more than a personal deduction.
- Every business action you take has a tax consequence; learn them.
- Take every deduction that's coming to you!

5

© Michael Moran 1997

"I am worth top dollar
and I demand top dollar
and won't consider anything less."

What Are You Worth? And How Can You Get It?

In the places where self-employed people hang out—home office forums on CompuServe and America Online, virtual newsgroups on the Internet, and in actual conferences, meetings, and even bars—the debate always gets spirited when talk turns (as it usually does) to money and fee setting.

Two camps emerge quickly. There's the "I am worth top dollar and I demand top dollar and won't consider anything less" camp, and the "I can work cheap because I work fast and use low-paying jobs to fill in between my better-paying clients" group. Both sides are fairly assertive, but only one is right. And that's the top-dollar group.

These people have figured out that in this hyper-competitive marketplace, they need to charge enough to cover the costs of doing business in a professional way. They need to be able to subscribe to appropriate publications to keep up with their field, to take vacations to keep their brains clear and creative, and to spend time marketing their businesses. They also know that they need to charge enough to convince the marketplace that they are worthy. The "I can work cheap" people almost always end up working sixty hours or more a week, just to make ends meet. And those ends sometimes barely graze each other.

SECRET: *Even though high-priced entrepreneurs say they charge top dollar, they don't always. They still cut deals for the clients they really want to keep. But they talk a good game and have figured out the true secret of the marketplace: If you act like you are worth a lot, people will believe you. On average, they earn more and are more successful longer than their colleagues who are always willing to accommodate every client's budget.*

A Tale of Two Writers

I know these two individuals personally. Both are highly competent writers and researchers. Both are self-employed in the same town. Both write the same kinds of commercial copy for the same kinds of clients. It would appear that they are in direct competition with each other, but they aren't.

One, let's call him Jeffrey, started his freelance writing business by advertising his rate at $85 an hour. He spent money setting up a professional computer system that allows him to modem and fax copy to his clients, and marketed to those business clients he thought could afford that $85 rate. He's been profitable since his first year; although occasionally, he takes jobs that work out to less than his stated minimum, he made $75,000 in his third year in business.

The other writer, Joanne, bills out at $15 an hour and can't get enough work to keep busy. She fills in by doing temp work. She doesn't have a computer, because she claims not to make enough money to afford one. She worries about charging more. There are so many writers in town, she's afraid she'll just price herself out of range of a lot of clients.

Probably she would. The lesson Joanne has to learn is that those are clients she'd just as soon not have anyway.

SECRET: *Here's a rash generalization: It's very difficult to make it in any business long-term unless you are charging your clients $50 an hour for your time. You may be able to charge less if you also sell products that you mark up, or you live in some place like Oklahoma City or Casper, Wyoming—deemed by experts as most affordable places to live in America. But if you are going to be long-term competitive and realistic, you have to charge enough to cover more than just your minimal living expenses.*

First, Get The Right Attitude

In a minute, we'll get to the formulas that will allow you to devise an appropriate fee structure. But first, read this to determine if you need an attitude adjustment. The biggest mistake many sole proprietors make, says Bernard Tennenbaum, who founded Fairleigh Dickinson University's Center for Enterpreneurial Studies, is in setting their fees not by what the market will bear, but by the minimum amount they think they need. If you work at home and not in a leased office, if you do all the work yourself and have no employees, if you wear sweatpants every day and don't need to budget for frequent pantyhose replacements, you can "afford" to charge less. But you shouldn't.

We self-employed workers are too often ashamed to charge what we should, because we're having so much fun. We feel a little guilty about it. Some of us, who dropped out of corporate America to live a downsized lifestyle in tune with our ethics, don't feel right charging high fees. Get over it!

If you make more than you need to live on, you can always give your money away. But to build a successful business, you have to act like a successful business, and you have to charge competitive prices.

SECRET: *You don't have to give your clients a discount, just because you're having fun, or not commuting, or wearing comfortable clothes. If it makes you feel better, you could act like you aren't having fun when you prepare estimates!*

Fee-Setting Formulas

So just how do you set those dignified rates? There are many formulas, the one that works for me was devised by my husband, self-employed writer Ken Norkin. When I asked him how he approached rate-setting, he said "YECH," as in Y(ou), the E(nvironment), C(ompetition), and (H)unger.

Fee Setting = YECH

This concept of fee setting provides a basis for an externally driven fee schedule. If you're leaving a business, think about what that business charged for your services. Then figure out what the market will bear by

chapter

5

What Are You Worth? And How Can You Get It?

joining professional groups that conduct earnings surveys; and ask friends who are in similar businesses what they have paid for similar services. Chances are, your colleagues will have formed a local network, perhaps only informally, where they can get together and chew over fees and services. Join, if you can.

Now, let's take YECH letter by letter.

❏ **You:** How much do you need to earn? If you already did a serious personal budget in Chapter 1, you know what number you are shooting at. How much were you worth at your last job? When you are figuring out your "need to earn" number, remember to include insurance costs, self-employment taxes, retirement contributions, overhead like supplies and telephones, and all of the other costs of being in business for yourself. A shortcut is to add between 25 and 33 percent to your target salary to cover such costs. If you want to make $50,000 a year, add another $14,000 or so to cover your expenses, so you'll be aiming at $64,000 a year in gross revenues. Remember that the You part of the equation isn't just about how much you need to make; it's about what you have to offer that's special. Are you the only one in your area who can put someone on the World Wide Web in under a week? Do you have years of experience? Special awards? Contacts or a reputation? These all feed into the fees you can charge.

❏ **Environment:** The underhanded way to factor this is to call your competitors, pretend you're shopping for their services, and find out how much they charge. It's not entirely kosher; a better way is to network. Many old hands are happy to share their numbers, both to help a newcomer get started, and to put a floor on the industry's prices. You can get a lot of pricing ideas online by chatting with colleagues who are too far away to be intimidated by you entering their field. The environment refers to how the economy is doing. Is your service a necessity or a luxury?

❏ **Competition:** How much is out there? And don't forget to consider competition from unexpected places. If you're setting up an accounting business, for example, don't just look around at other tax preparers. Think about how much tax software might eat away at your business. How much are your competitors charging and making? When you use your competitors to set your prices, remember this rule of thumb: Try to put your business in the top half of the range, but not at the very top. Never try to build a business by being the cheapest guy on the block; you'll always lose out on price to the next cheapest guy.

❏ **Hunger:** How bad do you really want this work? This is where you cut your deals. Maybe you've decided that $85 an hour is really where your prices should be set. But a potentially great client—a friend—has asked you to do one project that will net you only $60 an hour. Check your appetite. Will this job do a favor for a friend, bring in better work down the road, fill in a slow month? Maybe you're hungry enough to cut your fees that one time. Maybe not. Judge this on a case-by-case basis.

Billing By The Hour: How Many Hours Can You Bill?

Say you've gone through the preceding steps, and figured out that you want to come out of this year with a $50,000 salary, after you've paid business taxes, overhead, and put money in your retirement account. How much are you going to charge?

Remember that you are going to need at least $64,000 gross to get that net. A really simple way to set your hourly fee is to divide that figure by 1,000. Why? Unless you're an attorney steeped in the large law firm school of billing every minute, at least twice, you're likely to be able to count on only 1,000 billable hours a year. Work it out:

2,080 hours = 40 hours a week, 52 weeks a year

− 100 hours = two and a half weeks vacation

− 80 hours = 10 popular holidays

− 40 hours = one week of sick leave

Now you're down to 1,860 hours.

1,860 hours

− 419 hours = about 20 percent of your time in marketing

− 93 hours = administrative tasks, like reading trade journals, and doing your accounting

− 279 hours = the 15 percent of your time when you're willing to work, but have none

− 58 hours = that 15 minutes a day you'll waste (if you're lucky and disciplined!)

So now you're down to 1,011 hours. Round down to an even 1,000, and that $64,000 target comes out to a billing rate of $64. It's quick, it's easy, and it's close enough when used as a rule of thumb.

chapter

5

What Are You Worth? And How Can You Get It?

COMPUTER SOLUTION: CALCULATING A FAST DAY RATE

Here's a simple spreadsheet that shows you how much you need to charge if you bill by the day. You can vary the spreadsheet to show bigger or smaller profit margins, an optimistic or pessimistic number of days billed, and higher or lower than expected overhead.

First, key in your expected overhead and target annual earnings, in cells B5 and B6. Add them, then in cell B9, divide by the number or days you might expect to bill in a year. (To get the number of billable days, start by assuming you won't work weekends [260 days], will take three weeks off for vacations and illness [245] and will spend about one-third of your time on nonbillable tasks [160 hours].) Guesstimate that you'll do better, and then that you'll do worse.

Add in various profit margins to your minimal daily earnings in cell B11, and you'll see your minimal daily rate. The nine examples here offer an array of profit margins and billing scenarios. But the business owner of this spreadsheet can know that he or she shouldn't charge less than $351 a day and might need as much as $597. Depending on how she makes her bets, she'll know what to charge.

CALCULATING A FAST DAY RATE: Formula View (continued)

	A	B	C	D
1	**Figuring a Quick Day Rate**			
2				
3	Billing 160 days a year			
4		Low profit margin	Midrange margin	Biggest profit margin
5	Annual overhead	9500	9500	9500
6	Target earnings	64000	64000	64000
7				
8	Total	=B5+B6	=C5+C6	=D5+D6
9	Daily earnings	=B8/160	=C8/160	=D8/160
10	Profit margin	=B9*0.1	=C9*0.2	=D9*0.3
11	Daily rate	=B9+B10	=C9+C10	=D9+D10
12				
13	Billing 200 days a year			
14		Low profit margin	Midrange margin	Biggest profit margin
15	Annual overhead	9500	9500	9500
16	Target earnings	64000	64000	64000
17				
18	Total	=B15+B16	=C15+C16	=D15+D16
19	Daily earnings	B18/200	C18/200	D18/200
20	Profit margin	B19*.10	C19*.20	D19*.30
21	Daily rate	=B19+B20	=C19+C20	=D19+D20
22				
23	Billing 230 days a year			
24		Low profit margin	Midrange margin	Biggest profit margin
25	Annual overhead	9500	9500	9500
26	Target earnings	64000	64000	64000
27				
28	Total	=B25+B26	=C25+C26	=D25+D26
29	Daily earnings	=B28/230	=C28/230	=D28/230
30	Profit margin	=B29*0.1	=C29*0.2	=D29*0.3
31	Daily rate	=B29+B30	=C29+C30	=C29+C30
32				

chapter
5

What Are You Worth? And How Can You Get It?

CALCULATING A FAST DAY RATE: Data View (continued)

	A	B	C	D
1	**Figuring a Quick Day Rate**			
2				
3	Billing 160 days a year			
4		Low profit margin	Midrange margin	Biggest profit margin
5	Annual overhead	$9,500.00	$9,500.00	$9,500.00
6	Target earnings	$64,000.00	$64,000.00	$64,000.00
7				
8	Total	$73,500.00	$73,500.00	$73,500.00
9	Daily earnings	$459.38	$459.38	$459.38
10	Profit margin	$45.94	$91.88	$137.81
11	Daily rate	$505.31	$551.25	$597.19
12				
13	Billing 200 days a year			
14		Low profit margin	Midrange margin	Biggest profit margin
15	Annual overhead	$9,500.00	$9,500.00	$9,500.00
16	Target earnings	$64,000.00	$64,000.00	$64,000.00
17				
18	Total	$73,500.00	$73,500.00	$73,500.00
19	Daily earnings	$367.50	$367.50	$367.50
20	Profit margin	$36.75	$73.50	$110.25
21	Daily rate	$404.25	$441.00	$477.75
22				
23	Billing 230 days a year			
24		Low profit margin	Midrange margin	Biggest profit margin
25	Annual overhead	$9,500.00	$9,500.00	$9,500.00
26	Target earnings	$64,000.00	$64,000.00	$64,000.00
27				
28	Total	$73,500.00	$73,500.00	$73,500.00
29	Daily earnings	$319.57	$319.57	$319.57
30	Profit margin	$31.96	$63.91	$95.87
31	Daily rate	$351.52	$383.48	$415.43
32				

Project Billing: A Better Way

Now that you've learned to calculate an hourly fee, you're probably better off quoting it as infrequently as possible. Professionals as diverse as architects, accountants, gardeners, printers, and tile setters have found that they can win more business and earn more money if they quote project fees instead of hourly fees. Why? You can build extra hours into a project fee, and your clients will be none the wiser. And by guaranteeing them a flat cost for a project, you'll be protecting their budget and calming their fears about your project spinning out of control.

Of course, it takes a lot of experience to be able to confidently estimate a flat price for a project. Expect to lose money on some of them, while you get better about figuring out how many hours you'll really put into a job.

And when you quote a price for an entire project, you have to be extremely careful to define the project. Don't just bid a kitchen design, for example. Find out first whether your clients want rough drawings or buildable blueprints. And are they talking about a 1,200 square-foot-kitchen or a 12,000-square-foot kitchen? And how many redrawings will you do if they don't like your first attempt? The more you talk about these details early, the happier you and your clients will be.

Setting Minimums

If you are in a service business, it takes time to get in and out of a project. You have to drive to where the work will be performed; or at least clear your mind, desk, and a space on your hard drive. You have to think about the work you are about to do, do it, check it. You have to estimate it, bill it, deliver it, and collect on it. That's why you need to set a minimum figure for any job you take on. "This should only take a few minutes, not more than an hour or two," suggests a bargaining client. How does he know? And what about the time administering the project, and moving in and out of it? As you become more successful, you will naturally raise your minimums by rejecting smaller jobs because you are too busy with bigger ones. But even before you are busy enough to turn down tiny projects, you should think about doing that anyway. Better to spend that hour or two marketing to bigger fish than filling in with trifling work, unless it is trifling work you think will lead to something better.

What's a reasonable minimum? To start, perhaps a three-hour job. Or $200. Some workers, depending on their field, don't take projects they can't bill at least a day for. Others, like desktop publisher C. J. Metschke, say "If it doesn't have a comma in the estimate, I stay away from it."

chapter

5

What Are You Worth? And How Can You Get It?

How to Negotiate

Of course, imagining—or even calculating—a rate is a far cry from getting that rate. How do you get the money you're now convinced you need and deserve?

For starters, act professional and serious. Know your own bottom line. When a potential client says "That's way out of our league!" just say, "Sorry, maybe in the future we can work together."

If a client offers an assignment at a rate too low, try negotiating like this: "I'm sorry. I'd love to work with you, and this project sounds fun and exciting. But I just can't afford to do it for the amount you quote." There's no magic in that line, but it often works like there is.

There's another alternative: You can compromise. Take less money, but redefine the project so it fits the money being offered. If you are a newsletter editor, for example, and a client comes to you wanting a four-page newsletter for $700, you can try this approach. "Well, I'd really like to do this brochure for you, and I may be able to help you stretch that $700. If your staff can supply all of the research for the newsletter, and you can live with two photos instead of three, and you'll write the president's message yourself, I think we can work together."

Remember that politely turning down work that is below your going rate is a good business practice. It leaves you free time to pursue those clients more worth your while. And sometimes it lets you test the bottom line. Many a client has found room in the budget when the person he or she really wanted to work with couldn't (or wouldn't) budge.

Don't Give It Away

There's another problem that comes up with fee setting: If you are selling your expertise, you sometimes find yourself giving away what you're supposed to be selling. This happens to computer consultants, who get tied up on the phone with clients calling to ask emergency questions. Or to architects, forced to do creative designs just to win a job. Or especially to small advertising agencies in a field where it's the rule, rather than the exception, that you do the work before you get the work.

David Lawrence, a.k.a. "Doctor Mac," calls them the "hit and runs." He'll be sitting at his desk, minding his own Washington D.C. radio talk show and computer consulting business, and the phone will ring.

"Before they even give me their names, or ask about fees, they ask questions," he complained to me recently. "What's the best word processor under $100? What's the command for bold type in Microsoft Word? Why is my screen showing a question mark, even though I inserted a disk?"

COMPUTER SOLUTION:
SETTING PRICES FOR THINGS—
A FAST COURSE IN BREAK-EVEN ANALYSIS

What if you don't just sell time, you sell stuff? Pricing gets more complicated. The fast way is to figure out everything the item costs you to supply (including your labor) and double it to set the price.

For a more accurate price, you need to figure out how much it costs you to produce or obtain the products you are selling, and add a sensible estimate of what the market will bear.

Then it really helps to perform a break-even analysis. Usually, these are used by salespeople to figure out how much of a product needs to sell at a given price for the seller to break even on all costs. But you can easily use it to set your prices.

First, you need to figure out how much the items you sell cost you before you can price them. You need to calculate which costs are fixed, like the rent you pay or the computer on your desk. And you need to calculate which costs are variable, which means that they change depending on how many items you sell. For example, if you sell gift baskets, your electric bill will be more or less fixed, but the ribbons you buy will be variable. Then you need to make some rough guesses about how many items you expect to sell.

Here's the formula you'll use for the break even analysis:

```
Break even point =        Fixed costs
                       ────────────────────
                       1- Variable costs
                          ───────────────
                              Sales
```

Go back to the gift basket business. Let's say Johanna's overhead or fixed expenses are $8,000 a year. For every basket she makes, she spends $7 on materials. She can set up a break-even analysis on her spreadsheet, as follows, using different unit prices to see what her business would run like under the various prices.

chapter

5

What Are You Worth? And How Can You Get It?

SETTING PRICES FOR THINGS: Formula View (*continued*)

	A	B	C	D
1	**If Price is 25**		Units Needed	Baskets/Day
2	Fixed costs	8000		
3	Variable costs	7		
4	Sales	25	=B4/25	
5	VC/sales	=B3/B4		
6	1-VC/sales	=1-B5		
7	Break-even point	=B2/B6	=B7/25	
8	**To net $50,000**		=(50000+B2)/(B4-B3)	C8/160
9				
10				
11	**If Price is 30**			
12	Fixed costs	8000		
13	Variable costs	7		
14	Sales	30	=B14/30	
15	VC/sales	=B13/B14		
16	1-VC/sales	=1-B15		
17	Break-even point	=B12/B16	=B17/30	
18	**To net $50,000**		=(50000+B12)/(B14-B13)	=C18/160
19				
20				
21	**If Price is 35**			
22	Fixed costs	8000		
23	Variable costs	7		
24	Sales	35	=B24/35	
25	VC/sales	=B23/B24		
26	1-VC/sales	=1-B25		
27	Break-even point	=B22/B26	=B27/35	
28	**To net $50,000**		=(50000+B22)/(B24-B23)	=C28/160

SETTING PRICES FOR THINGS: Data View (*continued*)

	A	B	C	D
1	**If Price is 25**		Units Needed	Baskets/Day
2	Fixed costs	$8,000.00		
3	Variable costs	$7.00		
4	Sales	$25.00	1	
5	VC/sales	0.28		
6	1-VC/sales	0.72		
7	Break-even point	$11,111.11	445	
8	**To net $50,000**		3222	20
9				
10				
11	**If Price is 30**			
12	Fixed costs	$8,000.00		
13	Variable costs	$7.00		
14	Sales	$30.00	1	
15	VC/sales	0.23		
16	1-VC/sales	0.77		
17	Break-even point	$10,434.78	348	
18	**To net $50,000**		2522	16
19				
20				
21	**If Price is 35**			
22	Fixed costs	$8,000.00		
23	Variable costs	$7.00		
24	Sales	$35.00	1	
25	VC/sales	0.20		
26	1-VC/sales	0.80		
27	Break-even point	$10,000.00	286	
28	**To net $50,000**		**2071**	13

chapter

5

What Are You Worth? And How Can You Get It?

SETTING PRICES FOR THINGS (*continued*)

In this example, she puts one unit's variable costs in cell B3, and then the possible price for one unit in cell B4. This tells her how many baskets she needs to break even at that price. And, by setting up line 8, she also knows how many baskets she needs to sell at that price to net her $50,000 goal. The spreadsheet shows Johanna some different price options. And in column D, she learns how realistic they are. Assuming she works 160 days a year on making baskets, can she really make from thirteen to twenty every day? And sell that many?

Possibly Johanna needs to lower her fixed costs, raise her prices even further, or figure out how to trim that $7 in basket supplies. She can go back to this spreadsheet again and again to crunch those numbers.

In the bad old days, Lawrence used to answer every question, politely and completely. Then he noticed a trend. The people whose rapid-fire questions he answered on the phone were not the ones who became his best clients. He found himself spending a lot of time answering queries on the phone for free.

So he stopped. Now, if you call Lawrence out of the blue and start asking questions, he'll respond by asking your name and address, so he can send you a bill. He charges $1.50 a minute. And many clients are happy to pay it, just to get the fast answers they want. It's called "capture."

That's not to say that Lawrence never gives away information. He has regular clients who get free phone time, and he's happy to trade information with colleagues. But he's learned the basic lesson that all entrepreneurs must: You can't make money by giving away what you are supposed to sell.

How can you avoid giving away the country store? Here are some ideas that work.

❑ **Stop doing speculative work.** If you are an architect and your potential clients don't want to hire you without seeing your stuff, show them photos of your other work. Tell them you will be happy to do some preliminary drawings, but you will charge them your hourly fee for the quick sketches.

❑ **Offer an inexpensive, but not free, initial consultation.** To weed out serious potential clients from those who aren't, offer a one-hour consultation at your hourly rate.

❑ **If you sell creative work, be descriptive, but vague until you have the work nailed down.** Stuart Sanders runs a consulting group in Richmond, Virginia, that trains ad agencies in how to get business. He tells them to avoid doing mock-ups of designs to win jobs. "Instead use descriptive phrases such as 'a strikingly spare, black and white glossy cover,'" he says. This gives your potential clients a mental picture of what you'll do for them without you actually doing it. Or giving them a design they can copy without using you at all.

❑ **Help beginners sparingly.** Once we've established ourselves, we usually like to give others a leg up. But this can be very time costly. If you find yourself spending too much time giving away free advice, write what you know as a little booklet. Sell it for a nominal fee to everyone who calls to ask the basics. If you enjoy consulting, consider speaking at professional association seminars, or hold "office hours" like college professors, when you are available to take those calls.

❑ **Get something when you give it away.** If your business is slow, find the best project you'd love to do for a nonprofit and offer to do it pro bono. You'll expand your experience and your contacts, feel good, and know that even without the cash, you're controlling how you spend your time and resources.

Give Me My Money Now: How to Collect with Finesse and Results

If you want to get paid, you have to ask for money. That may not sound so tough, but many newly minted entrepreneurs make the mistake of waiting for their clients to pony up or of not pressing potentially valuable clients to pay past-due accounts.

Both behaviors are counterproductive. I once received a letter from a reader asking for advice on how to get paid. "Some of my clients offer to pay, but others take it for granted that I'm doing it for fun," he wrote, sounding as if he were having less fun all the time. Collections are a key part of your business. Not only do you need to learn how to ask for

chapter

5

What Are You Worth? And How Can You Get It?

money; you need to learn how to ask for it again and again, a little more stridently each time. You need to learn how to make it easy for your clients to pay. And you need to learn how to speed up those payments as much as possible, so you can keep cash flowing through your business in a timely way.

Develop The Invoice Habit

Even if your client promises to pay you without one, you'll get paid faster with an invoice. Here's how to adopt the invoice habit so you get paid fast.

- ❏ **Call your form a "bill" or an "invoice."** Unbelievably, some companies actually have policies that don't allow them to pay "statements," only "bills" or "invoices."

- ❏ **Include your terms.** It's typical today for most small businesses to allow thirty days for payments, although "due on receipt" is a popular runner-up. Some small businesses are now putting ten- and fifteen-day terms on their invoices.

- ❏ **Turn them in fast.** The longer you let an invoice languish on your desk or in your computer, the more vague the memory of your services become to your client, and the hazier your own recollection of the charges becomes. Bill as soon as the project is completed if not sooner.

- ❏ **Offer a payment plan.** Tell your clients that you will give them a 5 percent discount if they pay within ten days of receiving the invoice. You'll collect fast. (Of course, you can bump up your fees a bit so you aren't really taking less money.)

- ❏ **Carry a big stick.** Re-invoice monthly, and add late fees.

SECRET: *If you call your late fees "interest" you may find yourself subject to a lot of banking regulations you'd be better off not dealing with. Instead call them "rebilling fees," make them a flat $15 or $20 a month, and don't expect to collect them very often. Do expect them to speed your collections.*

- ❏ **Consider color.** When Xerox Corporation studied the efficacy of invoices, it discovered that those that use color to highlight the all-important "balance due" section are paid as much as 30 percent more quickly. This may not make it worth buying one of those color copiers or a color laser printer, but you could always use one of those collegiate yellow highlighters to draw attention to the details, or set your computer up to shade the key number.

❑ **Be very clear about what your client is supposed to do.** At the very bottom of your invoice, put "Please Remit" with the amount due. Clients who receive a lot of different invoices can get confused over formats.

❑ **Curtail details.** Did you know that most clients are more likely to pay a bill that says "Accounting Services, $500," than they are a bill that itemizes each fifteen minute period and how it was spent? The more details you provide, the more there is to argue about.

Take Credit Cards

Of course, you don't have to bother invoicing at all, if your clients pay up front with a credit card at the exact time they are ordering or you are providing a service. And it's not difficult to be a credit card merchant these days.

Banks and credit unions that looked down on sole proprietors just a year or two ago have started pushing their Visa and MasterCard programs to them. And American Express, which issues cards that have no credit limits, has always been comparatively easy for merchants who want to sign on. In addition, there are now a number of independent agents who act as intermediaries between banks and businesses. They'll approve you a little more easily—but charge you more too. Check, also, with your professional trade group; it may have a credit merchant program for which you are eligible.

How much will it cost you to take credit cards? Consider all of the following costs:

❑ An initial application fee that can run as high as $400.

❑ A credit card machine, which can cost you more than $1,000 to buy or as little as $20 a month to lease, depending on where you go. The latest technology includes credit card software that you can use with your computer and modem to take charges and get them approved.

❑ A per-transaction fee of $5.

❑ And extras: a $5 statement fee, a voice authorization fee, a check verification surcharge and more!

So accepting credit card payments is not cheap. But business experts suggest that adding a credit card capability will increase your sales by at least 10 percent and possibly a lot more. Moreover, it's a foolproof way of collecting from a recalcitrant client. When he or she says, "Gee, I really want to settle up, but I just don't have the cash this month," you can say,

chapter
5

What Are You Worth? And How Can You Get It?

COMPUTER SOLUTION:
USE SOFTWARE MADE FOR INVOICING

If you use one of the full-fledged business accounting programs on the market today, chances are it has invoicing and accounts receivable capabilities. You can also buy an inexpensive, freestanding invoicing program that will do both tasks for you. When you use invoicing software, you get clean, traditional looking invoices. You should also look for:

- Automatic accounts receivable aging, which means at the click of a key or mouse, you can find out who owes how much and when it was due.
- Tax calculations, if you are selling items for which you need to collect sales taxes.
- Customer records, which will track from one sale to the next the credit terms, shipping methods, and tax status of each customer.
- Easy billing by unit, hour, or project.
- The ability to bill separately for reimbursable expenses.
- The ability to match payments with specific invoices. Most programs now allow you to choose to which invoice you are going to apply a payment; the previous generation of software often automatically applied the payments to the oldest invoice.
- Automatic extras, like discounting for fast pay, extra fees for rebilling, and more.
- Recallable price lists and product codes.

In addition to the full-fledged accounting programs noted in Chapter 3, there are several invoice-specific programs. Among them:

- My Advanced Invoices, from My Software Co., 415-473-3600
- The Invoice Store, from Software Store Products, 516-244-6927
- OnAccount, from White Crow Software, 802-658-1270.

Every program is different, so make sure you find answers to all your questions before you buy an invoicing program. Make sure that the one you buy is created with your type of business in mind; it's hard to squeeze a service

USE SOFTWARE MADE FOR INVOICING (*continued*)

business into a "goods" invoice, and almost impossible to do the reverse. Below is a sample invoice from My Advanced Invoices and an accounts receivable report from QuickBooks.

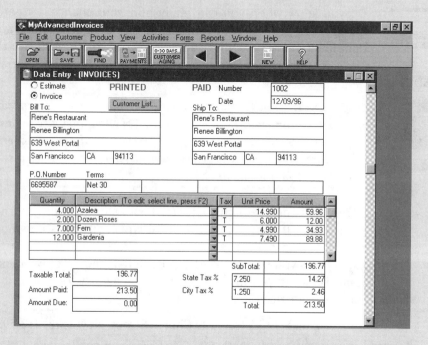

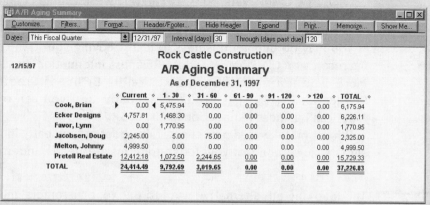

chapter
5

What Are You Worth? And How Can You Get It?

"That's okay! I take credit cards. You can charge it today and pay it next month when you get your cash."

Where can you find a company that will set you up? Try your own bank, credit union, or professional organization first. Then try Cardservice International, the nation's leading independent selling organization, at 800-948-6457.

Protect Yourself Early in the Relationship

Do you know when you can really hurt your chances of getting paid on time? When you sign on a new client. Your hunger for work, and the attendant failure to assess your clients can cost you. Before you do work for a new client, try to get the lay of the land; if possible get referrals.

SECRET: *Sad to say, but people like us—other independent sole proprietors—can make the worst clients. Too often, they use their own cash flow problems as an excuse to cause some for you. If you are approached by an entrepreneurial sort who comes without references, ask for a substantial percentage of your fee up front.*

How can you prequalify clients? First listen to your gut. Then use common sense. If they are in the local small business community, ask for referrals, and call others who have done business with them. If you expect that you will be doing a substantial amount of business with them, it maybe worth paying a credit reporting agency for a report on their past payment practices. Try:

- ❏ Dun & Bradstreet, 99 Church Street, New York, 212-593-6800;
- ❏ TRW Credit Data, 505 City Parkway West, Orange, California 714-385-7000. Ask for information about their business credit profiles.

You may do enough business to justify having your own credit reporting records on CD-ROM. American Business Information, Inc. sells data on more than ten million businesses on its Business Credit Reference Service for $1,295. It is updated annually, and you can order it from American Business Information at 800-555-6124.

When you take on a new client, talk about money early in the relationship. Make certain that your fees and terms are clearly understood.

Collect Fast

The following are alternative ways to put your customers' money to work for you fast.

❏ **Collect while you are working on a job.** If you are working on major projects, advance the concept of incremental billing, or billing in progress. You might set up a schedule, for example, where every month, you meet certain project objectives, and your client pays you a predetermined percentage of the whole time.

❏ **Don't lay out money.** Don't put yourself in the position of laying out money for a client if you can possibly avoid it. If you are asked to buy something for a client as part of a job, such as printing services, or materials, or advertising time, let your client know that you are a small business without the cash flow to lay out on large projects like that.

❏ **Call your client when a payment is late.** Or have someone else make those calls for you. You could hire a neighbor, friend, or college student to say, "I'm the bookkeeper for Joe Jones, and I'm cleaning up his accounts receivable for this quarter. Can you tell me when your bill will be paid?"

 *S*ECRET: *Use finesse, and give your client an out. For example, you can say, "I'd really like to do this next project for you, but your accounting department (or accountant, or bookkeeper, or whatever) is holding my payment. Can you give them a call and make sure they put through my last payment?*

❏ **Don't hang up without a commitment.** Ask your client how he or she will be paying the bill, and when you can expect payment.

❏ **If a client is habitually slow to pay, consider dropping him or her from your roster.** Work with no money is worse than no work!

❏ **Use your judgment.** There are times when a good client runs into unexpected financial difficulty, and you'll want to carry him or her. Just make sure it's not too often.

When All Else Fails . . .

You can sue, or just prepare to sue. One effective technique, if the amount of money you are owed falls under small claims court jurisdiction in your state, is to fill out the forms for filing a small claims suit. Send a photocopy to your deadbeat client with a date by which your client must pay the bill in full to avoid your filing the claim. Then make good on your word.

If your client owes you too much for small claims court but not enough for you to hire an expensive lawyer, you can have Dun & Bradstreet collect

chapter

5

What Are You Worth? And How Can You Get It?

the money for you. This financial reporting firm has two services. For $25, they'll send out two letters to your deadbeat client, reminding him that he owes you money and that D&B is watching. If those letters don't work, the firm supplies you with a list of local attorneys who specialize in collections.

The firm also will move to collect the money for you, pocketing a percentage for itself if it does. For more information, you can call D&B's Small Business Information Services at 800-552-3867.

If you are owed more than $10,000 from a single client, you may have to hire an attorney to collect the money. Or you can turn your "cold" invoices over to a collection agency, which will charge you as much as 50 cents on the dollar to find your former client and squeeze the money out of the rat.

Is all of this talk about rats and refusals making you nervous? Living on your own business income can be nerve wracking, especially in the early months when it's too early to detect the comforting cycles of your business. The next chapter offers techniques to help you calm your nerves while you're waiting for the invoices to be answered by checks.

YOU MUST REMEMBER THIS: LESSONS FROM CHAPTER 5

- You have to set prices carefully, and resist the temptation to charge too little.

- You can protect your fees by demanding them professionally, finding the right clients, and collecting with care.

- Computerized invoicing programs will help you collect quickly and track your receivables.

6

"Income that fluctuates weekly,
monthly, or seasonally
takes a lot of adjustment,
both financial and psychological."

Riding a Roller-Coaster Income Without Falling Off

Tracking the ins and outs of self-employment income takes the words "ebb and flow" to a whole new level. The money comes and goes in fits and starts, and that may be how you sleep, too—especially in your first couple of years when the midnight money crazies are at their worst. You know the "Oh my God, what if I never get another check for the rest of my life?" panic attacks.

In addition to those panic attacks, these symptoms of roller coaster cash flow may also seem familiar to you:

- ❏ You get a big project, and you think you're rolling in dough—until the estimated tax payments for the quarter come due.
- ❏ You've just come through a month of nonstop work, but there's no cash in your account to pay your rent or mortgage.
- ❏ Your income fluctuates by hundreds, if not thousands, of dollars every month.
- ❏ Your spouse or significant other wants to know why you seem to be working all the time, but no money is coming in.
- ❏ You discover that you have a huge tax bill for money you can't even remember earning.

❏ You have lots of cash, and decide to take a vacation. The month *after* your vacation, you can't pay your bills.

❏ Your income isn't just erratic, it's seasonal, too. You have to make your September collections last until April.

❏ In the previous month, you've gone through near psychotic ups and downs. You're a winner! You're a loser! You're a winner! And you can't take many more of the mood swings.

You get the picture. Income that fluctuates weekly, monthly, or seasonally takes a lot of adjustment, both financial and psychological. There are steps you can take to smooth the money bumps and mental bumps too. The cash flow management techniques you have read about in the preceding chapters will go a long way toward balancing the financial ups and downs. But they won't do it all. As you adjust to the roller coaster, your personal budget will feel some strain, and so will you.

The following are some money management tricks and psychological games you can play to minimize the misery of erratic income.

SECRET: *Don't forget you can also use that erratic income to your advantage. If you have a college-bound child, spend the most and make the least during the calendar year that starts when he or she is a high school junior, to be eligible for more financial aid. You can prepare a tight, live-on-less budget, and then devote extra chunks of income toward saving a down payment or burning school loans fast.*

First, Install Some Financial Shock Absorbers

Here's a baker's dozen techniques and tricks for smoothing out an erratic income. You can try some or all of them to even out your money cycle.

1. **Capitalize your business to start.** When Daniel started his financial planning business, he borrowed $20,000 to get it started. He put that reserve in the bank, and got a business line of credit to complement it. When money got low, either in the business or at home, he paid out of savings or even borrowed from the credit line. When money came in, he replenished first and spent second.

2. **Set a circumspect salary.** Figure out the minimum you need to draw from the business to keep food on the table. (You can do that using the spreadsheet in Chapter 1). Set that salary, and draw

it weekly, biweekly, or monthly from the business. Any excess, keep in savings. Daniel decided to take $2,000 a month.

3. **Save for estimated taxes.** Plan ahead, so that you only use about half of the money that comes into your business. Every time a check comes in, deposit half of it in a special account for federal, state, and local taxes. You won't miss what you never see, and you'll have enough on hand for those big quarterly tax bills.

4. **Budget.** Use all that information you learned in Chapter 1. If you have at least a rough idea of what you're going to owe, and when, you can schedule those payments in advance.

5. **Maintain one bread-and-butter client.** Be willing to cut your rate for the one loyal customer who will pay you a monthly retainer. They are out there.

6. **Market when you are really busy.** You have to force yourself to look for work when you're already busy with work. That's one way to smooth out the contrary pattern that is the bane of the one-person business. You know the drill: When you're really busy there's no time to market, so a slow period follows. During that slow period, you market like crazy. Then, all of the business comes in at once and you find yourself working like a dog, no time to market.

   There's a corresponding financial cycle, too. Given the lag of most client payments, if your work is too ebb and flow, your money will be too. That leads to some glorious slow times when the checks are piling in from your last work frenzy. But it also leads to very frustrating times when you are slaving away and there are no checks in the mail.

   Force yourself to take even a half a day a week when you are busy to send out new proposals, make phone calls or the sales pitches you need to bring in cash.

7. **Use the cash management techniques of big business.** You'll learn about them in the following chapters. But briefly, invoice promptly, collect conscientiously, and demand regular payments.

8. **Get overdraft protection on your personal checking account.** You'll need it. Sometimes you know a check is coming next week but the mortgage or rent and the insurance payments are due *this* week. Write the checks, play the float, and depend on the over-draft line in a pinch. (This is a perfect example of the type of financial advice that a regular wage earner shouldn't follow, but

COMPUTER SOLUTION:
THE MIDNIGHT MONEY REALITY CHECK

It's three a.m. and Annie is wide awake and worried. Her most important client isn't returning her calls. She's thinking about returning the color printer and giving up on her desktop publishing business. She never should have ordered that new letterhead! What if next week's checks don't come in on time?

She could wake Alan, her husband, but it would be the third time this week, and instead of him calming her, he's starting to get a little nervous, too. Instead, she rouses herself and Annie dials in to the online service of her choice. Whether she chooses, America Online, CompuServe, Prodigy, or goes straight to the Internet, she knows she'll find many like-minded colleagues who can offer consolation, perspective, and useful advice.

By networking online, Annie talks to other desktop publishers who can give her information about what their money flows are like. What they did when their calls weren't returned. She can find out how much her colleagues spent on letterhead and color printers.

The cyberworld is not as competitive as the neighborhood professional association, because often geography separates colleagues from the same clients. Online networking can generate dispassionate advice that is more worthwhile than a loved one saying "don't worry, honey."

To seek out fellow entrepreneurs, check out these online locations:

- On CompuServe, try the Work from Home Forum and the Entrepreneur's Forum.

- On America Online, visit the Entrepreneur Zone, Strategies for Business, and the Home Office Computing Section.

- On the Internet, start with a search engine like Yahoo http://www.yahoo.com) or Web Crawler (http://www.webcrawler.com). Look for keywords like "small business," "home office," or your kind of business, like "bookkeeper" or "architect." You'll find more than you know what to with.

- Try some mailing lists, too. On the Internet, sign up for ESBDC-L, a small business development center's mailing list. Or FAMBUS-L, the Family Business Discussion List.

THE MIDNIGHT MONEY REALITY CHECK (*continued*)

But remember to manage your online time. If Annie finds, herself surfing the Web instead of working, or having cybersex with a screen name instead of Alan, it's a sign she's gone too far.

And finally: just because the online environment holds value doesn't mean you should pay for everything you find there. There are a lot of online con artists hoping Annie will spend big bucks buying a "business opportunity" some wakeful night.

---

that a business owner may have to. Credit becomes another way to manage the flow.)

9. **Juggle a couple of credit cards and learn the grace periods.** Another example of for-entrepreneurs-only advice. If you know your MasterCard closes on the fifteenth of the month, and you are short of cash, charge your expenses on the sixteenth and seventeenth. It will buy you a month to raise the cash. Then pay the bill in full when it comes.

10. **Pay bills infrequently.** Set up a personal bill paying schedule whereby you write checks only once or twice a month. Let your savings build until then, collect all the bills that are due, and pay them all at once. You won't have to worry about the short-term fluctuations in your income; the longer you can wait between bill-paying sessions, the more chance your money has to even out.

11. **Pay personal bills when you have the cash.** In your personal life, forget about the business cash management techniques that tell you to hold every dollar until the last possible second. Stick to your regular bill paying schedule, and if you have extra money in your bank account, pay some bills ahead. This may cost you a bit of interest—pay your $1,500 mortgage a couple of weeks early and you'll give up about $7.52, by my count. But you'll pick up some peace of mind, knowing that the bill is paid.

12. **Don't pay personal bills when you don't have the cash.** There's a logical list of creditors to pay in a hurry and those you can stall.

Don't defer credit card payments, because issuers tend to be quick to report your payment problems to the credit monitoring agencies. Don't defer your rent or mortgage payment, for similar reasons. And don't defer insurance premiums, or your policies may be canceled. Everything else is fair game. In a pinch, your electric, phone, water, and gas utilities will carry you for a month or longer. Your dentist, doctor, accountant and lawyer will carry you even longer than that, or may let you work out a level payment plan.

13. **Rely on other cash that comes in.** Do you have a spouse who gets a paycheck? That's a major money-smoother right there. Or if you receive regular interest or dividend payments, you can use them to smooth the flow of cash coming in from your business. Just remember to replenish what you use.

Keep Your Emotions on an Even Keel

The real problem with erratic income isn't the occasional late fee; it's the cycles of exhilaration and self-doubt that accompany it. To some extent, we all tend to measure our self worth in dollars. During a bad week, we feel like chumps who work day and night and still don't bring in what the nine-to-five slacker next door earns. When we raise our rates and make other necessary financial adjustments, we can feel guilty for profiteering. Conversely, a really good week can find us treading dangerously close to the Master of the Universe syndrome, which Tom Wolfe described so aptly in Bonfire of the Vanities.

Moreover, personal relationships suffer too. Friends and family may resent a business that seems to consume so much of the your time without returning much in the way of income. But there are practical ways to minimize the emotions that come with the ups and downs of your income. Here's another baker's dozen for riding the emotional roller-coaster.

1. **Stay grounded in reality.** If you can't afford a new color printer, it doesn't mean you are a loser. It means that this month you can't afford a color printer.

2. **Draw your own line in the dust.** Don't let your business creep into every aspect of your personal life. You don't have to discuss whether to buy a new printer with your friends; you have

professional advisors for that. If you are married, this can get tricky; some entrepreneurial spouses like to discuss every paper clip; others don't want to know the details as long as the business brings in the cash it's supposed to. Learn to put your business in a box, so that you can shut the lid when business worries are taking over too much of your personal, social or family life.

3. **Set nonfinancial goals for your business.** Are you in business so you can see your kids after school, provide a service to the community, or perform a job you've always wanted to do? Remember to count those benefits along with a fat checking account.

4. **Do the right thing financially.** If you budget and employ cash management techniques described throughout this book, it is bound to reduce your anxieties.

5. **Make a list of 100 ways to access money in a pinch.** Everything from the Visa card, to your brother-in-law, to nighttime waiting on tables, to mowing lawns. If you start to feel hopeless, a look at the list should remind you that backup money is always available.

6. **Make another list of people you really admire.** How many of them have lots of money and safe steady incomes?

7. **Look at the carnage in the Fortune 500.** Remind yourself that a nine-to-five job doesn't assure you security these days either.

8. **Give yourself the occasional reward.** Once in a while when work is slow, blow off an afternoon and play. It will remind you of why you work for yourself.

9. **Practice selling.** Especially if you are shy. If you force yourself to market, market, market, you will feel a sense of empowerment. And you'll bring in business, eventually.

10. **Schedule your dread.** Allow yourself what debt maven and motivational speaker Jerrold Mundis calls "five minutes of self-pity and terror." Get away from your desk, and just wallow in how bad it could be. Think up worst-case scenarios about your future failures. Then set them aside. Get back to work, and if worries creep in, say, "I already dealt with that today."

11. **Be personally supportive.** Try not to transfer all of your anxieties to those closest to you. When business is slow, spend time with those you love.

12. **Budget a break.** Make sure your business budget allows for an annual vacation. You need it for renewal.

INSTANT ANALYSIS! YOUR MONEY PHOBIAS CURED!

Most of us have some idiosyncratic behaviors and beliefs about money. If you let your money worries determine how you run your company you can sabotage your financial future .

But relax: this table succinctly delivers many hours of psychotherapy. Find your personal hangups on the left, then cure them yourself by following the advice on the right.

 SECRET: *In truth, this table can be boiled down even more. The essence of money psychotherapy is this: Go against instinct. You'll see.*

Don't be too hard on yourself! Volatile self-employment income can take years to master, so use as many of the management techniques as possible and give yourself time to adjust.

And remember that one of the best ways to stay in control of your money, and your money-driven emotions, is to squeeze every penny. In the next chapter, you'll learn how.

Your Condition	Your Symptoms	Effects on Your Business	The Cure
High Anxiety	You worry about money too much; you think you're one purchase away from living on the street.	Your business can choke to death without adequate spending.	Whenever you start to worry, market instead. Check with friends and colleagues to make sure you are spending enough.
Still Sixties	You love self-employment, but secretly believe money is evil. You hate charging your friends, and since everyone is your friend, they all get discounts.	You can scramble for years at unprofitable levels. You can give away the store.	One of the hardest problems to treat! Force yourself to spend a little on yourself, up your prices and if necessary, donate profits to the charity of your choice.

INSTANT ANALYSIS! YOUR MONEY PHOBIAS CURED! (continued)

Your Condition	Your Symptoms	Effects on Your Business	The Cure
Identity Crisis	You *are* your money. When you spent a lot, it means you're important. When business is light, you're a loser.	Your behavior makes those money cycles worse. When business is bad, you hide; when it's good, you overspend. Your business lurches along with your moods.	Give your business a name that is different from your own name. List your personal characteristics and outside interests that have nothing to do with your business or your money.
Delusional	You forget that you aren't working for that Fortune 500 company anymore. So you still spend like you have an expense account and supply closet at your disposal.	You can ruin your business spending what little money you have on lavish lunches, showy office furniture, and other less-productive trappings. Or you can lose clients waiting for your assistant to photocopy something before you remember: You have no assistant!	Budget, in whatever way works for you. Set up a procedure for approving expenses, before you incur them. Keep your budget on your desktop.
Artistic	It's what you do that you love. You don't want to be bothered with invoices, spreadsheets, and all that other stuff. Somebody probably gave you this book and you are reading it under duress. Anyway, money just makes you nervous when you think about it.	You lose money because you don't know how to ask for it, or forget who owes it to you. Checks bounce when you don't bother to make deposits that are in your desk drawer.	Hire a bookkeeper. Do what he or she tells you.

INSTANT ANALYSIS! YOUR MONEY PHOBIAS CURED! (continued)

Your Condition	Your Symptoms	Effects on Your Business	The Cure
Irreconcilable Differences	You and your spouse or business partner disagree often about money. You have dramatically different styles of dealing with it.	Your spouse or your partner or you can sabotage the business, refusing to pay bills for costs incurred, or by spending unnecessarily to make a point.	Agree to disagree. Put the more circumspect one in charge of doing the books, but compromise on big spending decisions. Talk a lot. If it is severe enough, it's better to find out early.

---

13. **Remember this basic truth:** There is not one business development out there that will fix your life. And no business loss that can ruin your life. Your life is bigger than your business. Make sure it stays that way.

YOU MUST REMEMBER THIS: LESSONS FROM CHAPTER 6:

- Use cash flow techniques to smooth out the peaks and valleys in your income.
- Play "mind games" to smooth out the psychological bumps that volatile checkbook balances can cause.
- Train yourself to ignore the inevitable slow periods: You never know when you'll get your next break!

© Richard A. Goldberg 1997

"Every penny you spend
in your business should increase
your business income."

You Have to Spend Money to Make Money

Setting fees, invoicing, and collecting money is only part of the successful cash-flow formula. The other half is spending. To run a business successfully, you also have to control the money flowing out the door. You have to make sure that it is allocated where you need it most; that is, spent on smart buys, and ultimately sent on its way as slowly as possible.

When money from your business flows directly into your personal budget, you have another layer of decision-making to worry about. Which is more important, to buy a new copier for the home office, or to repair the leak in your roof? It may not be possible to make that judgment; they are both important. But it will be easier to allocate business and personal expenses if you remember the two bedrock rules of business spending:

Never spend one unnecessary cent.

Every penny you spend in your business should increase your business income.

Never Spend a Penny...

I once tried to write a magazine article about business people who regretted starting their businesses on the cheap. I couldn't find anyone to interview, so I gave up the article. Business experts agree on this subject: squeeze every dime. Businesses fail when their owners borrow to look big. They lease too much space, hire too much staff, or spring for too much advertising air time. When the money doesn't come in as fast as they hope, they have little leeway to forestall payments due. So they fail.

That's what almost happened to Margaret Janis, a management consultant in Alexandria, Virginia. "I made some very large business mistakes. I borrowed money and overextended." She bought $50,000 worth of top-of-the-line equipment, leased office space, accumulated colorful artwork, rented plants and picked up a fast $200,000 payroll. "I hired staff in anticipation of work that never developed," she remembers.

Janis almost lost her business. She and her husband had to draw on personal funds to repay her business debt. She returned the plants, shrank her staff to three and started rebuilding very, very cautiously. She cut her expenses to the bone, and only spends a dollar when it's absolutely, positively, necessary.

She's learned the most fundamental rule of entrepreneurship: A lean, mean budget buys you time.

It buys you time to get through a slow sales period (hence the entrepreneur's slogan: cash will get you through times of no work better than work will get you through times of no cash). It buys you time to line up the kind of work you want. And it buys you time and savings to spend on the sectors of your business that really matter.

Of course, none of this means you should be a notorious cheapskate. Nothing will lose you business faster than saying things like, "Well, I was going to call you back but I don't make long-distance calls during peak hours." Or, "I'm still using my dot-matrix printer from 1987, so call me back if the fax is too light to read."

Productivity, Please

The things that really matter are those that will boost your bottom line. So buy a high-speed modem that will cut down on your America Online bills. Or hire an assistant who can clear away paperwork so you can bill more hours of creative work. Or invest in a mailing list that you expect will bring you new customers.

For the vast majority of small businesses, you don't need to spend money on designer furniture, or a plant-watering service, or original artwork. It's nice to make your surroundings pleasant, both for you and for your clients, and if you run a retail business, it is crucial, but be extremely careful to separate success spending from "trappings of success" spending.

When to Scrimp and When to Splurge

Here are a few rules to keep in mind when you are considering business expenses.

- **Splurge on anything that will save you time.** Benjamin Franklin was the first one to equate time and money, and he didn't have to worry about billing in six-minute increments or buying online time by the second.

- **Scrimp on staff.** Don't hire an employee until you absolutely, positively have to. There are many alternatives. You can pay an independent contractor who has his or her own business to do your clerical work; use part-time teenage labor, non-profit sheltered workshops of handicapped workers, and free interns. But make sure there's a job and a half before you get involved in meeting regular payroll.

- **Splurge on services.** You're probably better off staying in your office and paying a delivery service $15 to carry your proposal across town; or chatting up clients while somebody else does your books, or cleans your office. Don't do everything yourself.

- **Scrimp on furnishings.** Reward yourself with the rolltop desk *after* you have had a really good year. For starters, collect sturdy, but not flashy furnishings wherever you can find them.

- **Splurge on equipment.** It won't be long before you wish you had a hard disk with a greater capacity, or a speedier processor, or a fax machine you didn't have to stand next to and feed, sheet by sheet. Get the very best equipment you can possibly afford.

- **Scrimp on advertising.** Advertising is really, really expensive. It works, but until you've "made it," you can't really afford it. Instead, explore nontraditional ways of putting your name out there: post flyers, network at meetings, sponsor a soccer team, or try to get free press by sending out press releases.

- **Splurge on networking.** Most small businesses make it on word of mouth. Money spent on professional associations will be repaid in better contacts, better knowledge, and, ultimately, better referrals.

- ❏ **Scrimp on the trappings of image.** You may need a business card that looks more substantial than the ones you print on your own laser printer, but do you need four colors, raised lettering, and metallic ink?

- ❏ **Splurge on forging a corporate identity.** Put time, as well as money, into picking a name for your business and a look for all of your printed materials. You can hire an artist to design a classy two-color logo, and still save money on the fancy print job.

- ❏ **Scrimp on anything unnecessary.** Client lunches, for example, are not the attractions they once were. Most of your clients are as busy as you are, and would just as soon conduct a quick phone call as dawdle for hours over pastry and a project.

- ❏ **Splurge on phone service.** This might be the most important expense a small business can have. Don't try to economize by sharing a voice and data line, or by using an old finicky answering machine.

*S*ECRET: *In an informal survey of home-based business people, many of the same products and supplies turned up on almost everyone's "favorites" list, items that were found to be well worth spending money on: fax software and modem; a second phone line for data; computer checks that work with your accounting program; a telephone headset; removable disk labels; professional dues; seminar fees; voice mail (as opposed to an answering machine); a zip drive for extra computer storage and backups; a coach to help you market, sell, or speak; a good Internet access account; automated backup software; a strong file cabinet with weight-balanced drawers; and clerical help.*

Cutting Your Best Deals: How to Sweet-Talk Your Suppliers

Once you know what you are prepared to buy, you still need to know how to get the best deal on it. There's a special art to winning a favorable price when you are a small business. On the one hand, you may not have much leverage. General Motors buys sheet steel in the millions of tons; that's leverage. Your annual supply order may not even cause the local Office Depot point-of-purchase screen to hiccup.

But small businesses have their own deal-making advantages. You can network like crazy, have great flexibility, and are often winsome enough to win some concessions. You can build relationships by sharing your entrepreneurial vision. If your supplier is a struggling company, point out how you hope to be in business together for a long time. Tell the vendor that you plan to make referrals and will bring in your friends. Don't mistake this investment of time for idle chitchat: It will position you to learn when good deals come along, help you to gauge where to set your prices in negotiations, and find out whom you can tap for referrals.

Consider the example set by Naimah Jones, who launched Naimah Cosmetics with little more than a great idea, unbridled enthusiasm, and clever coordination. Without a product or final packaging, she talked buyers at a California department store into agreeing to place an order worth $80,000 if they liked her samples. With that promise in hand, she persuaded a manufacturer to make the samples. And when the department store buyers saw the samples, they placed the order. Jones then took that purchase order and her selling ability back to the manufacturer, who agreed to supply the cosmetics and wait for his money until the department store paid her.

While the manufacturer was lining up the job, Jones found a package designer, who agreed to slash his rates and hold his invoice until she got paid, and a photographer, who took promotional photos at cost. Now, Jones is leveraging that first big order to garner TV publicity. And the manufacturer, photographer, and graphic designer all got in on the ground floor of something big.

Here are some strategies for finding and working with the best suppliers:

❑ **Hang out on campus.** Many college-based business incubator programs are developing lists of affiliates who need some help but not full-time "incubation," notes Glenn Doell, director of the program at Rensselaer Polytechnic Institute in Troy, New York. Doell's incubator clients get subsidized Internet access, low-cost use of the college's graphic arts department, and access to top-flight libraries.

❑ **Deconstruct every deal.** Sometimes, you can save money by splitting your business between suppliers. For one computer consultant, this means buying computers at a local service-oriented store that will give him a good price, but going to the superstore down the street for the modem, cables, and other accessories, that the local shop marks up.

❑ **Don't get talked into buying extras.** If you are spending $200 extra to get a hard drive loaded with $1,000 worth of software you don't really need, it's not such a bargain.

❑ **Ask for a professional discount, even if you don't know whether one exists.** For example, art supply stores are in the habit of giving discounts to professionals who know enough to ask for them.

❑ **Buy it when you spy it.** If you see a good deal on an item you know you'll use, scoop it up. Paper, pens, tape, and disks are worth stockpiling for two reasons: You can buy them at a favorable price, and you won't be caught short, so you won't be pressed to pay an exorbitant price because your shelf is empty and your report is due at three P.M.

❑ **Join buying cooperatives.** Most professional associations offer discounts on office products and insurance. Some, like the highly regarded Independent Business Alliance in Windsor, Connecticut, exist for just that purpose. Contact them at 800-450-2422. Or form your own buying cooperatives with colleagues. You can buy disks, pens, notebooks, and copy paper in bulk and then split them up with your entrepreneurial friends.

❑ **Toot your own horn.** Are you in a position to influence buying decisions? You are if you are a consultant, and that's why many software programs have special rock-bottom prices for consultants. If you are active in any small business networks, let others know that you will pass on your recommendations.

❑ **Work with your professional advisors.** Ask your insurance agent how you can trim premiums, your accountant how to cut his or her retainer. You'll be surprised what they come up with. Ask other professionals where they get their supplies: The artist knows the best paper sources, the computer consultant can find savings on software.

❑ **If you don't like the prices you see on technology products, wait a couple of weeks.** In the '90s, everything goes on sale.

❑ **Quote competitors.** "We'll match any offer" is a rallying cry now. Take advantage of it.

❑ **Offer exclusivity.** Like this: I promise to buy all of my baskets from you, if you'll give me a special deal on the baskets. And I buy 2,000 baskets a year!

❑ **Always ask about competitive upgrades.** Software sellers are so anxious to put their products on your hard drives they will give you a cut rate to come over from the competition.

❑ **Ask for an additional cash discount.** It costs the merchant to take your credit card. If that doesn't work, find suppliers that will invoice you, giving you time to use your money on other business needs. And if you're buying inventory to sell, find a supplier who'll carry you until you resell the goods.

❑ **Propose to pay early.** Tell your supplier you would be happy to pay your bills early in return for a 2 percent discount. Not only will this save you the 2 percent, it will enable you to build a really strong credit record, which will enable you to cut other deals down the line.

❑ **Don't pay state sales taxes when you don't have to.** If you sell items, and not just services, you can get a state sales tax exemption for the parts and materials that you buy for resale. Contact your state treasury department for a resale number, and use it when you buy supplies. You will not be charged tax on them, but you will have to make sure you collect state sales taxes on the items you sell. Can you use your ID to avoid sales taxes on all of your business expenses, even if they aren't for resale? You're not supposed to.

❑ **Don't be a jerk.** Remember that relationship thing! Getting ugly and pushing someone to the wall for one good deal is counter-productive, as is developing the buy-use-return habit or the this-is-trash-so-charge-me-less negotiating posture. Avoid well-known lies like "the check is in the mail," "my cat ate the invoice" and "oops! did I forget to sign that check?" Pay on time, call if you can't, and remember to ask nice.

Doling Out the Dollars

Of course, there's a proper way to pay, once you've made your deal. And the main rule is, not before you have to. Keep track of bills and pay them on a schedule that saves you time and money. You can, for example, write all of your checks twice a month, but only send them out a couple of days before they are due. That keeps the money working in your account (or available for your emergencies) as long as possible.

Cash or Credit?

As a general rule, it's better to avoid borrowing money on a credit card, but a business budget is different from a personal budget. For starters, business interest is fully deductible as a business expense, so when you charge something for your office and pay it off, the effective interest is roughly half of what you are paying.

And businesses do need to worry about cash flow as a separate concern. You need to be able to pay all of your business bills in March, and you don't know for a fact that every client will pay on time. So it doesn't make sense to drain your account in February to pay off the new equipment.

When you are buying business equipment, it sometimes makes sense to finance it, either through the company you are buying it from, with a bank loan, or on your own credit card. Pay it off in regular installments, and you'll build a credit rating you can use further on down the road as your business continues to grow.

But make sure that you don't tap out all of your personal accounts running up business charges. You need personal borrowing power in case of emergencies.

SECRET: *Buying equipment on credit is a good way to cut your tax bill in a hurry. In December, charge next year's fax, phone, computer, modem, software, and copier, and write them off on this year's taxes, even though the bill might not arrive until next year. Then you can spend Christmas week setting them all up; nobody works then anyway. By New Year's Day, your new setup is ready to go. Caution: The one problem with this strategy is remembering that all of the checks you write next year to pay off the charge won't be deductible again.*

To Lease or to Buy? Not an Easy Question with Cars and Computers

This used to be a no-brainer. Until just a few years ago, buying was almost always better. Leases tended to be outrageously expensive (or even fraudulent), and equipment lasted long enough to be worth owning. End of story.

But that was then, and this is now, when entrepreneurs have a new lease on . . . well, leases. Automotive companies are using their own leasing firms to subsidize sales and make luxury cars more affordable. Computer equipment becomes so obsolete in three years it's hard to give away. Consumers have become more demanding about lease terms; big reputable companies like General Electric have gone into leasing in a big way; and state regulators have cracked down on lease fraud.

That said, at the end of the day, you usually still come out ahead if you buy equipment (including a car) instead of leasing it, but the dollar differences have tended to converge. You might spend all day immersed in cash-versus-credit-versus-lease spreadsheets and discover that you're only a few dollars off either way.

The lease-versus-buy decision often comes down to this: Which type are you? Some people are more comfortable owning; others prefer to rent. You can save yourself a lot of calculations if you just follow your nature.

And you can save yourself some dollars if you follow these basic guidelines:

❏ **If you really need to protect your cash, lease.** A typical lease will require a month's payment up front and no other down payment. You can keep your money in the bank and go for the monthly payment.

❏ **If you get a lot of use out of your purchases, buy.** If you expect to keep a car longer than three or four years, a computer longer than three years, you'll come out far ahead by buying. Leases are based on the theory that you never live without payments. If you can pay off a computer in three years on a credit card and squeeze another payment-free year out of it, you might as well buy it.

❏ **If you drive a lot, buy your car.** Automobile leases charge extra for mileage (typically over 15,000 miles a year), and can fine you at the lease's end for returning a car not in pristine condition. Larry Peterson, a former car dealer and president of the Consumer Automotive Resource Services in Eugene, Oregon warns that the dealer's idea of good condition and yours might (and probably will) differ. And when you return a car that needs repairs, the dealer isn't going to offer you any discounts on fixing it.

❏ **If you're not sure, buy.** It's actually cheaper to buy a car or a computer, decide it's a mistake and sell it than it is to try to get out of a lease early. Leases tend to be front-loaded like the loans they really are; you can end up owing almost the whole lease if you bail out one-third of the way through, reports Charles Hart, author of Expert Lease Software. If you're not sure, rent a car or computer for a couple of weeks before you commit to the long-term lease.

❏ **If you qualify for an immediate write-off, buy.** The Section 179 deduction lets you immediately write off up to $18,000 of business equipment annually. If you haven't used it up, buy that computer. There's no great leasing tax break that will be better than that.

❏ **If you live in a state with high sales taxes, lease.** Typically, you don't pay sales taxes on something you are leasing, unless you buy it at the end of the lease Then you often have to pay taxes only on the amount you are paying for it then.

COMPUTER SOLUTION:
CRUNCHING A CAR LEASE ON YOUR COMPUTER

Expert Lease Pro is software aimed at automotive consumers. Creator Charles Hart took a basic economic lease-versus-buy calculator and stuffed it full of current car data. It comes loaded with invoice and retail pricing for all new vehicles, the latest car dealer rebate incentives, and automotive lease guide residual value data. You can use it to decide whether to lease or buy any particular car, but you can also use the information to help you find the best deal on a car.

Sean bought the software when he was looking for a J-30 Infiniti, a car with a suggested retail of $39,000. His dealer offered him a lease that had an up front payment of $1,995 and 36 monthly payments of $399. Sean ran the lease through Expert Lease software, and discovered that the dealer had built the full retail price into his calculations. He went back and negotiated a new car price that led to monthly payments of $387 with no money down.

Expert Lease Pro compares lease/buy decisions by figuring out the future value of the deal, including the value of the car at the end and the interest lost on cash spent. In the case of Sean's Infiniti, the ultimate value of the lease after three years when he gives the car back would be $17,147. If he bought the car outright and sold it at the end of three years at its expected value, he'd have spent $23,951 over three years. If he bought the car on a 7.5 percent loan, his final cost, over three years, would have been $24,496. If Sean is certain he wants a new car in three years, he'd do better with the lease.

❏ **If you will be forced to depreciate your equipment, lease.** You'll be able to write it off faster. If you divide your use of the equipment in question between personal and business use, you'll still have to prorate the tax deductibility of your lease.

❏ **If you think leasing a luxury car for your business affords you a much bigger tax break, check again.** Federal tax rules limit depreciation on luxury cars, and match those limits for leasers

CRUNCHING A CAR LEASE ON YOUR COMPUTER (*continued*)

The Expert Lease Pro is available for $129.95 from Chart Software in Largo, Florida, 800-418-8450.

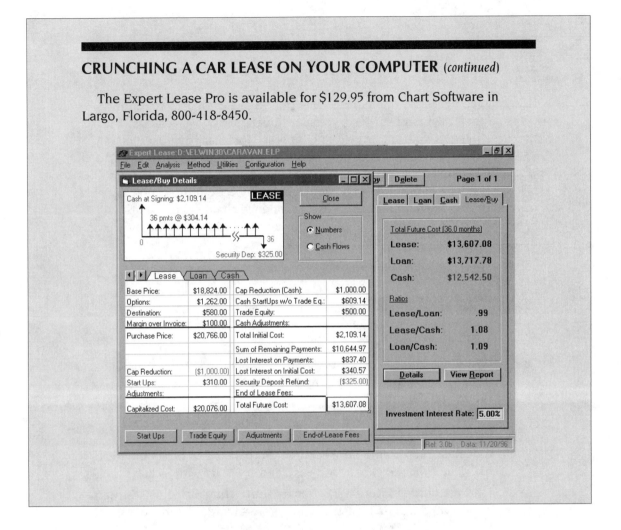

with requirements that you add part of the lease's value to your income.

Deconstruct Your Lease

The key to getting a good lease is to bring maximum knowledge to the negotiation. Often, computer stores and car dealers build their biggest price into a lease on the theory that you'll never be able to find it. Prove to them that you can by asking them to deconstruct their lease proposal so you know what product price it is built on.

QUICK CALCULATION: THE CAR LEASE

How can you figure out the hidden costs buried in a car lease? Accounting firm Coopers & Lybrand suggests you go through the following steps. The firm uses this example: a thirty-six–month lease for a car advertised at a $17,000 purchase price. The residual value (what the car ought to be worth when the lease ends) is set at $11,340. The lease calls for a $1,000 capitalized cost reduction payment (a down payment, in lease terms). Monthly payments are $199 month, plus an excess mileage charge of ten cents a mile over 12,000 a year. Here's how to analyze the lease, Coopers & Lybrand style:

1. **First, figure out your total cost.** The lease payments add up to $8,164.

2. **Figure the capitalized cost.** That's the price of the car that the dealer is using to work out the lease. In this case, use the $17,000 advertised price.

3. **Check the fairness of the residual value.** In this case, the $11,340 three-year residual value represents 59 percent of the manufacturer's standard retail price. That's not bad, according to the Kelley Blue Book Residual Value Guide, available at your local library, bank, or direct if you dial 800-258-3266.

4. **Calculate reasonable depreciation.** In this case, subtract the residual value from the capitalized cost, and come up with $5,660.

5. **Find the hidden interest.** Do this by subtracting the $5,660 depreciation from the $8,164 lease payments. Total interest turns out to be $2,504.

6. **Figure out the interest rate.** Here's the formula:

$$\text{Interest rate} = \frac{\$2{,}504}{(\$16{,}000 + \$11{,}340)/2*3}$$

7. In that formula, the $16,000 is the car price reduced by the $1,000 you are paying up front. The $11,340 is the residual value. The 3 is the number of years in the lease. The 2 is a constant. And the underlying rate? 6.1 percent.

QUICK CALCULATION: THE CAR LEASE (continued)

8. **Put it all together.** The total payments add up to $8,164. That's the equivalent of a depreciation charge of $5,660 plus $2,504 of interest charged at 6.1 percent. It's not such a bad deal. If it were, the interest rate at the suggested price and turn in value would have come out far higher. But if the dealer is offering a special 3 percent rate on car loans, or you expect to drive it for more than three years, you still might prefer buying the vehicle.

SECRET: *Before you even go down the lease/buy lane, determine the best price on a product. After you have negotiated that deal, talk about a lease separately. If you don't like the lease the store has, call in a third-party leasing firm (look in the yellow pages to find one.) Often, however, the store or its leasing affiliate will have a better incentive to get you the best plan.*

Crunch, Crunch

The bottom line, of course, is the bottom line when it comes to making the buy/lease decision. You have to sit down and compare your final costs of leasing to your final costs of buying on a case-by-case basis to figure out which makes the most sense. Consider:

> your out-of-pocket costs
>
> the after-tax costs
>
> the opportunity costs of tying up money. (That's the money you don't earn because the money's not available to invest elsewhere in your business, or in an interest-bearing account.)
>
> whether you'd buy the equipment with cash, or on a loan
>
> the after-tax cost of the loan

The easiest way to crunch all of this is to use software. Many programs offer lease/buy calculations. One example is Prosper, a program from Ernst and Young, the accounting firm, that will compare loans and cash to leases. Once you know the steps involved, you can easily tailor your own spreadsheet to give you the ultimate answer.

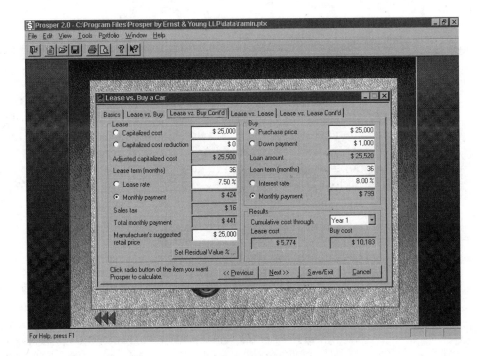

Here's a typical lease/buy analysis: Say you are considering a new $10,000 setup, including a computer, color printer, scanner, digital camera—the works. If you have the cash on hand, you could buy it outright. If you live in a state that has a 5 percent sales tax, your cost would be $10,500. Assuming all the items are deductible business expenses, and that you are in the 28 percent tax bracket and pay 15.3 percent self-employment tax, you'd reduce your taxes by $4,546 (roughly, this doesn't account for the fact that you lose a bit of that savings when you reduce your self-employment tax deduction on your 1040.) So the final cost of the deal would be $5,953. But in three years, you'd be shopping for new equipment.

But wait! What if you took that $10,500 and invested it at the beginning of the year, and earned 7 percent on your money? You'd earn $2,946 on your money over three years, the amount of time you expect you could use this equipment before you'd have to buy a new system. That's the opportunity cost of using your cash to buy the equipment.

Okay, what if you lease the equipment? You can get a three-year lease for $338 a month. That's a total layout of $12,168; there's no sales taxes because you aren't actually buying anything. It's all deductible, so at the same tax rate, your deduction saves you $5,268 and your after tax costs

BONUS!
100 STRATEGIC SAVING SECRETS
OF THE SELF-EMPLOYED

The key to stretching your business cash is to spend it wisely. If you know how to go about it and adapt personal penny-pinching tips to business costs, you can save on just about anything you might need to buy for the office. Consider the pages that follow a book-buyer's bonus: 100 tips that can save you thousands of business dollars. Scan them before you get to Chapter 8 and learn how to raise money for your business: You may need to raise less than you think!

Save on the Phone

- Get serious about cutting your long-distance costs by signing on with a third-party telephone reseller that charges low rates and bills in six-second increments. The Telecommunications Resellers Association will send you a list of agents who represent several different companies, and can crunch your calls for the bottomest line. Reach them at 1155 Connecticut Avenue, NW, Washington, DC 20036, or online at resellers@aol.com. Annual savings, for a conservative $100-a-month phone bill: $240.

- Alternatively, put all the major carriers through their paces and find the best small business calling plan for you. Some have rates as low as sixteen cents a minute, compared to full fares that run thirty cents or more. Contact the Telecommunications Research & Action Center (TRAC), P.O. Box 27279, Washington DC 20005, (202) 462-2520. For $5 and an SASE, they'll sell you a thorough report detailing all the small business long-distance plans.

- Dial 800-555-1212 before you make a long-distance call to find out if there's a toll-free number. Better yet, get a set of toll-free number phone books and use them.

- Join the cyberphone frontier. Two software packages, Internet Phone by VocalTec of Northvale, New Jersey, and Net Phone, by Electric Magic, in San Francisco, allow you to use the Internet for actual phone calls; you'll end up spending about $1 a hour to talk through

100 STRATEGIC SAVING SECRETS (continued)

your computer mike to your Internet friends' speakers, once the rest of the world is wired.

■ Use Biz*File and Phone*File on CompuServe to look up long-distance phone numbers. At an average cost of twenty-five cents per number, it beats directory assistance. If you look up ten numbers a month, that's $60 a year you save.

■ Alternatively, call 900-555-1212, AT&T's long-distance information service and get two listings for seventy-five cents.

■ If you're making multiple long-distance calls from the road, press the pound key (#) after you complete your first call. It will give you a dial tone for a second call, and you won't have to punch in your account number again. You'll also avoid new connect charges that can run fifty cents or more per call. Do this 100 times a year and save $50.

■ West coasters should start early and east coasters should call late: You have a better chance of catching your cross-country colleagues at their desks and you'll save as much as 60 percent on your phone calls, reports Kimberly Stanséll, publisher of Bootstrappin' Entrepreneur newsletter. East coasters who dial between five and eleven p.m. will save thirty percent; West coasters who can work before eight a.m. will save even more on the same bill.

■ If your business name is your name, get a second residential instead of a business listing. You won't be listed in the yellow pages, but you won't be paying an additional 7.2 cents per call either. If you make twenty calls a business day, you will save $360 a year.

■ Alternatively, get that business line, put a two-line phone on your desk, and use your residential line to make all of your outgoing calls.

■ Use one of those new phone debit cards, but only when you are making expensive calls from public phones.

Save Online

■ Learn the Internet for free. The National Public Telecomputing Network, P.O. Box 1987, Cleveland, OH 44106; (infor@nptn.org) will

100 STRATEGIC SAVING SECRETS (continued)

get you on Free-Net, a community computer system with free Internet access. In some locations, it may be limited and you may have to go to your local library to use it.

■ If you're a light online user, go through one of the commercial providers, like CompuServe or Prodigy. For $9.95 a month, you can use five hours of the Net a month.

■ If you can't get enough online, sign on for an "all you can eat" Internet access account for about $20 a month from a local provider. If you are online twenty hours a month, (not that much), your annual savings will be $119.

■ Remember, with many online accounts, the first month is free. Use it up exploring every nook and cranny.

■ If you publish an e-mail address and get tons of mail, get two e-mail addresses. Put the busy one on your unlimited service; keep a second private account on your commercial service. This will prioritize your mail-reading time and save you on reading all your mail on Prodigy, for example, which charges you $2.95 for every hour over five a month that you're online. If you spend one and a half hours each business day combing through general mail, you'll save $991 in a year.

■ If you're a regular researcher, learn to love Knowledge Index, the off-peak alternative to costly databases. On CompuServe, for a flat rate of forty cents a minute, it can save you plenty over databases that charge $12.50 a search or more. Do two five-minute searches a week and save $100 a year.

Save on Equipment

■ Furnish creatively. You can buy a cardboard shoe shelf for $9 at any discount store, and use it as a paper/document sorter.

■ Stay a year out of date. Today you can buy a total MacLC system for $890; it's a little slower but will handle just about anything a

---

100 STRATEGIC SAVING SECRETS (continued)

comparable new Performa can crunch. Savings: $609. You can buy an IBM Think Pad for $700.

- Upgrade! You can turn that LC into a Power Mac for another $699, and still save; $500 if you buy and upgrade, $1,000 if you already own an upgradable computer. The savings are comparable for IBM/PC models

- Save less. Unless you do design work, a fiften-inch screen is big enough, especially staring at you across a narrow desk. You'll save $400 over a seventeen-inch monitor.

- Shop the components of your computer system separately. For example, computer from a local discount store, monitor from a mail-order house, modem from a different mail order house. The savings: $300 on the computer, $40 on the modem, and $200 on the monitor; total: $540.

- Buy recycled cartridges for your laser printer. Try RDS in Poughkeepsie, New York 800-344-9951, or try a local supplier. If you replace once a quarter, you can save $146 a year.

- But don't bother buying those recycled cartridges for your inkjet printer. A recent comparison found the Hewlett-Packard new color inkjet printers at Staples Office Supply run $5 cheaper than the recycled ones.

- Buy your new computer through the mail. The state sales tax you save will more than make up for the shipping. On a $5,000 system in a 5 percent tax state, with a typical $60 shipping charge, you'll save $190.

- Save $24.50 for every incandescent bulb you replace with a fluorescent, says money-saving expert Lucy Hedricks.

- Think of the environment and buy recycled batteries. Battery Express (800-666-2296) will save you $35 on a battery for an IBM ThinkPad 700. Take two; they're small, and save $70 a year.

- Buy used stuff. Contact the National Materials Exchange Netlink (509-466-1532), a Spokane clearinghouse of business materials and equipment to find industrial materials, including paper, medical supplies, wood, plastic and the like that other businesses are trying

100 STRATEGIC SAVING SECRETS *(continued)*

to lose. Aaron Rents & Sells will sell you a Hewlett-Packard Model 950 plain paper inkjet fax for $350. You'll pay $600 for it new if you find it on sale somewhere. Savings: $250.

- Slash utility bills by installing motion sensors, which automatically turn off lights when you leave a room.

- Use shareware. There are lots of nifty free and cheap programs available for download from the Internet or on disk collections you can buy cheap.

- Ask for special competitive upgrade prices before you buy new software. Sometimes the deals are so good, it's worth buying an old piece of software just to upgrade.

- Create a business purpose for your personal trips. It won't make them any cheaper, but it will make them at least partially deductible.

- Buy stuff the government is selling. Contact the Consumer Information Center (Department 71, Pueblo, CO 81009) and ask for the Guide to Federal Government Sales.

- Relabel all of those America Online disks you keep getting in the mail and reuse them. Save the one you need for reinstalling it on your computer.

Save on Business Practices

- Incorporate online via The Company Corporation (corp@incorporate.com.) Instead of a $500 plus attorney's bill, you'll pay around $45; savings: $455. Or buy Incorporate software from Unabridged Software in Houston (800-248-7630). It will provide all the forms and addresses you need so you can file them yourself, for $69.

- Ask around until you get the name of a sales rep who already reaches the kinds of customers you are looking for. Then piggyback: since he or she is already making those sales calls, he or she might be willing to distribute your brochures for free, or at a very reasonable cost.

100 STRATEGIC SAVING SECRETS (continued)

- Target your marketing dollars by paying attention to where your existing clients come from. Then market in the same places for more.

- Swap mailing lists with colleagues who don't directly compete with you.

- Abandon fax cover sheets whenever possible; instead, use those tiny stickies or just type "Fax for Marcia or John" on the top of your page. If you fax long-distance five times a day, that can save you $312 a year in long-distance costs.

- Ask those faxing to you to abandon those covers as well. You'll save $56 a year in fax paper.

- Give your favorite clients gifts instead of buying them meals. Gifts are fully deductible up to $25 each, while meals are only 50 percent deductible. For the same amount of money, you'll save $6.38 in taxes on each $25 expenditure. Spring for 20 at Christmas and save $127 in taxes.

- Set your fax to send at standard mode rather than fine mode. Save about half the time in transmission. That's roughly fifty cents on a five-page fax, or $250 if you fax ten pages a day.

- Split your broadcast fax list into local and long-distance lists. Send the local ones yourself, but hire a service to broadcast the long-distance ones. At charges around eighteen cents a minute, you'll save time, effort, wear and tear on your machine, and long-distance charges. If you fax two pages to a list of 500 eight times a year, that's $720.

- Give up your car phone and use a pager instead. You'll still be reachable in an emergency, and you won't be paying hefty 40-cents-a-minute fees for your calls.

- Forget the fax and just do it all through your computer with a fax modem and nifty new software. Save the $500 you'd spend on a decent fax.

- Exhibit at a trade show to attract potential clients in bulk. Pay just $107 per lead instead of $230 you'd spend on individual sales call,

100 STRATEGIC SAVING SECRETS (*continued*)

according to Marilyn and Tom Ross in their book, Big Ideas for Small Service Businesses (Buena Vista, 1994, Communication Creativity).

■ Lower your thermostat one degree and save as much as 20 percent of your heating bill, says financial planner Barbara O'Neill. Good for your computer equipment and your productivity!

■ Remember your grade school art teacher? "Please use both sides of the paper." Keep a box by your printer for printer tests, notes, and other uses. If you use a ream a month, you'll save $30 in a year.

■ While you are at it, buy all that paper at once and get a quantity discount. Instead of paying $5.99 a ream one at a time, buy ten at once and pay $4.99 at Quill Office Supply. If you run through enough paper to buy (and store) 100 reams at once, the price drops another dollar. Savings, for those who can only keep 10 reams at once: $12 a year.

■ Are you a writer? Many computer companies, including IBM and Apple, may lend you a full system to write your book or latest project. Save $3,000 at least, more if they'll go top of the line.

■ If you take lots of photos in your work but don't need high-quality results, buy cheap film. Many local discounters sell their brands at about 25 percent less than Kodak or Fuji. If you're shooting one roll a week, that's $50 a year.

■ Lower the density on your laser printer for everyday copies; your cartridges will last about three months longer. If you usually replace them once a quarter, you can save $143 a year.

■ If you regularly submit work on disk to clients, or sell a product on disk, it pays to buy cheap disks. And don't pay for high-density disks if you are only going to use a little corner of them. Switch to cheaper and less capacious double-density disks and save $24 every time you buy 100.

■ Never subscribe to a magazine until you find out if it has professional rates for your type of business. One example: U.S. News and World Report charges the hoi polloi $39.45 annually, but certain professionals can get it for $19.89. Savings: $19.

100 STRATEGIC SAVING SECRETS *(continued)*

- Of course, you can hit up your librarian for the year-old copy of the reference book you love. Many of the names and addresses will remain current. You can save $50 on a good, standard directory.
- Share subscriptions with your friends or colleagues.
- Cadge supplies at your local bank. The tellers are often happy to get rid of the paper clips and rubber bands they accumulate during a day.
- Dog big downtown offices for furniture and equipment. When a company relocates, there's lots of furniture to get rid of in a hurry.
- Get fancy preprinted foil labels, and use them to dress up cheap file folders when you are delivering work to clients.
- Ask for prompt payer and cash discounts whenever you shop.

Save at the Bank

- If your business name is your personal name, you can get around the high fees for a business checking account by using a second personal checking account instead. If you need an account with a business name so you can deposit client checks, try a business savings account first. Often, there are no fees with a minimum balance, and you can transfer money as you need it into that personal checking account. A bonus: You'll earn some interest on your money.
- Use a money market mutual fund instead of a checking account for your business emergency fund. There are no monthly charges, and the yields are far higher (currently about 5.5 percent). Two that are particularly friendly to check writers are United Services Government Securities Savings Fund (800-873-8637) and the new E-fund (800-533-3863), which has a $35 annual fee, but also gives you a debit card.
- Take money out of your savings account to pay off your charges. Then keep your balances at zero.
- Insist on a no-annual fee credit card, and save the $25–40 you've been paying.

- If you run card balances, look for the lowest rate card by contacting Ram Research at (301-695-4660; http://www.ramresearch.com) for a list.

- Buy checks through the mail. You can expect to pay $32 for 400 checks from your local bank; Checks in the Mail (800-733-4443) charges about $10 for the same order.

- Ignore all the frequent flyer promos and just find a credit card that kicks back a 1 percent rebate. Charge everything; pay it off monthly, and pocket $240 a year if you charge $2,000 a month.

- Pay bills in advance. If you know you're going to be sending in a $25 cable TV check every month, send in four months worth. You'll save on stamps, envelopes, and time, and give up only a pittance in interest.

- Refinance your home, if you own instead of rent. Loan rates have been low for years; if they currently run more than 2 percent below your rate, get a new loan.

Save on Travel and Entertainment

- Get one of the new restaurant discount cards. Transmedia (800-422-1231) gives you 25 percent off your total tab, including drinks, at many member restaurants.

- If you travel anyway, why not get deep discounts and the occasional ticket free by being a courier? Contact the International Association of Air Travel Couriers (407-582-8320).

- Book hotel rooms through a reselling consolidator. When you book through Quikbook (800-789-9887), you could save $104 a night on a basic hotel room in Manhattan and $85 on a room in San Francisco.

- If you want to take advantage of the stay-over-Saturday discounts on the airlines, but you don't want to stay, buy two sets of tickets and throw half of each pair away, suggests Sylvia Blishak, who runs Accent on Travel USA in Klamath Falls, Oregon. Fly from New York to Miami using this plan and save a total of $510, she says. You'll save

100 STRATEGIC SAVING SECRETS (continued)

so much on the Saturday-stay tickets that two sets will be cheaper than one.

- Live with a little inconvenience. Save an additional $268 from New York to Miami for example, if you're willing to fly with an airline that will have you switching planes. Let your agent know you're willing to adjust your schedule for maximum savings.

Hire Help and Save

- Hire consultants initially, then do the grunt work yourself. You can pay a public relations writer $300 to write a press release for you. Or you can pay him or her for an hour of time to teach you the essentials of press release writing, and write it yourself. Pay an organizer $500 to rearrange your file cabinet. Or pay him or her for a couple of hours of strategy planning on how to arrange your files and then do that yourself. Choose carefully, of course; everyone can't do everything.

- Hire your spouse if you're married, and provide family insurance benefits to him or her (see Chapter 10 for complete details). It's a perfectly legal, if circuitous, route toward total health insurance deductibility for the self-employed, as long as your spouse really performs a legitimate function in your business. You can provide not only insurance, but fully reimbursable health spending accounts, so family orthodonture, well-baby visits, and the like are covered. And these expenses are deductible from your business return, not your family return.

- Hire your kids, too, if you have them. It's time they learned that work ethic and understood what you do in the basement all day, anyway. Pay them a legitimate rate for legitimate work and keep track of their hours. You'll be able to deduct their salaries from your business, avoid Social Security (self-employment) taxes on the money, and pay them up to $3,800 before they start owing taxes themselves. Annual savings for one child: $1,862.

- If you bill out at $50 an hour, you can find reasonable assistance at $10 to $15 an hour for filing, correspondence, research, errands, and more.

100 STRATEGIC SAVING SECRETS (*continued*)

- Teach an intern from the local college your business. If you offer serious work experience and some guidance and grading, you may not have to worry about the paycheck. One semester's worth of fifteen hours a week work, even if you pay $5 an hour minimum wage, saves you $2,250 when you compare it with the $15 hourly fee a non-student might charge.

- Reward your workers with noncash perks. Give them extra time off when business is slow; or let them use your business library; or provide parking and an easygoing atmosphere at work.

- Barter with other professionals to get work done around your office: You can write a brochure and they can set up your bookkeeping system, or vice versa.

Save on Printing and Publishing

- Bring your own paper and envelopes to the printer. For 1,000 6 x 9 envelopes, save $32. This adds up if you publish a newsletter. Supply your own paper for 1,000 copies of a monthly twelve page letter and save $1,704 a year.

- Print lots! You can get 500 two-color business cards for $213 or 1,000 business cards for $218, because the printer's main cost is in setting up the job and making the negatives.

- Instead of hiring a service bureau to produce camera-ready art of your letterhead and the like, print it out double-sized on your laser printer. Then have the printshop shoot your art at 50 percent. You'll get crisp output that's double your laser printer's normal dpi (dots per inch) resolution, with smaller dots, and save about $15 a sheet. Do your letterhead, mailing labels, business cards, and some small ads this way, and save about $45.

- Market with postcards instead of letters. They are attention-getting and cheap.

100 STRATEGIC SAVING SECRETS (*continued*)

Save on Freight

- Get the U.S. Postal Service to clean up your mailing list, free. Submit your list in ASCII format and the post office will flag incomplete addresses, add zip plus four to them, and make you eligible for its bar code discounts. Contact 800-238-3150 for details.

- Use e-mail. Encourage your clients to accept reports online, and save yourself courier and overnight fees. Give up one overnight delivery a month and save $156 a year.

- Split mailing costs with a buddy. If you're an accountant, find a lawyer, an organizer, and a marketing consultant to go in on a mailing with you. You can each put a flyer in the envelope, send out 10,000 pieces, and save $3,750.

- Hire a mailing house to do your mass mailings. With their bulk rate permits, they will charge you roughly 52 cents per piece. That's about what you'd pay for the stamps and envelopes on your own, not counting the labor.

- Alternatively, collect kids from the neighborhood to stuff your envelopes. Even if you throw in pizza, you'll save.

- If you are serious about your mailing, get your own bulk mail permit. It costs $85 a year, but postage is 22.6 cents per piece. You'll save $855 in a year if you bulk mail 10,000 pieces.

- If you love and don't want to give up FedEx, start checking the Next Business Afternoon box on your sheet instead of Priority. You'll save about $3 a delivery and your packages still will get there the next day (and often by 10 a.m.).

- Keep all kinds of postage stamps on hand. And weigh everything you mail. The cents you save by not putting extra stamps on envelopes will add up eventually.

Save on Your Insurance

- Raise the deductibles on your insurance. With a regular Blue Cross/Blue Shield plan, a family of four can save $1,500 a year in

---

100 STRATEGIC SAVING SECRETS (continued)

premiums by moving from a $200 deductible to a $1,000 deductible. Even if you end up spending the deductible, you're ahead.

- Adjust the stop loss on your health insurance. You know the part where you agree to pay, say, 20 percent of all charges up to $5,000? Instead, go with a plan that requires you to pay 50 percent of all costs up to $2,500, says Rockville, Maryland, insurance pro Martin Rochkind. In the worst case, your out-of-pocket costs go up $250 a year, but premiums for an individual drop by $324.

- If your car is old, drop your collision coverage. Save at least $100 a year.

- If you work at home, call your auto insurance company and tell your agent you don't commute. He or she might give you a discount.

- Skip most "one-purpose" insurance. That includes cancer insurance, life insurance that only pays your home mortgage or credit cards, and insurance that only covers maintenance on one piece of equipment. Generally speaking, these policies are really stacked against you.

- Just buy term life insurance for your family protection needs. Invest in cheaper ways than through whole, universal, or variable life policies.

---

are $6,899. And don't forget you can leave that $10,500 in the bank or mutual fund earning interest while you dole out the $338 a month. You'll earn less than $2,946 on the money, but you only have to earn $1,000 to break even with the purchase.

There is a third alternative. You buy the computer, but put the $10,500 on your Visa and pay it off over three years while you pay 14 percent interest. You end up paying $358 a month which is more than the cost of leasing it, but only marginally more. Pay it off a little quicker, or get a better rate on your card, and the advantage starts to go to you. Squeeze a fourth year out of it and you really come out ahead by buying. And so what if the computer's completely outmoded then? You can at least use it to calculate whether you're going to lease or buy your next system.

SECRET: *You can always save money on a credit card purchase by paying it off faster. In the example above, bump the payments up to $508 a month and you'll pay off the computer a year earlier, and save $696 in interest. Switch over to a lower-interest credit card and save more: If the card charged 12 percent interest instead of 14, you could save another $14 a month, or $336 over the two year life of the loan.*

Before You Sign

Even if you like the terms of a lease, make sure you read the fine print and consider all of the angles before you lock yourself into it. Don't sign a lease that lasts longer than the warranty on the underlying product (if you don't want to replace an engine in a car you own, you really don't want to replace one in a car you are renting), and look for a lease that is "closed end." That's like built-in insurance that covers you from having to pay the lessor to take the car, computer, or copier back if the value has fallen more than you both expect.

Strategic Savings Secrets of the Self-Employed

Finally, remember that you can save a lot of money without compromising your work style or your lifestyle if you learn to think like a penny-pincher. Analyze every expense to determine whether there is a cheaper way to do it. And get inspired by the Strategic Savings list on page 151: it's a bonus of 100 strategic tips that other entrepreneurs have used to save tens of thousands of dollars every year.

YOU MUST REMEMBER THIS: LESSONS FROM CHAPTER 7

- You do have to spend money to make money, but far less than you think!
- Don't part with a dime unless you have to.
- Even after you've decided to buy something, you have choices about how you pay for it. Make them carefully.

© David Wink 1997

"Any banker will tell you
that the best time to line up a loan
is when you don't need one."

Money, Money, Who's Got the Money?

Money is blood for a business, and sooner or later we all need a transfusion. The trick is in matching the right type of loan to the need. Go to a venture capitalist seeking $5,000 to buy a computer, and you'll be laughed at. If you ask your suppliers for longer credit terms, when what you really need are the megabucks that can take your business national, you're collecting drops in a bucket. And if you are looking for those first few dollars to get your business off the ground, you probably will waste your time no matter who you ask, unless they are relatives.

When your business is new, it may be impossible to separate your personal identity from your company's financial needs. A bank will expect you to guarantee a business loan, if you're lucky enough to be granted one. But use this to your advantage: If your business and personal life converge, use that fact to get the cash you need at the best price. And then move the cash around to put it where you need it most.

When Should You Borrow Money?

Maybe never, but start now anyway. Any banker will tell you that the best time to line up a loan is when you don't need one. You look good on paper, you are confident about the future, and your creditors will be, too. When you are in business for yourself, it is always a good idea to get a line of credit that you can draw down at your discretion. It can carry you through those bumpy periods of slow-paying clients, enable you to buy a new copier when your old one dies, or expand your business, all without having to ask for cash in the clutch.

Some lines of credit to pursue include:

- ❏ **A business line of credit from your bank.** Hard to get at first, but the cleanest in terms of its business connection. Business credit also helps to establish a credit history that will enable you to borrow big bucks down the line.

- ❏ **A home equity line of credit.** The good news is, the rates are lower and the interest is usually deductible regardless of whether you use the cash in your business or your personal life. The bad news is, if you blow it, you can lose your house.

- ❏ **Credit cards.** Entrepreneurs have always used credit cards in a pinch, and with some new cards boasting rates in single digits, this isn't always the awful idea it used to be. Keep a couple to use if you have to. Remember them as a last resort: because their interest rates are typically higher than other money sources, credit cards are not a practical source of long-term money.

The key to these credit lines is that you don't necessarily have to use them, and you certainly shouldn't rely on them or run your business on them. They are standby, backup, and emergency sources of credit that you should establish just in case.

As far as actually borrowing money, that requires you to perfect more of a balancing act. You can starve a business without adequate cash flow, so don't be too shy about borrowing to grow. But you can also bury a promising business with heavy debt burdens. Borrow only when you absolutely have to, and then borrow smart.

Some good business reasons to borrow include:

❑ You have lots of orders, but not enough cash to buy the supplies and hire help you need to get them out.

❑ You need to upgrade your business equipment.

❑ Your business is seasonal and you need to borrow money now, to put supplies, equipment, and people in place for your busy period.

❑ You and your business are ready to grow, but that takes more money than you have.

Before you borrow, figure out as exactly as possible how much you need and what you need it for. Use the budgeting techniques and cash flow projections you learned in Chapter 1 to calculate how much you'll be able to afford to pay back monthly. Then explore these classic and alternative ways to raise cash.

Use Personal Resources to Raise Money

Before digging into the pockets of others, you usually have to dig deep into your own. There are many different ways to borrow from yourself; here are the main ones, along with considerations about using them.

Borrow Against a Retirement Fund

If you are still employed outside of your business, and have a 401(k) plan, or have a working spouse with such a plan, there's a good chance you can borrow against it easily by filling out a few forms in the company benefits office. These loans are limited by law to the lesser of half of the money in the plan or $50,000. If you borrow only those funds that the employer deposited, the interest is deductible as a business expense; but it isn't deductible if you borrow money you or your spouse contributed.

This is a good way to borrow money, because the interest you pay goes directly back into that retirement account, so it's like paying interest to yourself. But these loans can get called in a hurry when the job ends, so if you're planning to quit to run your business full-time, don't borrow

THE HUNT FOR CASH

If you're on a hunt for cash, consider the example set by Susan Anderson, dubbed by *Home Office Computing* magazine as "the Queen of Guerrilla Financing." Based in Minneapolis, Anderson started her business Kit Company with an idea, but as in many cases, not much cash. Her idea, providing companies with cleaning kits for their business equipment, required a large amount of cash to finance the costs of engineering, formulation, manufacturing, packaging, advertising, and distribution of her product.

Anderson began by running up $20,000 in Visa bills, supplementing her income with consulting fees, and in a speculative move, when there was a shortage of latex gloves in New York due to the AIDS epidemic, Anderson tracked down suppliers on the West Coast and then sold the latex gloves back East. The profits made from this venture were funneled back into her Kit Company projects.

Anderson then convinced Citibank to lend her $15,000. She negotiated deals with her suppliers, chemical, packaging, printing, and bottle companies to supply products on 90-day credit terms. Anderson put in so many requests for credit that Dun & Bradstreet, the financial rating firm, called her to find out who she was and why they were getting so many calls about her. Anderson also took advantage of a contest sponsored by a women's venture-capital program backed by the National Association of Female Executives. She won a low-interest $50,000 loan.

The money she raised to get her company off the ground and running elevated her status to the big leagues. The name of her company was changed from Kit Company to Planna Technology, Inc., reporting about $500,000 a year in sales.

At last report, Anderson was looking for $1 million to $2 million to fund a national sales effort. She was talking to investment bankers about selling part of her company in exchange for cash in a transaction known as a "private placement" of shares. Next stop for Anderson and Planna Technology? Perhaps the New York Stock Exchange.

On the accompanying table is a handy hierarchy of where you can go for cash when you need it, depending on how much cash you need.

THE HUNT FOR CASH (*continued*)

Money Steps					
The Source	**How Much?**	**Good News**	**Bad News**	**Best for**	**Concerns**
Friends or relatives	<$20,000	Favorable terms; easy application	The friend/relative may try to take over; stress to relationship	Start-up costs	Can they afford it?
Credit cards	<$30,000	Do it yourself	Expensive	In a pinch	Using up and, perhaps, ruining your credit
Customers (collect up front, sell services in packages)	<$50,000	You don't lay out for them; helps you plan your work	No room to maneuver; you owe the work	Business with a loyal following	Under-charging to get the cash in early
Suppliers (stretch those payments!)	Depends on the size of your business; $5,000 to $500,000	Buys you some float time; may be no interest	Short-term money; not a viable way to expand	Business with lots of cash flow	Suppliers over-charging to pay for the float
Borrow from employed spouse's retirement fund	<$50,000	You end up paying interest to your spouse	If your spouse leaves the job, you must repay the loan immediately	People who aren't close to retire-ment	Spouse losing income on the money you borrowed
Home equity line	<$75,000	Easy; do it yourself	Putting your house on the line	Secure individu-als with safe busi-nesses	Losing your house

THE HUNT FOR CASH (continued)

Money Steps					
The Source	**How Much?**	**Good News**	**Bad News**	**Best for**	**Concerns**
Factors (sell your receivables)	> $20,000 a month	No more worry about collections	Expensive	Goods businesses	Your customers may frown on the practice
Raid your retirement fund	The average is $35,000	Do it yourself	You may pay penalties, plus taxes, to get it	Borrowers with total confidence in their future	No safety net if your business fails
SBA microloan	<$25,000	Small, friendly	Short supply	Small start-ups	Limited availability
SBA loan	$150,000 to $750,000	The feds qualify you	Many SBA hoops to jump	Growing businesses shut out of bank loans	Lengthy application process
Basic bank loan	>$100,000	Easier process than SBA	Hard to get for small companies	Big businesses	May require cosigner
Angels	From $5,000 to $1 million	You get an advisor, too	Can be difficult to dissolve	Specialized businesses	Risky relationship with a stranger
Venture capital	>$250,000	Expert advice included	You give away part of your company	Big and fast-growing companies	Lose control of your firm

---

THE HUNT FOR CASH (*continued*)

Expect that your sources of money will change and grow as your business and your need for money expands. A cash source that might not work at the beginning of your business can work well once you get bigger.

In the next chapter, we'll explore another way your business might grow from a one person enterprise to a company with its own staff!

---

money this way. And remember, if your interest rate is lower than what your 401(k) was earning elsewhere, you're stinting your retirement fund.

Liquidate Your Retirement Plan

You can, of course, cash the rollover IRA you took from your last job, or take money out of your Keogh account. But this is a costly way to go. You'll pay income taxes on all the funds you withdraw, as well as a 10 percent penalty if you are under fifty-nine and a half. And don't forget, you're gutting your nest egg.

There is one exception, but it probably won't net you enough money. You can avoid penalties if you are under fifty-nine and a half, as long as you make withdrawals in equal amounts designed to let the money last your or your beneficiary's lifetime. Even then, you still will pay income taxes on the money.

*S*ECRET: *If you control your own IRA or Keogh, you can make yourself a quick and painless sixty-day loan. Federal regulations allow you to withdraw money from an IRA or Keogh, and then give you sixty days to roll it over into a new account elsewhere. If you are having a real cash flow crunch, and know the money will be in your hand within that two month period, you can take money out of your IRA or Keogh, use it to pay bills, and then replace that cash within two months by opening a rollover IRA or Keogh elsewhere. You can do this only once a year, and be sure that you can replenish it, or you'll get stuck paying those taxes and penalties and running through your retirement security.*

173

Take Out a Home Equity Loan

Especially with interest rates as low as they are these days, this is not a bad way to borrow money. It's easy to qualify, and the rates are likely to be much better than you could get on a business loan. There are three choices: You can take a home equity line of credit, a second mortgage, or refinance your original mortgage. The credit line gives you more flexibility; the second mortgage (or refinanced first mortgage) lets you lock in today's rates for the long term. Of course, this doesn't help you build a business credit rating for the time when you need big money. And you are betting your house on your business. But if you are disciplined and careful, it's an easy and cheap way to get start-up money in a hurry.

Tap Your Life Insurance

If you've accumulated cash value in an old-fashioned whole or universal life insurance policy, you can lend it to yourself cheaply. Policies that are twenty years old or more often carry very low interest rates, in the 4 to 5 percent range, so this can be an ideal source of financing for older entrepreneurs seeking to build second careers. If your children are grown, your spouse is self-supporting, and you no longer need the death benefit, there's a hidden bonus here: You never have to repay the loan.

Use Your Credit Card

With a good credit rating and a lot of cards, you could probably push this up around $75,000, but you don't want to. Credit card debt remains expensive, unless you shop hard for low-interest cards. This approach does give you instant money, with no questions asked, and might be the best bet if you need to buy a computer or bookcase immediately. But be aware that most credit cards now carry variable interest rates, so credit card debt can quickly bury you in interest if rates move up. And if you run into a personal financial emergency, you might already be tapped out, with no plastic to depend on.

SECRET: *Wachovia Bank in Georgia is consistently the issuer of the lowest interest rate credit card (800-842-3262). For a comprehensive list of low rate cards, contact Ram Research at 301-695-4660, or visit its Web site at http://www.ramresearch.com.*

The First and Last Resort: Borrow From Relatives or Friends

This can be the best or the worst route to take. If things go bad, you can lose your business, your buddies, and/or your brother-in-law.

But, when it goes well, a personal loan can be a winning act of love and faith for all concerned. For example, Maria can borrow money from her parents to buy the equipment she needs to start her computer consulting business. She can arrange to pay them back at 7 percent interest. That's less than she'd have to pay at the bank, but more than her parents would get from the bank. Eliminating the banker this way thus allows Maria and her parents to both win from the same transaction. As long as Maria really pays them back, her parents don't use the loan as a reason to meddle, and the loan doesn't strain their own finances.

To arrange a personal loan that works for everyone, follow these pointers:

- ❑ **Pick the right friend or relative.** The best choice is someone who believes in you and your business, who is comfortable in a business relationship, who is not personally in crisis, and who can comfortably afford to lend you money. Avoid anyone who will do what sociologist Jan Yager calls "extracting psychic payment for a loan." Avoid, too, those relatives and friends who are not risk-takers. Suppress the urge to ask friends who have suddenly come into money—perhaps through an inheritance—and are wary of any financial requests they are getting.

- ❑ **Make sure your benefactor can afford it.** Parents or grandparents may have money put away but might be living on the interest. Friends who seem to have money may not be in control of it—perhaps their funds are tied up in trust funds or retirement accounts or managed solely by others.

- ❑ **Test the waters.** There *can* be harm in asking. Talk in general terms first to see if you can extract the person's attitude about lending money.

    Jan Yager suggests that this preliminary conversation can help you figure out how your friend or relative feels about personal

A PROPER PROMISSORY NOTE

If a friend loans you money, be sure to write a promissory note. There are two important reasons for this. A note puts your arrangement on paper, for the benefit of both parties, establishing the terms of the agreement. It also establishes that you have a bona fide loan, so you can deduct the interest payments as a business expense.

In a proper promissory note, include the following: names and address of the parties; the amount borrowed; the date(s) on which it must be paid; the name and address to which payments will be made; a payment schedule including interest payments. Some lenders might ask you to include a "call" provision—a clause that lets them request the money back whenever they want or need it.

Here's a sample note:

I, **(your name)** promise to pay to the order of **(lender's name)** the sum of **($XXX.00) (amount in words)** dollars.

Interest on the principal shall be charged at an annual rate of **(X%) (percent in words)** percent. This note will be paid in monthly installments of **($XXX.00) (amount in words)** dollars, beginning on **(month, day, year)** and due on the **(date)** of each month thereafter, until the principal is paid in full. Those payments will be made to **(name and address of lender)** .

Should interest not be paid when due it shall thereafter bear interest at the same rate as the principal.

The holder of this note retains the right to call the entire amount of unpaid principal and accrued but unpaid interest due after 60 days notice to the signer of this note.

I, the undersigned, agree to pay costs of collection, including just and reasonable court costs.

(Name of borrower)

(Address of borrower)

(Date)

(Location)

(Signature of borrower)

A PROPER PROMISSORY NOTE (*continued*)

Of course, different loan arrangements will be constructed in other ways. Several excellent sources of fill-in-the-blanks promissory notes are available, including:

Nolo Press, Berkeley California, 800-992-6656, publishes a simple Loan Agreement Kit which includes seven different promissory notes as well as comprehensive instructions on how to structure the arrangement and calculate interest and payments.

Legal LetterWorks is a motherlode of legal documents on disk. It includes promissory notes, as well as documents for writing your will, leasing equipment, hiring employees, and incorporating. Import the document you want into your word processor, and fill in the blanks. To order, contact Round Lake Publishing, 31 Bailey Avenue, Ridgefield, CT 05877, or call 203-431-9696.

---

loans in general. You might bring up someone you read about who launched a business on his mother's (or uncle's or friend's) dime, just to see what the reaction will be. If your relative says "what a heartwarming story," go ahead and ask for the loan. If, instead, he or she says "it's terrible to take advantage of a friend that way!" you'll know his or her attitude about inside lending.

Sam Mouallem, a Montreal product broker who launched his Simex Equipment Inc. with a $11,000 loan from his uncle, tested the waters first by asking his father for an objective opinion. "Do you think it would be a good idea to ask Uncle Maroun for the money?" he asked. His father thought his uncle would welcome the opportunity to help Sam build his business, and told him so. Only then did Sam ask his uncle for the loan.

❏ **Be completely honest.** When you do ask, lay all your cards on that table. Be very businesslike. If you really want a gift, don't ask for a loan. Tell the truth about how your business is doing. If you expect it to take a couple of years before you are able to pay back the loan, say so.

AWARDS, GRANTS, AND PRIZES

Before you borrow or give away equity, or beg your in-laws, or cash in your retirement account, why not investigate money out there with few strings attached?

A number of companies and organizations sponsor cash awards, grants and prizes for small businesses that need money to grow. Here's a list of the biggest and best, so get out that letterhead, and don't drag your feet: Even give-away money is getting harder to find; several special grants have been discontinued in the last year.

Best of America Awards. The National Federation of Independent Business Education Foundation and Dun & Bradstreet Information Services give four awards to recognize excellence in small business. To qualify you must have fewer than 250 employees; at least three years in business; and demonstrate growth, innovation, and community involvement. First prize is $25,000; three runner-up prizes are $5,000 each. Contact: Best of America Awards, NFIB Education Foundation, Suite 700, 600 Maryland Avenue SW, Washington, DC 20024.

Partners for Growth. AT&T Capital Corporation and the American Institute of CPAs sponsor this city-specific program. Currently, they are offering $50,000 in grants to Baltimore-based startups that combine social responsibility with solid business planning. Awards have already been given in Philadelphia and Houston. Contact: Partners for Growth, 800-822-8632.

Elizabeth Lewin Fund (ELF) Award. The National Chamber of Commerce for Women sponsors these grants for male and female entrepreneurs who want to develop a high impact profile in their industry, need help, and ask for it. The grants range from $500 to $15,000, and are project-specific. Business owners can ask for cash, products, or services or a combination. For example, someone who wanted to start a newsletter for home-based businesses could ask for $500 to rent a mailing list and hire part-time staffers to assist with the first mailing. Applicants must detail their projects and budgets when they apply. Contact: National Chamber of Commerce for Women, Suite 6H, 10 Waterside Plaza, New York, NY 10010, 212-685-3454.

Indian Business Development Grants. The Bureau of Indian Affairs provides seed capital for Native American entrepreneurs to build profitable

AWARDS, GRANTS, AND PRIZES (*continued*)

businesses and create employment on or near Indian reservations. The grants run as high as $100,000 for an individual business, but recipients must have other sources of funding as well. Contact: the nearest Bureau of Indian Affairs office (listed in the government section of your phone directory).

Great Idea Contest. Seed money, scholarships, trademark searches, federal patents, and more are awarded by the Inventors Workshop International Education Foundation to anyone who comes up with an innovative idea that can be turned into protectable intellectual property. Awards are given in seventeen categories, including arts, construction, electrical, energy, agriculture, furniture design, chemical, transportation, education, food, tools, medical, toys, games, and ecoenvironmental. Cash prizes totaled $15,000 last year, and typically run from $1,000 to $3,000. Contact: Inventors Workshop International Education Foundation, 818-340-4268.

Small Business Innovation Research (SBIR) Grants. Technologically based businesses can get megabucks from their favorite federal agency through this program, which funnels money through the Departments of Agriculture, Commerce, Defense, Health and Human Services, Transportation, and Environmental Protection, as well as the Nuclear Regulatory Commission, the National Science Foundation, and the National Aeronautics and Space Administration. These agencies give Phase I research grants up to $50,000 to determine the feasibility of a project or technology; Phase II grants, to develop technologies and specific products, go up to half a million dollars. The competition is fierce, with only 10 percent of proposals recommended for funding each fiscal year. You can get information from the SBA at 202-205-6450.

Women of Enterprise Award. Avon Products, Inc. salutes five outstanding women entrepreneurs who have achieved success despite significant personal or economic hardships. Candidates must have been profitably self-employed for a minimum of five years after developing a business in the face of significant personal or economic challenges. The winners get $1,000, an all-expenses-paid trip to New York City, speaking engagements, and national publicity. Contact: Women of Enterprise Awards, Avon Products, Inc., 9 West 57th Street, New York, NY 10019.

AWARDS, GRANTS, AND PRIZES (*continued*)

Publishers Grants. The National Endowment for the Arts still has money for small publishers. If you're starting a literary magazine or a small press, consider these grants. The NEA awards $4,000 to $12,000 to support literary magazines that have matching financial support and $4,000 to $15,000 for small presses that have matching money. Contact: Literature Program, Room 722, National Endowment for the Arts, Nancy Hanks Center, 1100 Pennsylvania Avenue NW, Washington, DC 20506-0001, 202-682-5451.

SECRET: *If you don't find an appropriate source on this list, go to a library and ask to see Awards, Honors and Prizes, published by Gale Research. This directory lists more than 20,000 prizes, many of which carry cash awards, in every field from the Abrasive Engineering Society to the Zonta Amelia Earhart Fellowship awards for women in aerospace. And contact your local professional society, too; most give annual awards that can get you recognition, contacts, and perhaps enough money to put a new top on your lap.*

❏ **Write the agreement down.** Putting it all on paper makes the terms crystal clear. It also can come in handy should anything happen to you or the lender before the note is repaid. The lender holds the agreement (though the borrower should also keep a copy.) This is a negotiable financial instrument, just like a bond or certificate of deposit, and should be stored just as safely.

❏ **Use the tools of the trade.** There are many shareware programs that will guide you through calculations of simple and compound interest or full loan amortization, so you can give your benefactor a full payment schedule.

❏ **Reward the lender.** The lender is giving something up to let you use his or her money, so it's a good idea to give something back. For a relative, perhaps write a personal thank-you note along with a business-related gift: Do some work gratis, or find some useful item that expresses your appreciation.

More likely, though, the lender will expect financial rewards in the form of interest. Bank spreads between depositors and borrowers are wide enough for you to split the difference and both come out happy.

❏ **Consider the tax aspects.** The interest you pay is deductible as a business expense, but make sure that your lender is actually declaring it as income before you fill in your tax forms. Personal loans that are forgiven fall into the category of gifts, and tax law limits tax-free gifts to $10,000 per year for each donor and recipient. So, your mother could give you $10,000 and your father could give you $10,000 before gift taxes kicked in. The same limit applies to friends. If the loan is repaid, but no interest is charged, the IRS would view the interest income given up by the lender as a gift.

❏ **Consider the worst-care scenarios.** Your business fails and you can't pay it back. The lender falls on hard times and needs the money back in a hurry. One or the other of you divorce or die, and the new (or former) spouse or heirs are uncomfortable with the arrangements. Your mother forgives the loan, but your siblings find out about it after her death and want you to pay back her estate. Probably none of this will happen to you, but sorting out possible consequences now mean you won't have to worry, fight, or become estranged over it later.

❏ **Stay in touch.** The lender who calls every day to find out how your business is doing can be annoying (especially on days when it's the only phone call you get), but he or she has a moral right to ask. You shouldn't wait for your benefactor to call. You should keep them apprised of what is essentially an investment in you.

Borrow from Suppliers

If you resell inventory or sell goods that you manufacture, your suppliers can ship goods and give you sixty or ninety days to pay for them. Many will do this, just to help give you a leg up; after all, the health of your business contributes to theirs. A small business might float $1,000 to $5,000 this way, while a big manufacturer with orders in hand can get millions.

When Bernard Tenenbaum started a small chain of stereo stores in Long Island, New York, he made the rounds of wholesalers who stocked the products he would be selling. "I begged and pleaded," he remembers. "We are going to do great things together. Would you give me three weeks to pay?" One supplier eventually agreed. "A supplier like that is money in the bank, " says Tenenbaum. He then filled his store with that supplier's merchandise and quickly sold it with sales and special promotions. He took the profits and bought other merchandise. By the time the three weeks were up, Tenenbaum had leveraged the supplier's willingness to wait as if it were a bank note.

This approach puts you and your suppliers in partnership, and gives you two or three months to collect receivables without spending money on short credit lines to tide you over. But remember that your suppliers need to make money, too, and may not charge rock bottom prices if they know they have to carry you for three months.

Get Your Customers to Carry You

It's often good policy to collect money up front anyway, just to safeguard yourself from clients who stiff service providers. But a loyal following can go further to build you a little operating cushion. You can bill annually for year-long service contracts, collect payments in advance for shipping products, or offer special prerelease discounts or incentives for customers who buy your software, newsletter, birdhouses, or the like before they actually are published, manufactured and shipped. An attorney or financial planner can sell clients a year of consulting in January, and raise more than $100,000. A newsletter publisher might raise $5,000 or so through early subscriptions, just enough to get the first issue printed, and the first promotional effort mailed.

This approach also precludes having to pursue clients who don't pay on time. And this approach can get you a better class of client. Customers willing to pay up front, have faith in you and believe they are a part of your success.

When aviation enthusiast Henry Holden decided he wanted to self-publish his fourth book, *Ladybirds—the Untold Story of Women Pilots in America*, he knew he'd have to come up with about $6,000 to pay for the production costs of the book including the printing bill for the first 2,000 copies. He had $3,000 of his own money, and decided to try a different approach to raise the remaining $3,000 dollars.

Holden obtained a specialized mailing list containing the names of female aviators and sent out approximately 200 fliers offering his book at a special pre-release price. Buyers could take $4.00 off the $19.95 cover price if orders were placed by a certain date. As an added incentive, those who purchased early would also receive a First Day Cover—a specially postmarked envelope with the new postage stamp of Harriet Quimby, the first woman to get a pilot's license.

"The mailer sold 354 books in a couple of weeks," Holden remembers. "I ended up receiving about $5,000 from that mailing, more than what I needed for the printing."

The danger is, of course, if you sell a project too early and the project fails to get off the ground, you will have to refund money you don't have or face fraud charges. Make sure your early-pay incentives make financial sense. If you undercharge to bring in the bucks, you will spend all of your time on work that doesn't earn you anything.

Find a Factor

A factor is a company that will buy your receivables (the money people owe your business) at a discount. This enables you to get cash fast and not worry about making collections.

Factoring is typically used in large product-focused businesses, such as retail apparel, though smaller businesses desperate for cash can sometimes find spot factors to buy their invoices just once. Brad Wright, a northern Virginia regional representative for the Commerce Funding Corporation, says his company will buy invoices that are about $300 each, though the firm typically lines up clients who can offer a steady stream of invoices running about $15,000 a month.

How much of a discount will have you have to give? If you have a big cash flow and a ready-paying clientele, you can sell your invoices to factors without giving up too much of the bottom line. Some big-name retailers may pay as little as four cents or five cents on the dollar to get cash on their invoices. A small company with a one time need for a factor can pay as much as 30 percent, and that's for invoices that are current.

That's not the only bad news. Your clients may start to view you in a less favorable light if they suddenly start getting billed by a third party. And the short term nature of most factoring arrangements means you may be operating without much of a comfort cushion.

The bottom line? Unless you are in a traditionally factored industry, consider this cash source a short-term desperation move. To find out more about factoring, or to find a factor that would be interested in your invoices, contact the Commercial Finance Association in New York, 212-594-3490.

Tap the Small Business Administration

SBA loans were instituted because many small businesses don't qualify for regular bank business loans. The SBA typically guarantees the loan will be repaid, so banks will lend the money. And SBA terms let you stretch out your repayment longer than you would be allowed under a typical three- to five-year bank loan. The bad news is, the SBA usually requires lots and lots of paperwork, and the loans are so popular that the agency may run out of money long before the lending year is over.

For more information call the SBA Answer Desk at 800-827-5722. Or surf over to the SBA's comprehensive Web site at www.sbaonline. sba.gov/index.html. The National Business Association, a nonprofit small business trade group, also offers a free computer disk called First-Step Review, which gives an overview of SBA offerings, and you can get a rough idea of whether you'll qualify.

The SBA offers dozens of nifty free and cheap software programs to help you crunch your loan costs. Download them from the World Wide Web at www.sbaonline.sba.gov/shareware/finfile.html.

Here are some of the SBA's loan programs:

❏ **SBA microloan program.** This is the agency's only direct lending program. It offers loans up to $25,000 through a series of small, local, entrepreneurial nonprofits, such as the Flint Community Development Corporation in Flint, Michigan, or the Center for Business Innovations Inc. in Kansas City, Missouri. Typically loans are accompanied by small business advice, moral support, and a minimum of unfriendly paperwork. But be forewarned, there aren't enough microloans for all the businesses that apply.

❏ **SBA guaranteed bank loan.** This is a bank loan, up to 75 percent of which can be guaranteed by the SBA. Typically, applying for this type of loan requires lots of paperwork, but if you make it through the application process, you'll be awarded a loan that generally runs 2 percent over prime and permits you many years to repay. You may find it worthwhile to pay an SBA loan consultant to walk you through the process. Finally, be aware that these loans are for big small businesses—the minimum loan amount is typically $150,000. But you can't even apply for an SBA guaranteed loan until you have been turned down for a bank loan.

❑ **"Low-Doc" loans.** The SBA's new low documentation loan program eliminates much of the paperwork of its guaranteed loans. With a "Low-Doc" loan, you can get between $50,000 and $100,000 by filling out a one page application and copies of your tax return. Some banks are promising to turn these applications around and get a check in your hand (if you qualify) within two or three days.

Go to the Bank

Banks are notoriously reluctant to lend to small businesses. Traditionally, you had to prove that you would never need the money you were asking to borrow; and the bigger you were, the better. But opportunities are improving. In a recent survey by the Consumer Bankers Association, 74 percent of members said they were planning to increase small business funding. Recently, Wells Fargo Bank created a special credit line for small businesses, and promoted it through the same kind of direct mail solicitation it used for credit cards. It's an expensive line, but it's a beginning.

A bank business loan can be a line of credit or a fixed amount to cover a specific purchase or expense. Typically, these fixed loans are amortized over five years, with monthly payments, like a home mortgage. Expect, at the least, to have to put up collateral. And don't be surprised if your banker asks for a cosigner.

Here's what you need to know to get the best deal on a bank loan:

❑ **Bankers trust those they know.** That's why cultivating a relationship with your banker *before* you need money is recommended. Find out who is on the loan committee, how often it meets, what it looks for, and the like. Invite your banker to visit your business.

❑ **Bankers like facts.** The more financial information you provide, the better you look. And even if you like to crunch your own numbers, your application will carry more weight if an accountant helps prepare it.

❑ **Bankers are not impressed with big deposits.** That huge check you just received for the six-month project you finished last month won't convince your banker of your solvency—and it might

185

COMPUTER SOLUTIONS:
FIGURE YOUR LOAN PAYMENTS FAST

Chances are, if you have a computer, you probably have some sort of loan calculating software on it. Most spreadsheet programs come with their own amortization schedule, which will show you how much you have paid in principal and interest, and how much you still owe on a loan of any term or amount.

But here's a quick do-it-yourself spreadsheet if you'd like to guesstimate how much you'll pay on varying terms; the formula view is below and the data view is on the following page. Enter the annual interest rate as a decimal, the years of the loan, and the amount borrowed (as a negative sum). You'll quickly see your monthly payment at the bottom line.

This spreadsheet is good enough to help you devise a payment schedule for a private loan from a friend or relative. It can also help you compare different loans—say a 15-year mortgage with a 30-year plan at a higher rate/.

Formula View

	A	B
1	Annual interest rate	.12
2	Monthly interest rate	=B1/12
3	Years of loan	3
4	Total number of payments	=B3*12
5	Amount borrowed	-10000.00
6	**Your monthly payment**	=Pmt(B2,B4,B5,0,0)
7	Total payments	=B4*B6
8	Total interest	=B7+B5
9		
10		

FIGURE YOUR LOAN PAYMENTS FAST: Data View (*continued*)

	A	B
1	Annual interest rate	0.12
2	Monthly interest rate	0.0100
3	Years of loan	3
4	Total number of payments	36
5	Amount borrowed	($10,000.00)
6	**Your monthly payment**	$332.14
7	Total payments	$11,957.15
8	Total interest	$1,957.15
9		
10		

make you look like a lousy cash manager. Smooth cash flow is what bankers like to see. If your money comes in big chunks, try switching your clients over to an incremental billing arrangement that will smooth out your money flow.

❏ **Bankers want ratios.** Most have books on their desk, called the Robert Morris Associates statement studies, which reveal average key ratios for different types of businesses. Be prepared to provide your debt/equity, inventory turnover, current and quick ratios (more on this in Chapter 14).

❑ **Never ask "How much can I borrow?"** This demonstrates to a loan officer that you don't know what you need. It's like asking an English teacher how long the book report has to be.

❑ **Banking is a seasonal business.** Most banks try to maintain a lending ratio of loans to deposits of about 75 percent, but during different times of year they might fall above or below this. If you review your bank's quarterly financial statements, you can get an idea of the time of year your bank has more cash on hand. Many rural banks, for example, get tapped out in the spring, when farmers borrow planting money, but they are flush in the fall. City banks that run big retirement-account programs may be cash-rich in late winter and early spring as customers feed their Individual Retirement Accounts.

❑ **Make it personal.** Bankers like to go beyond the numbers and hear the exciting story of your business. Bring them in on an emotional level.

❑ **Rates may be negotiable.** Once a bank agrees to lend you money, try to find out how much that bank is paying for its money. A good measure is its ninety-day certificate of deposit rates. Then check the bank's most recent annual report to see what their typical interest margin is. Apply that margin to the current CD rates, and try to get your loan for the resulting rate.

Dance with an Angel

Some growing concerns get funding from the "angels:" older, wiser, richer private individuals who know the business and buy into small companies to seed start-up growth. Usually, angels view their contributions as investments and hobbies. An angel who really knows your field—typically a retired businessperson—can really be heaven sent. He or she can give you sound advice along the way as you build your business. But keep in mind that most "angels" will have strong opinions about how you should run your company. If you don't "click," conflicts can arise that may be difficult to resolve.

How do you find a guardian angel? The best way is often through a local venture capital club, which you can find through your Chamber of Commerce. The MIT Venture Capital Network in Boston, Massachusetts (617-253-7163) boasts a comprehensive database of would-be angels and entrepreneurs in need of divine help, and does matchups on the basis of geography, industry, and other factors. A $250 fee will get you listed for a year.

Venture into Venture Capital

You're not into traditional venture-capital territory until you are looking for more than $250,000, and that's not easy to find in today's tight money markets. These professional firms will buy a piece of your company to help you grow it, and this is often the last step before you take your company public. When you go for venture capital, you essentially sell a piece of your company—sometimes the biggest piece—to someone who will have his or her own ideas about how to run it. They will also have a cadre of experts in finance, marketing and more, to help make your company grow. This, obviously, is a very serious step to take, since you can end up losing control of your baby. Remember the venture capitalists' slogan: "10 percent of a watermelon is better than 100 percent of a grape!"

SECRET: *Use your computer to find a venture capitalist. VenCap DataQuest is a list on disk of venture capitalists. Order the eastern or western versions, and get at least 400 deep pocket names for $89.95. You can sort them by fourteen criteria, including preferred industries and investment levels. To order, contact AI Research at 2003 St. Julien Court, Mountain View, CA 94943, or call 415-852-9140.*

Seek Your Own Shareholders

Finally, if you are really thinking big, you can hire an investment banking firm, get registered with the Securities and Exchange Commission, sign up with a stock exchange, and have your own initial public offering. In today's heady markets, you can raise huge amounts of money this way if you have a unique and trendy business and aspire to a major national presence.

But by doing this, you'll lose control of the company. SEC forms and shareholder meetings can keep you too busy to run the business, and your clean and dirty laundry will be hung out for all to see. This is a genie that's virtually impossible to put back in the bottle, so consider this option with extreme caution (and a book far more advanced than the one in your hands.)

YOU MUST REMEMBER THIS: LESSONS FROM CHAPTER 8

- You need a lot of money to build a business
- There are sources of cash all around you; don't dismiss any of them
- Look for nontraditional sources, but structure your arrangements cautiously and professionally.

9

© Janet Street 1997

"Hiring help can boost your income
and save your sanity,
but it can also get complicated."

Hiring
Help

You'll know when it's time to hire help. Maybe it will be another midnight, when there's no one else around and you still have got two hours of work to do by tomorrow. Maybe it will be that drawer full of checks, bills, and other financial papers you don't want to deal with. Perhaps your moment will come when you find yourself confronted with too much work—and you don't want to turn any of it down. Or maybe you don't have enough work, and you suspect that hiring someone to sell for you will give you the business you need.

The finances of hiring help can be daunting. It's not cheap: An employee costs a minimum of $4.25 an hour, and you aren't going to get anyone very skilled for that. Add in 7.6 percent Social Security and Medicare taxes; state and federal unemployment up to $432 a year, and worker's compensation costs; and the space and equipment an employee will need to do the job for you. And don't forget the time you'll spend administering, training, and being a boss.

But think of it this way, too: Let's say you bill out your consulting services at $50 an hour. How much does it cost you to write a form letter, stuff envelopes, buy stamps, or make routine phone calls? What if you hired someone at $5 an hour to do 10 hours of clerical work a week? You'd only have to bill a little more than one extra hour a week to pay for that help. Isn't that worth it?

Well, maybe and maybe not. Nothing can kill a business faster than high overhead. And nothing can keep you tossing and turning at night like failing to meet payroll. So...

SECRET: *Be decisive when you hire; but don't do so until you absolutely, positively can't get it done any other way.*

Help for What?

You probably already know that you or your business needs help. But keep in mind that the happiest people are usually those who hire help to do what they don't like to do or can't do. So if you like fiddling with figures, for example, do your own bookkeeping, but hire someone else to write your letters, or to research, type, shop, or schedule appointments, or all of these. In short, hire help that can free you to do what you are best at.

Sales Help

Few men or women succeed when they hire someone to sell for them. It's a temptation, for sure, because selling yourself is hard. Chances are if you're self-employed, you are an artist, or a consultant, or an architect, or an accountant, not a salesperson. So why not hire a pro to line up work for you, so you can just hide at home and do the work?

To be blunt, it rarely works out. A good salesperson, in the first place, costs a lot of money. And many small businesspeople sell themselves directly to generate good chemistry between them and their clients. If you hire someone to build your business, make sure that person really knows your business. Otherwise the subtext of their message will not ring true to your potential clients, and you'll spend a lot of money for nothing.

There are some fields where salespeople thrive. In construction, for example, job estimators sell the job but don't do it. At advertising agencies, the account executive brings in the work and turns it over to the creative staff. If you are in that kind of field, and can find a really strong candidate who really believes in your approach, give it a try. But expect to put a lot of time and money into the relationship before it starts paying for your business.

How to Avoid Hiring Help

Knowing you need help doesn't mean you have to run out and hire an
employee. Explore these other methods of getting help before bringing a
bona fide employee into your company:

- ❏ Hire another business as an independent subcontractor.
- ❏ Take on an intern from a local college.
- ❏ Use sheltered workshops—nonprofit organizations that hire
  handicapped workers—to do work for you.

Use an Independent Subcontractor

One of the best ways to get help is to hire someone like yourself: an
independent contractor. You can hire a writer, researcher, accountant, typ-
ist, secretary, or artist who has his or her own business. Then you don't
have to worry about withholding taxes, paying benefits, or providing
workspace. And it may be easier to find the qualified professional you
need at an amount you need to pay, because you will only be buying a
portion of their time.

To hire an independent, seek out others in your network first. Perhaps
you get together with other professionals who use the same bookkeeper.
Perhaps you've already worked with a researcher or writer or artist in one
of your own assignments, and liked the work that he or she did. Or why
not mix and match? You can work for Marsha on Mondays and
Wednesdays, and she can work for you on Tuesdays and Thursdays. On
Fridays, you can form a partnership to go after Mr. or Ms. Big.

There are, however, a couple of disadvantages to going the independent contractor route:

- ❏ **You'll pay more.** A professional businessperson necessarily costs
  more than a staff employee. But you only pay for your project or
  for the hours worked on your project.
- ❏ **You hire a contractor for one purpose only.** Unlike an employee,
  who can answer your phones in the morning, run errands at

midday, and do a mailing in the afternoon, you can't usually find a contractor willing to go above and beyond. You could hire an answering service, a go-fer, and a writer, but that's probably three different contractors.

❏ **The IRS has cracked down on people who hire employees and then call them "independent contractors" as a ruse to save on taxes and benefits.** You must be able to demonstrate that your contractor really is independent and runs an independent company. Otherwise, you may have to withhold taxes and provide benefits.

Proving Your Contractor Is Independent

IRS examiners make case-by-case decisions, and follow a series of guidelines to determine who is a staff member or an independent contractor. If you or your contractor are suspected of violating the independent contractor/employee rules, you will receive form SS-8 in the mail. This form has twenty questions, though in true IRS style, most of the questions have a, b, c, and d components (and question 18 goes from a through n!).

But the 20 questions can be boiled down to one: Who really controls the time, effort, and expenses of the employee/contractor? In a paper called "Keeping Independent Contractors from Being Reclassified," Chicago attorneys Stuart Duhl and Donna Shaw identified fourteen steps employers can take to make sure their help is legally qualified as an independent contractor and not an employee. Here they are:

1. Sign a contract that explicitly identifies the worker as an independent contractor and not an employee.

2. Identify the exact nature of the independent contractor's.

3. The independent contractor should not be prohibited from providing service to others. (This is a key consideration for the IRS. Your contractor should also work for others.)

4. The independent contractor is responsible for all state and federal income and Social Security and unemployment taxes on his or her income earned under the agreement.

5. The agreement should state a definite term, and contain no unlimited automatic renewal provision.

6. The independent contractor must supply the necessary tools, equipment, and materials required for his or her job.

7. The contractor is responsible for his or her own business expenses.

8. The contractor should be paid on a commission or job basis, rather than on a unit of time, like weekly or monthly.

9. The independent contractor should not receive bonuses or fringe benefits.

10. The independent contractor should be prohibited from incurring obligations or open charge accounts in the company's name for normal business expenses.

11. If the independent contractor is paid advances against the work done, he or she is responsible for repaying those advances if the arrangement ends in deficit.

12. The company should not provide excessive control over the contractor. Specifically, you should not tell the contractor where to work, when to work, or how to work. You should not train a contractor to work "your way" or provide a workspace.

13. Always provide contractors with 1099 tax forms at the new year, showing how much you paid them in the previous year.

The IRS also wants to know that your contractor can have a profit or a loss in business, and that either of you can terminate the relationship at any time without incurring a liability. If you cover your contractor's overhead, and protect him or her from losses, the arrangement starts to look more like employment and less like an arm's length contract. The IRS is particularly focused on identifying contractors who do the vast majority of their work for one company, which can be measured by time or by income.

Making the Most Out of an Intern

Public relations pro Don Dorsey never thought about hiring an intern until his trade association, the Public Relations Society of America, asked him if he would be willing to put his name on a list of members willing to use interns, which would circulate to colleges near his Dallas home office.

"Why not?" he thought. He always had bits and pieces of research, writing, and phone work that always seemed to clog his "to do" list, and he thought that having to organize his business well enough to explain it to an intern might help him clarify his own plans. He decided to give it a try.

That was half a dozen interns ago. Since then, Dorsey has moved to Washington, D.C., and brought his intern habit with him. Through the local colleges, Dorsey has found student workers to conduct library research, write press releases, handle initial client meetings, return phone calls, and, in one case, generate a new assignment.

"I've had more interns call me than I can use," says Dorsey, who doesn't pay his interns, but gives them substantive work and writes evaluations for their professors. "I've brushed up on my own management abilities and caught their enthusiasm. I've worked with people who were so good I know I wouldn't have been able to afford them once they were out of school. And my interns are never disappointed. They tell me they learn more in one semester here than in any class they ever had."

Talk about a win-win situation! The right intern can boost your business without unbalancing your budget, and leave you with the warm fuzzies because you know you've helped someone else get a leg up. Sadly, of course some internships are not successful. Especially, if you haven't structured the internship carefully, you can end up spending all of your time teaching, get no business benefit, *and* still feel exploitative in the process.

Here's how to bring in an intern and make the relationship work:

❏ **Be broad-minded.** You don't have to find an intern in your field; someone with a complementary interest might work better. For example, if you are a computer consultant, you might want to mine the marketing or accounting fields for an intern who can fill in your knowledge gaps.

❏ **Define a finite project.** Internships work best when the job is specific. For example, you might have your intern compile marketing mailing lists, design packages for new products and set up payrolls for summer youth employment programs. Here are ten other good job assignments for an intern:

1. Design and produce the packaging for your next product.

2. Develop a mailing list of new business prospects and write direct mail letters aimed at those prospects.

3. Set up your business accounting system.

4. Line up public speaking jobs for you.

5. Do primary research for a report or article you have to write.

6. Investigate media for a local advertising campaign.

7. Write a report for one of your clients.

8. Business-specific jobs: If you are a caterer, let your intern plan and price a menu; if you are an architect your intern can do rough sketches, come up with his or her own plans, or—if you really trust them—do measurements on the job sites.

9. Create a database that tracks your business.

10. Set up a permanent internship program for your company.

❏ **Ask local colleges for recommendations.** There are several routes to finding the best interns. You can go directly to a department head or professor, but many schools have career centers that coordinate internships for the whole campus. Ask for the office that handles "cooperative learning" or "experiential education" or "field experience." Another place to look is the entrepreneurship office that many universities have established.

❏ **Prepare to teach.** Even if your intern is a self-starter, don't forget that he or she wants a learning experience. Expect to spend about ten percent of your time teaching your intern how to do the tasks that are routine in your business. And don't forget to invest time in the beginning teaching your intern how to use your fax, phone, and other equipment.

❏ **Keep one eye on the calendar.** If you're looking for a college student, be mindful of the semester schedule. It's best to make your request *before* the semester starts. Make your calls in July and August for the fall semester, and in April if you're looking to line up summer help. And design a project that can be completed within one ten week semester. Many students do internships for classroom credit; they can't do that if the class has ended and your project is still chugging along.

❏ **Don't forget about exams.** When you're setting up a schedule with a student intern, try to plan around periods of maximum stress. And if you want your intern to stay on as an employee after the semester is over, tell him or her early, before he or she lines up another job for the next term.

❏ **Accentuate your entrepreneurship.** Don't assume that you can't compete with the big employers who offer enticing training programs. Some students would rather work for a one-person business than a big company. Others ask specifically for entrepreneurial opportunities.

❏ **Set a fixed schedule.** Don't just tell an intern to show up when it's convenient. Set regular working hours.

❏ **Pay them . . . maybe.** There's some disagreement about how important this is. Some employers feel it is exploitative to get free work, and it's true that the best interns go to those who pay. But others believe a good internship is worth more than money to a student. Indeed, a well-crafted internship for which a student gets college credit may go unpaid. Remember, though, that the student is probably paying for those college credits and is on a limited budget. Some employees at least offer stipends to cover transportation or lunch on the job.

❏ **Be explicit about everything.** Set up the job like it's a classroom syllabus, and coordinate with your student's professor or supervisor when you do. Lay out the terms of the job and the workload. Include when your intern is supposed to work, how much he or she will be paid (if that's part of the deal), and exactly what work he or she will perform. Describe the project, the order of work, and the expected finished product and due date.

❏ **Know your liability.** If you work at home, make sure you've increased your homeowner's policy to cover accidents and injuries that may occur during the conduct of your business. You'll also have to withhold income taxes and pay workers' compensation insurance if you're paying your intern as a regular employee. Every state has different rules about workers' comp, so check locally to see if a short-term internship might fall beneath the requirements.

❏ **Let your intern do important work.** This doesn't mean that everything your intern does should be challenging and professional. But don't stick your intern in a boring clerical job either. If all you need is help with the paper crunch, you (and your would-be intern) would be better off if you just hired a temp. If you have a lot on your plate and you're not sure what to turn over to the intern, ask what kind of work he or she is most interested in.

❏ **Invest in another computer, and another phone.** Your intern needs a place to work. Even if you can't spring for a full office, another computer and phone set up in a corner of another room really doubles productivity. And you can use the backup if your computer fails.

❏ **Before one intern leaves, ask him or her to help you with the next one.** Every intern has ideas about how to make the experience better for the next time person. Your intern can help design the next internship project and find the right person.

SECRET: *One of the best ways to find an intern is to go into the classroom yourself. Offer to speak to a college class about your business, and let the instructor know that you will be looking for talent. Barbara Hemphill, a professional organizer from Raleigh, North Carolina, barters her own expertise for classroom exposure. As president of the National Association of Professional Organizers, she is a frequent public speaker. She offers to speak to a college class about entrepreneurship in exchange for the chance to "advertise" in her speech for the right student.*

Sheltered Workshops

As founder and director of Conscious Singles Connection in Ulster County, New York, Joan Goldstein receives thousands of inquiries a month. She sends an information packet in response, but how does she get thousands of packets stuffed in thousands of envelopes every month? She does it for the cost of a few pizzas. The local Association for Retarded Citizens, a sheltered workshop, runs a program called DayHab. People of all ages come to the center, where they can watch TV, play games or—if they want to—work. Many of them prefer to work, even though they don't get paid. Joan stops by with pizzas or another treat; the day-care clients feel busy, useful and involved, and Joan gets her envelopes stuffed.

Not all sheltered workshops are "free." That is, they expect their workers will be paid modest amounts for their efforts. But the pay is usually far cheaper than you would offer an independent employee.

To find sheltered workshops near you, start with the yellow pages, and look under Social Service agencies. Or call one of these resources: Job Accommodation Network, P.O. Box 468, Morgantown, WV 26505, 800-526-7234; or President's Committee on Employment of the Handicapped, 1111 20th Street NW, Washington, DC 20036, 202-653-5044.

Going for the Employee

Let's assume you've considered all of the alternatives and decided that you are ready for a bona fide employee, someone to really learn your business and fill a specific role within it. Someone whose time is yours while he or she is there.

COMPUTER SOLUTION:
LEARNING TO LOVE A PAYCHECK PROGRAM

Nothing, short of having your own accountant, takes the pain out of doing payroll like using a payroll or small business accounting program. All you have to do to set up a new employee in one of these programs, and payday becomes a point-and-click affair, as does tax day.

QuickBooks is a typical program. Set up each employee with his or her base rate. The program will account for extras only. It can accrue vacation days or sick days, for example. It will automatically set up the appropriate withholding levels for federal and state taxes (though if you live in a county that also has a local income tax, you may have to add that rate manually during the setup.)

It will also withhold any other miscellaneous deductions you'd like from your employees. So, if you've set up a pension plan or health program that your employees pay into, the accounting program will easily accommodate it.

When it is time to make your payments, click on the names of the employees. You can adjust their hours or approve a regular salary. Direct the program to print the checks and the checks get printed. All of the various withholding amounts are posted to the right accounts.

Four times a year, implement the program to print out the quarterly reports. It will also print out your annual report and tell you how much to pay for all of the taxes and insurance policies that are paycheck-derived.

Some programs, such as the stand-alone PayCheck, which retails for $49.95, or the Ultimate Payroll ($199.95), both from Aatrix, include modules that let you put your employees on an electric time card system.

The facing page shows typical task screens from Booksmith. These programs are so much fun, they might even make you want to go out and hire somebody! (And his or her first job can be to set up your payroll.)

LEARNING TO LOVE A PAYCHECK PROGRAM (*continued*)

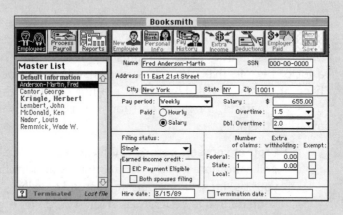

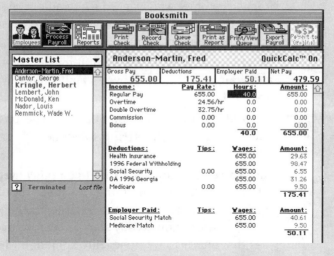

What do you have to do? You have to hire smart, and then you have to follow the myriad federal and state laws and tax requirements that are your responsibility once you become a real live employer.

Hiring Smart

"If I were to do one thing differently in my business, I would be much stricter in my hiring policies," a court reporter once complained in an online session about business mistakes. "It seems I have hired and fired a lot of people over the years, and mainly it has been related to their lying about their skill levels and me not checking deeply enough." Bad hires are painful, for them and for you. Here are some suggestions for avoiding them:

- ❏ **Protect yourself before you hire:** Take the time to interview several candidates, and ask questions that pertain specifically to your business. For example, instead of asking, "Where do you see yourself in five years?" ask "How would you handle a phone call from a customer who wanted a guaranteed delivery date you didn't think you could meet?" Or "Where, specifically, would you go for information about...?"

- ❏ **Don't hire anyone on the spot:** It makes you look too desperate, and your potential employee's faults may become more apparent upon reflection.

- ❏ **Don't hire yourself:** The point of hiring help is to complement your skills and abilities. Hire someone who enjoys doing what you hate.

- ❏ **Hire someone who has a small-company mentality:** "Not in my job description" is something you never should hear in a small business. After all, you're the owner, and chances are you sweep floors, answer phones, buy stamps, and do every other menial task that needs to be done. Hire someone who loves the idea of entrepreneurship, who wants to learn everything, and who is willing to do what it takes to get the job done.

Forms and Taxes, Taxes and Forms

Once you bring in an employee, you graduate to a new level of complexity in your legal requirements. You will have to withhold state and federal income taxes and Social Security and Medicare taxes. You will also have to pay federal and state unemployment taxes for your employees. You will also have to file forms and pay taxes quarterly and annually for your employees. Follow this: step-by-step process to ensure that you don't overlook anything:

1. When you decide to hire an employee, file federal form SS-4, Application for Employer Identification Number, to the IRS.

2. Let your state tax office know that you are seeking employer status; they probably have another ID number for you, too, along with its own list of requirements.

3. Have your new employee fill out a W-4 form. He or she will use this to figure out his or her tax status and number of exemptions. You can use that form to calculate the proper withholding.

4. Order Publication 15, Circular E, Employer's Tax Guide from the IRS. That will tell you how much to withhold for federal income taxes.

5. Remember, too, to withhold 6.2 percent of your employee's salary (up to $65,400 of income) for Social Security taxes, and 1.45 percent for Medicare taxes. Match those for a total payment of 15.3 percent.

6. Pay Social Security, Medicare, and income taxes according to the schedule published by the IRS that fits your business. You can make your tax payments quarterly if your quarterly liability is under $500. If you have a bigger payroll, you may have to make deposits to a payroll tax account as frequently as you write paychecks.

7. File Form 941, Employer's Quarterly Federal Tax Return by April 30, July 31, October 31, and January 31 to the IRS.

8. File Form 940 or Form 940-EZ, Employers Annual Federal Unemployment Tax Return with your federal unemployment taxes by January 31 of each year. They come out to 6.2 percent of wages up to $7,000, for a max of $432 per employee per year. Your federal unemployment taxes will be reduced by the amount of state unemployment taxes that you pay.

9. File Form 945, Annual Return of Withheld Federal Income Tax by January 31 for the previous year.

10. Every year, by January 31, give your employees W-2 forms, Wage and Tax Statements, which show exactly what they earned, what you paid, and what you mailed to tax agencies on their behalf.

11. Call your insurance agent and make sure any additional liabilities will be covered by your existing policies. If not, make the necessary adjustments.

12. Check your benefits packages, including your retirement plan, to find out if and when you need to bring your employee(s) into the

program. If your current retirement plan would be overly generous to new hires, you can usually end it and start a new plan.

*S*ECRET: *If you don't want handle this process yourself, you can hire a payroll company to do it for you. Paychex, for example, recently offered to do a payroll of up to five employees, including tax payments and report filing, for about $35 a month. You can find the firm in the local phone book, or call 800-322-7292. Another company big in this field is ADP 201-994-5003.*

*S*ECRET: *If you hire employees who don't work many hours, consider paying them monthly instead of weekly or biweekly. When you pay them monthly, it gives you more time to collect the money you will pass on as wages. It also enables you to withhold fewer tax dollars; the monthly withholding tables are lower than the weekly or biweekly ones.*

A final warning about payroll taxes: Don't spend your employees' money on other items between the time you collect it and the time it is due: Small businesses that use their payroll taxes for other items and then can't pay taxes for their employees are considered the lowest of the low by IRS standards.

Making It Worthwhile to Hire Help

To go through all of this, you have to really make it worthwhile to hire a permanent employee. To do so, develop long-term and profitable relationships with your employees. Treat them fairly and in a friendly manner. Lay down specific objectives for their jobs, and design a grievance procedure before you need to use it (and hopefully you won't ever).

And, if you're married, read on, to find the secret to the most profitable hires: your spouse and children. If you hire your family members, you can ease up on many of the federal requirements. And earn tons of tax breaks.

A Family Affair

As a self-employed businessperson, it can be very satisfying to include your family in your work. Think of the psychic rewards: Your family can bond while you are all working side by side toward a common goal. Then there are the financial rewards: You can save buckets of money traveling with your spouse on the business, paying your kids in pretax dollars, and writing off family health care.

All of this is legal and justifiable, as long as they perform actual work and you pay them a reasonable wage. Of course the reasonable-wage-for-reasonable-work is a judgment call, but there's a lot of leeway. Here are some examples:

- ❏ Barbara Brabec, self-publisher and editor of Barbara Brabec's *Self-Employment Survival Letter*, hired her retired husband. She pays him a small enough salary so that he still qualifies for his Social Security benefits. But now the family gets fully paid health care on the business. And they enjoy those business trips!

- ❏ Craft entrepreneur Jane Bucy is watching her kids grow up in her decorator sewing business. Christine and Michelle started at four and six: emptying the trash and sweeping fabric scraps off the floor. Now they vacuum, label files and update prices on the computer. Soon, if they follow the path started by the older daughters of Bucy's former partner, they will be sewing balloon shades and dust ruffles. For every $1 Bucy pays her daughters she saves about 50 cents in taxes.

- ❏ Seattle money manager Paul Merriman hired his infant grandson to model for a photo that graced his sales brochure. He paid him $2,000, and had the child's parents use that money to open an IRA for the baby, so the money could compound tax-deferred. By the time junior is 65, Merriman expects him to have more than $3 million to play with, just from that one deposit.

What's the deal? The U.S. tax laws are somewhat skewed against owners in favor of employees when it comes to benefits. Yet those same tax laws favor family businesses. Here's how:

- ❏ You can provide health insurance for your employees and deduct the full cost of that insurance in your business, which you can't do with your own insurance. But you can hire your spouse, provide a family policy (that covers your spouse's spouse and kids—and we know who they are), and write that off.

- ❏ Children who work for their parents are exempt from Social Security and Medicare taxes on those earnings.

- ❏ Children's income is tax-exempt up to the $3,900 personal exemption. Then their income is taxed at the lowest 15 percent rate until it reaches $24,000 a year.

❏ Spouses and children who are employees are typically exempt from federal unemployment taxes.

❏ Spouses and children who are employees are typically exempt from state unemployment and worker's compensation taxes.

❏ If you hire your spouse, that may qualify your family for the child care credit.

❏ A child who has a salaried position can have his or her own Individual Retirement Account.

❏ You can provide life insurance for your employee spouse and write it off in your business.

Hiring Your Spouse

If you are running a small or home-based business, chances are your spouse already makes significant contributions. Maybe you are married, as I am, to the kind of person who understands your computer's operating system and is there to fix crashes and to tell you what kind of equipment to buy. Maybe your better half keeps your books and acts as a sounding board for your ideas. Or helps with your newsletter, stuffs envelopes, talks to your clients on the phone, and generally supports your business in a lot of different ways.

Pay him or her for it.

When you put your spouse on the payroll, you reduce your net business income by the amount of his or her salary, including benefits, Social Security, and Medicare taxes. And you can provide health insurance and up to $50,000 of life insurance to your spouse. You may be able to take trips, use the child care credit, and save more for retirement. First the lecture, then the rundown on family members.

The Lecture

Be reasonable and be legal. Don't pay your spouse $30,000 a year to do one hour a week of typing. Don't provide $80,000 of fringe benefits for a $7,000 salary. Or pay your spouse so much that your business loses money on paper. And don't do anything really dumb, like paying your spouse "under the table" but then deducting all the benefits. To put your husband or wife on the books, really put him or her on the books. Follow the rules previously described, to make sure he or she is getting a legitimate paycheck. Withhold payroll taxes for your spouse just as you would any other employees. End of lecture.

The Health Benefits

The self-employed already have health insurance deductions. You can take a percentage of your health insurance premiums off your 1040 form. But why stop there? That percentage doesn't cover your full cost. And deducting the premiums from your 1040 does nothing to reduce your business income, which is subject to self-employment taxes beyond the income tax. Corporate employees can get their health insurance tax-free, and companies can write off the insurance they buy for their workers.

When you hire your spouse, you can agree to provide health insurance for him or her. You will be able to write your family's health insurance premium check on your business account and call it a business expense. You will report the expense on your tax form as employee benefits. This takes the deduction off of your 1040, where it is marginalized, and makes it a fully deductible against income and self-employment taxes.

> **C**AUTION: *With this benefit and most others, you can't discriminate against other employees. So, if your spouse is not your only worker, you'll have to examine your benefits package more carefully. Unless you intend to provide health insurance and other benefits for everyone on your staff, this might not work for you.*

To deduct health insurance premiums and make total out-of-pocket medical expenses 100 percent deductible you'll have to set up a medical reimbursement plan under Section 105 of the Internal Revenue Code. This allows you to pay almost all of your family's health costs to your spouse/employee and write them off in your business. That includes eye-glasses, braces, well baby care, prescriptions, and most other out-of-pocket medical expenses. How?

You can write your own plan, but without a background in benefits consulting, you probably don't want to chance it. One company, AgriPlan/BizPlan, of Madison, Wisconsin, and Adel, Iowa, has made a name for itself writing these plans. The company started as a service to farmers who had family businesses; now it is branching out with many small business customers. For $175 for the first employee and $50 for each additional employee, the company will establish a legal Section 105 plan for you and audit your medical expenses under it every year. The firm guarantees its plans are "audit proof" and promises to pay penalties and interest if you follow its directions and still end up with plan problems.

Most AgriPlan/BizPlan customers get this through their own accountants or attorneys, or ask your financial professional about this program. For more information from the company directly, call 800-626-2846, or

COMPUTER SOLUTION:
HOW MUCH CAN YOU SAVE
WHEN YOU HIRE YOUR FAMILY?

The following spreadsheet quantifies how much you can save when you hire your spouse and/or your children.

These factors and assumptions are built into it:

■ You pay self-employment taxes on your own net business income (line 6), but deduct half of that on your 1040 (line 7). Note that the Social Security portion of those taxes (12.4 percent) tops out once your business income passes a certain level. In 1997, that level was $65,400. But the 2.9 percent Medicare tax has no ceiling. Once your business income passes that Social Security "taxable wage base," the spreadsheet gets more complicated. You have to account for the reduced tax rate at higher levels of income.

■ When you take your health insurance premiums into the business (line 4) you lose the 40 percent of health insurance write-off from your 1040 form that self-employed taxpayers get (line 10).

■ In this example, Sarah earned $50,000 last year and spend $6,200 on health benefits. She expects to pay her kids a total of $6,000, and her husband $7,800. Her federal tax rate is 28 percent and her state tax rate is 5 percent. She'll save $4,855 by putting them all on the payroll! That's an extra $400 a month in spending money. And that doesn't take into account family excursions she can take on the books.

You can use the formulas given in the spreadsheet to set up a spreadsheet for your own business. Then play around with potential salaries for your family and see how your bottom line changes.

HOW MUCH CAN YOU SAVE WHEN YOU HIRE YOUR FAMILY?: Formula View *(continued)*

	A	B	C	D
1		Current Situation	Employ Children	Employ Spouse and Children
2	I pay the kids		6000	6000
3	I pay the spouse			7800
4	I write off health benefits			6200
5	My business net	50000	=B5-C2	=B5-D2-D3-D4
6	Self-employment tax	=(B5*.9235)*.153	=(C5*.9235)*.153	=(D5*.9235)*.153
7	(Less deduction)	=(B6/2)*.33	=(C6/2)*.33	=(D6/2)*.33
8	**Net SE tax**	**=B6-B7**	**=C6-C7**	**=D6-D7**
9	**Regular income tax**	**=B5*.33**	**=C5*.33**	**=(D5+D3)*.33**
10	**Health insurance write-off**	**=D4*.30*.33**	**=D4*.30*.33**	
11	**Added SS taxes**			**=D3*.153**
12	**Half deductible to business**			**=D11/2*.464**
13				
14	Tax burden	=B8+B9-B10	=C8+C9-C10	=D8+D9+D11-D12
15	**Savings**		**=B14-C14**	**=B14-D14**
16	**Savings of spouse alone**			**=D15-C15**
17				
18				
19	Assumptions:			
20	State Rate: 5%			
21	Federal Rate: 28%			
22	Health benefits			
23				

HOW MUCH CAN YOU SAVE WHEN YOU HIRE YOUR FAMILY?: Data View (continued)

	A	B	C	D
		Current Situation	Employ Children	Employ Spouse and Children
1				
2	I pay the kids		$6,000	$6,000
3	I pay the spouse			$7,800
4	I write off health benefits			$6,200
5	My business net	$50,000	$44,000	$30,000
6	Self-employment tax	$7,065	$6,217	$4,239
7	(Less deduction)	$1,166	$1,026	$699
8	**Net SE tax**	**$5,899**	**$5,191**	**$3,539**
9	**Regular income tax**	**$16,500**	**$14,250**	**$12,474**
10	**Health insurance write-off**	**$818**	**$818**	
11	**Added SS taxes**			**$1,193**
12	**Half deductible to business**			**$277**
13				
14	Tax burden	$21,581	$18,893	$16,930
15	**Savings**		**$2,688**	**$4,651**
16	**Savings of spouse alone**			**$1,963**
17				
18				
19	Assumptions:			
20	State Rate: 5%			
21	Federal Rate: 28%			
22	Health benefits cost $6,200			
23				

write: AgriPlan/BizPlan, National Sales Office 210 North 10th Street, P.O. Box 267, Adel, IA 50003-0267.

The Retirement Benefits

If you are at the high end of the income spectrum, it can pay to put your spouse on the payroll to maximize retirement benefits.

Here's how it works. Maybe you're making so much money in your business that you could shelter $50,000 or more in a Keogh account, but you're limited by law to $30,000. Employ your husband or wife in your business, give him or her enough hours to qualify for your retirement plan, and you can both shelter megabucks for your golden years.

Other Insurance

Presumably, your spouse already has life insurance. You can deduct the cost of up to $50,000 of term insurance as an employee benefit. If his or her policy is for more than that, prorate it and pay that $50,000 portion out of your business.

Don't provide disability insurance for your spouse on the company. If he or she is ever unlucky enough to have to use it, all of the benefits will be taxable to him or her because you, the employer, paid for the coverage. Disability insurance is best paid out of personal after-tax dollars.

The Child Care Credit

Picture this scenario: You are self employed. Your husband or wife doesn't work in your business, but stays home with the kids. But he or she is always helping out, for free, while the little dears run circles around all four of your legs. If he or she becomes a bona fide employee of the company, you can get that deductible health insurance, pay for your spouses retirement, *and* qualify for the child care credit. That credit can cut your taxes more than $1,000 by giving you between 20 percent to 30 percent of your child care expenses up to $4,800.

The Glamorous Lifestyle

Once your spouse is a legitimate part of your business, you can put more of your family travel and entertainment on the books. You can go out to lunch once a week to discuss your marketing and production plans for the following week. You can travel to distant cities to do research about how others in your business operate. You can find a conference to attend once a year, which will get you both charged up for work, while your expense account gets charged up for those travel deductions.

But don't get greedy: It's pretty hard to justify anniversary dinners and second honeymoon cruises as business expenses. Keep good records, be honest about integrating business purposes into your travel and entertainment plans, and be too legit to audit.

Watch Out! This Can Cost You, Too

The biggest break of hiring a spouse disappeared a few years ago when Congress enacted a requirement that spouses pay Social Security and Medicare taxes when they work for each other. In fact, this provision may result in *higher* taxes when you hire your spouse. Unless you are going to reap the tax savings from health insurance, retirement accounts, or the child care credit, it would not be worthwhile to hire your spouse. And if you have a high income, you may end up paying much more in Social Security taxes.

Here's why: Congress gave entrepreneurs a break in figuring their self-employment taxes. Instead of paying the 15.3 percent self-employment tax on your entire net business income, you first multiply your business income by .9235. So you're actually only paying self-employment tax on about 90 percent of your income. Why? To equalize your tax burden with that of corporate employers who get to deduct the Social Security and Medicare taxes from their business income.

When you hire a spouse, and transfer part of your income to him or her as salary, he or she still has to pay 7.6 percent in Social Security and Medicare taxes on income. And as the employer, you also have to pay the other 7.6 percent. None of that gets cut by 10 percent!

Furthermore, the tax code's so-called marriage penalty against two-earner couples can backfire if your spouse only works for you. Your income tax burden on the same amount of income can end up heavier.

High earners are especially vulnerable. The 6.2 percent Social Security taxes stop once your income exceeds $65,400 (for 1997.) If your business earns more than that and you hire your spouse, you might find yourself transferring earnings *not* subject to the Social Security tax into earnings that are subject to the tax. And it can take a fair amount of health insurance to justify that.

The Last Word

There's no quick and easy way to figure out if you are better off hiring your spouse. Use the spreadsheet in the Computer Solution on pages 211 and 212 to see if it will work for you. Even then, all you have are the numbers. Employing (or being employed by) the person you sleep with isn't always easy or smart. Think it through before you pad that particular payroll.

Finding a Job for Junior

The tax breaks are clearer when you hire your children to work in your business. If they are under eighteen, they don't have to pay Social Security or Medicare taxes. At incomes up to $3,900, they really don't have to pay taxes at all, because they can use the standard deduction. And after that, their tax rate is likely to be 15 percent, unless you pay them a lot. And they can put $2,000 of their earnings in an IRA.

Here's what happens when you put it all together. Say you give your daughter a summer job and pay her $9,000. Instead of you having to pay $4,140 in taxes on that income, it all passes out of the business and to her. She pays nothing on the first $3,900, and defers taxes on the next $2,000, which she puts in an IRA. That leaves $3,100 for her to pay taxes on, and she does—at a combined 20 percent federal and state income tax rate. Her tax bill is $620. The net family savings? $3520, or enough to pay at least a piece of that expensive freshman year.

Of course, be reasonable when you are hiring your child to do work for you. Don't pay a ten-year-old a $20,000 salary for sorting index cards, or you'll buy yourself a heap of tax troubles. And don't treat your child like a slave, either. Remember that any employee has strong and weak skills and prefers certain tasks over others. Construct a job that is appropriate for your child, helps you, and would pass an auditor's test of reasonableness.

Your children will get more than money out of the arrangement. They will develop a sense of responsibility and learn you are depending on them by the business tasks they accomplish. You and your child may also develop a closer relationship by working together. And remember, when they watch you on the job, you'll be teaching by example, fostering a positive ethic while you work.

They Can't Keep Their Rooms Clean

You'd be surprised what kids can and will do when you wave a paycheck at them. Treat the job you're proposing like the real position it is, and most likely they will respond. Keep the tasks and the times allotted appropriate to the age of the child.

And don't worry about their youth. Tax courts have upheld deductions of wages to children as young as seven. (Paul Merriman hasn't had any complaints about his grandson, the model!) Following are some ideas of what children can do in a home-based family business.

❏ **Ages five and under.** Not much, unless you have a need for models. You can always pay your cute kid to have his or her picture taken for the cover of your annual report or catalog.

❏ **Ages five to eight.** Menial: Take out the trash. Sweep the floor. Dust the desk. Reshelve books.

❏ **Ages eight to twelve.** More than you think. File. Label file folders. Stuff envelopes. Collate papers, copy computer disks, clean and organize stationary, work on assembling craft projects, entertain the children of your clients when they come calling, and all of the above.

❏ **Ages twelve to eighteen.** You name it. Today's teenagers are very bright. They can become your company "Webmaster," putting you online if you aren't there already, or checking your e-mail. They can be taught accounting work. They can teach *you* database work. They can answer phones, run errands, and do all of the above.

How to Make the Arrangement Work

There are some common-sense secrets to success to keep in mind when working with your children. Treat them like real employees. That means that you have to separate work and personal time. It's probably okay to have a generic "how was school?" talk while you're sorting mail. But avoid nagging them about their homework while they are on the clock. And avoid complaining about the quality of their professional work while they're doing their homework.

Discuss chores with them and set regular hours and/or tasks, so they are well aware of their responsibilities. Make them fill out timesheets. (See example that follows.) Don't pay your child out of the business for personal chores, like lawn mowing and emptying the dishwasher. And don't use a paycheck as a substitute for a family allowance. They are two different things. And remember, your children need to be reminded that they are valuable and contributing members of the family even if they don't work for you.

And—this may be the hardest part—let your kids spend some of the money. Pay them regularly, and establish a percentage that they must save for college, cars, or whatever you both agree on. Then allow them to blow some of it, even if you hate the way they do it. Don't forget, it's their money, and part of the grand employment experience involve their learning how to manage it.

A TIMESHEET FIT FOR A KID

When you hire your child, it's important to keep good records about what he or she does for you, not only for the IRS, in case you ever need to demonstrate that you were paying a legitimate wage for a legitimate job but, more important, for your child. This simple timesheet is a good way to teach him or her about business practices and the value of the work. You can fill out a sheet like this for a five-year-old, and with help, a seven-year-old can do one.

Set up a timesheet form in your computer and print one out for every pay period that your child works. Keep them together, so you can review the kinds of work he or she does for you.

Employee's name:		
Pay period:		
Date	Hours worked	Tasks performed
4/12/96	1.5	Bought stamps; stamped letters.
4/14/96	2.0	Cleaned desk; vacuumed office.
4/15/96	0.25	Organized letterhead.
4/17/96	1.0	Filed.
Total hours	4.75	
Hourly rate	$5.00	
Total	$23.75	

SECRET: *Pay your children monthly. Withholding is lower, and the paperwork is limited. A monthly schedule gives your kids greater impetus to budget their money, as well as bigger chunks to budget. And it gives you more time to meet that payroll if the money coming in is irregular.*

As your children get older, you can teach them about different aspects of your business. They may even like it enough to stick with it. But don't be surprised if they don't. Familiarity often breeds contempt—or extreme boredom—in a professional sense.

SECRET: If your child really dislikes working in your business but wants a job, consider trading with a friends. You can hire their child and they can hire yours. The disadvantage of this arrangement, however, is that the Social Security tax breaks your kids get by working for you don't exist if they are working for someone else. But there are advantages, too: Your children will learn about different kinds of businesses and different kinds of employers. And you'll avoid the interpersonal squabbles that can arise when you try to tell your offspring what to do. On the other hand, your children may really get into this self-employment thing. If they become fully contributing partners, consider opening a branch of the business. Or ask them to continue doing some work remotely from their dorm room when they go away to college, easy by modem, if they've got the time and the interest. This can cut college expenses and allow more write-offs of the back and forth traveling you'll both do.

SECRET: If your children go so far that they establish their own spin off, have them check out the Outstanding High School Entrepreneur Contest, run by Johnson & Wales University, 8 Abbott Park Place, Providence, RI 02903, 800-343-2565. Ten high school seniors compete for $250,000 in scholarships, including a four-year tuition to the University's College of Business.

Don't Forget That Kiddie IRA

The tax money you save on hiring your child may be enough to cover the entire $2,000 IRA contribution (which your child probably doesn't want to make). You can also use personal funds to match their money. Say, for example, that your son earns $5,000 for the year. He wants to put it all in his bank account to save for a car. You want him to stash it in an IRA, where it will build, tax-deferred. You can give him $2,000 of your money to put in his bank account. He can invest $2,000 in an IRA.

SECRET: Don't even bother with the kiddie IRA if your child isn't earning enough to pay taxes. You'll end up converting tax-free money into money that is taxable when he or she retires and takes it out.

This is not an insignificant investment. Mary Flood, a financial planner from Bountiful, (a good sign!) Utah, has figured out that a fifteen-year old who puts $2,000 in an IRA for ten years and never contributes again, will have $1.8 million dollars when he or she turns sixty-five, if the money goes into a mutual fund that earns ten percent a year. That's slightly below the long-term appreciation of stocks, so it's not out of the question.

The trickiest part about opening an IRA for a minor is finding a mutual fund company that will take your money. Because IRAs are legal contracts, and kids are not legal contract-signers, some firms frown on setting up these accounts. Among those that will according to Kiplinger's *Personal Finance Magazine*, are Benham, Invesco, Janus, T. Rowe Price, and Vanguard. All are solid, no-load fund families.

There are real advantages to hiring employees, whether it be from outside sources or family members. Either approach presents its own set of complex circumstances. Complicated business and personal lives require serious thought about risk management: protecting yourself from anything that may go wrong. The next chapter (the grown-up chapter of this book!) will discuss how you can use insurance to manage the risks of self-employment.

YOU MUST REMEMBER THIS: LESSONS FROM CHAPTER 9

- Hiring help can boost your income and save your sanity, but it can also get complicated.
- There are many alternative arrangements to try before bringing your first employee on staff.
- There are many personal and financial advantages to hiring your relatives.

10

"You must protect your business from the
crises that can befall families, and
protect your family from the problems
that sometimes beset businesses."

Risky Business: Protecting Your Livelihood and Your Lifestyle

When you run a business, especially a home-based business, assume nothing. When your client falls on your front walk while delivering materials for a project, don't assume that your homeowner's or renter's insurance policy will pick up his or her doctor bills. Don't assume that when fire guts your office and all of your customer records go up in floppy disk smoke you'll receive a penny from the aforementioned insurer. Don't assume said company will give you anything more than the value of said floppy disk (about 97 cents), should it agree to cover your business property at all.

Neither should you assume that if a prospect trips over your laptop's power cord while you are visiting her office she won't sue you for pain and suffering, as well as her chronic back pain; and don't assume that you won't be held liable. Don't assume your auto accident will be covered because you were delivering a business report when the brakes failed.

And above all, don't assume that all those insurance companies advertising on TV will even want your business once they find out you are self-employed. And if you are a self-employed businessperson with a family, you need to know at least twice as much about insurance as your single colleagues. You must protect your business from the crises that can befall families, and protect your family from the problems that sometimes beset businesses.

The Good News

The insurance marketplace is a far friendlier place for the self-employed than it was four or five years ago, particularly on the liability side of the industry. Property and casualty insurers (those that provide liability insurance, like homeowner's insurance,) recognize home-based businesses for what they are: gold mines. Most agents are happy to sell some business liability and add-ons to homeowner policies that cover computer equipment. And most insurance companies have crafted special small business policies for low-risk, home-based businesses that can be bought for (as they say in the trades) pennies a day.

The Bad News

All of that good will and opportunism doesn't translate to disability and health insurance for the self-employed, who are the forgotten of the health care calamity and even worse in the disability industry. You have to make the best of what's available, even if it doesn't stack up, which it won't, to what the big corporate employee next door can get.

And peace of mind doesn't come cheap. *Creative Business*, a newsletter for writers and graphic artists, estimates that a 35-year old male can expect to spend about $10,422 a year buying life, disability, health, and liability insurance to cover a home-based writing business.

The Details

Everything you need to know about insurance can be broken into three categories, by what you are seeking to protect:

❑ **Your "stuff."** You need insurance that will cover your computer from theft and fire, and that will safeguard your assets against the claims of others. Liability insurance comes under this category.

❏ **Your income.** This category covers life insurance, disability insurance, and also business interruption and key person coverage.

❏ **Your health.** Catastrophic illness and accident are too catastrophic to face unprotected. You need health care policies that will cover you better than those revealing hospital gowns.

Let's look at them one at a time.

Protecting What You Own

Probably you already have a homeowner's or apartment renter's policy that covers the items in your home. And maybe you've already done the right thing and inventoried everything in your home. But are you aware that most homeowner policies don't cover computers and other business equipment over $1,000 or $2,500? That they don't cover you at all if the liability is business related (your client hurts him- or herself delivering your check)?

There's a spectrum of products designed to protect your business equipment, and your personal assets from business liability. You increase the coverage, depending on how big and risky your business is and how much coverage you want to buy.

Sean Mooney, senior vice president of the Insurance Information Institute, a trade association sponsored by insurance companies, offers the following "hierarchy" of business coverage:

❏ **Level 1: Your homeowners plan.** You may already be paying $400 a year or so for this plan. It includes no coverage for business liability, though it may offer limited coverage for your computer equipment. This may be enough if you run your business out of a post office box and never receive clients or deliveries at your door.

❏ **Level 2: Endorsements added to the policy.** These cover added equipment or simple slip-and-fall business liability. They can cost as little as $15 to $50 a year, for each add-on.

❏ **Level 3: Specialty products.** New home-based business policies, like the one described later in the sidebar offered by State Farm, or CNA's "homeworks" policy. They expand coverage to off-premises property loss, damage, and liability; add more business liability insurance for items such as libel; and may include coverage that pays the business if your work or your collections are interrupted by fire or theft. For most home-based businesses, this is a good choice, and isn't too expensive: You should be able to add it for $200 or less.

❑ **Level 4: A full-blown, business owner's package.** These can start at $500, and are what you need if you manufacture or fabricate products, work with hazardous materials, or have more than one site and several employees.

When looking for liability coverage, make sure that you are dealing with a good-sized, well-known, and highly-rated company. Find an agent who already handles others in your field, and be honest about the uses of your equipment and the hazards involved. There's no point in paying for a policy that won't cover you for the way your business actually operates. Avoid policies that pay only for "listed" perils.

Car Insurance

Your auto probably is already insured and if you only use it occasionally for business purposes, it's probably covered for that, too. But don't take chances; the mark-up for business use of a car is minimal. And if you have a home-based business, you may even get a discount for *not* commuting in your car. The Government Employees Insurance Company (GEICO), for example, charges an Atlanta Toyota driver $48.20 a year extra for full coverage of business use of his car.

Computer Coverage

One company, Safeware, has built a business on insuring computer equipment against everything from fire and theft to too much Jolt Cola being spilled on the keyboard. But you may not need this added coverage, especially if your computer is covered on your homeowner's or renter's policy. You may, however, like what Safeware's sister company has to offer. The Computer Insurance Agency (800-722-0385), will insure your laptop and personal digital assistants, no matter where you take them. If you're on the road a lot, this may be worthwhile.

SECRET: *There's insurance and there's insurance. Don't underestimate the value of a good, fireproof safe for storing important papers and valuable objects. Or the value of a serious back-up habit for your computer data. An insurance policy isn't the best answer for every problem.*

Protecting Your Income

If the money you bring in sustains you, your business, or other family members, you need to protect yourself from its interruption or end. Consider these four types of insurance to ensure the money never stops flowing (nobody has yet invented insurance for money that stops coming in because business is slow, so don't look for that kind of protection).

❑ **Life insurance** protects your personal income if you die.

❑ **Disability insurance** protects your personal income if you become incapacitated and unable to work.

❑ **Key Person insurance** protects the cash flow of your business if you—they key player—dies or becomes incapacitated.

❑ **Business interruption insurance** protects the cash flow of your business if an accident or disaster disrupts your company's ability to function.

Life Insurance

Listen to an insurance salesperson for even a few minutes and you'll come away convinced of one thing: Life insurance is insanely complicated and you don't understand it, but you think you better buy some quick. Self-employed people, in particular, are targeted by an industry that would have us believe its policies are the tax-favored ticket to comfortable retirement, college funds, and the orderly transition of small businesses. They'd like to sell you a policy without even mentioning the words "death benefit."

But don't invest in life insurance unless you need that death benefit. Life insurance carries commissions, fees, and charges (including the so-called mortality charge that pays for the death benefit) that most mainstream investments do not.

Still, death benefits are what life insurance is all about for workers, self-employed or not. If you have a family that depends on you, you do need life insurance. That's not so complicated, is it? If you already know you need life insurance and want to add a few investment wrinkles, there are products that do that. Just make sure that you focus first on the death benefit.

A SAMPLE POLICY

State Farm Insurance was one of the first major companies to recognize the home-based business market. Currently, it offers a series of low-priced alternatives for policyholders who work out of their homes. These policies represent state-of-the-art home business insurance, and can be viewed as a sample of what's out there from other companies as well. This sample quote is for people in low-risk home-based businesses—Avon sales representatives and freelance writers, for example. If you have a staff of twelve who work in your iron smelting business, this is not the policy for you. And if you are an obstetrician or architect, you no doubt already know that you need separate liability (malpractice) insurance from a carrier who specializes in your occupation.

You first must decide if you want special riders added to your regular homeowner's policy, or if you want a separate business policy. In most cases, when the business provides primary income, State Farm recommends the separate business policy.

NOTE: *The following quotes are samples that were available when this book was being written, but may have changed by the time you read this. Use them as a guide only, and shop around if you are looking for this type of coverage.)*

For about $150 a year, (more in some big cities, less in the hinterlands), here's the coverage you get in a business owner's policy.

- Up to $10,000 of business property, including your laptop, is covered for damage and loss, both in your home office and away.

- Your income stream is protected for up to a year, should flood, fire, or similar events interrupt your ability to earn money.

- Up to get $300,000 of business liability coverage, with $5,000 of medical payments coverage for that delivery person who slips on your steps.

Business liability insurance in such a policy is far more valuable than that which comes with your homeowner's plan. In addition to property damage

---

A SAMPLE POLICY (continued)

and bodily injury, it includes advertising and personal injury, such as libel, slander, and defamation.

If, instead, you opt for the cheaper additions to your homeowner's policy, your coverage is more limited. Loss or damage to body and equipment are not covered unless they fall under a list of "named perils," including fire, aircraft crash, smoke, falling objects, and the like. If some peril not on the list befalls your home-based business and all you have is a rider to your policy, you may not be covered. And the personal policy riders don't cover any of those business blunders, like libel or defamation of character.

With that caveat, here's what State Farm is offering in the way of additions to a basic homeowner's policy. If you're in a low-risk business that is "incidental" to your house's use as a home, you can pick up any of these for about $15 or $20 a year:

- **Option BP (Business Property):** Increases the $1,000 standard policy sublimit on business property to either $2,500 or $5,000, for on-premises coverage. Off premises coverage remains restricted to $250. This doesn't include computer equipment.

- **Option HC (Home Computer):** Increases the standard policy sublimit on computer equipment and media from $5,000 to $10,000 to cover workstations in the home. If there is frequent off-premises usage of a laptop computer, you'll need a separate policy.

- **Option IO (Incidental Office):** Provides an additional $5,000 of business property coverage, which you can use instead of Option BP, or in addition to it. This doesn't apply to computer equipment or sample merchandise. An added $1,000 of off-premises coverage is provided on other business property.

How Much?

You can figure your life insurance needs the hard way or the easy way. The hard way: Calculate your personal expenses and then inflate that number into the future to determine how much money you will need in five, ten, or fifteen years. Subtract the amount of money that would be available if you weren't around (such as other income and the Social Security death benefit) from the total needed, and buy insurance to cover the difference.

Or use this rule of thumb: Buy five or six times your annual earnings. Buy more if you have kids to send through college, or if your business is substantial enough that your heirs would have to pay inheritance taxes just to keep it running.

What Kind?

There are five different kinds of life insurance, but they break down into two basic types: term insurance or permanent (also called cash value) insurance. Term insurance is the kind of coverage you get for your car: You make annual premiums and get coverage for a year, or for the "term" of the policy. You are simply buying coverage. Cash value insurance builds up extra money, which is invested for you and which you can tap throughout the life of the policy by taking loans against it. Which do you want?

Term life insurance Term life insurance is the quickest, cheapest, and easiest way to buy life insurance. Every year you pay for the insurance you buy. But if you stop paying, the policy lapses and nobody owes anybody anything. If you buy term insurance, make sure it is renewable. Premiums may rise (typically on an annual or five-year schedule), but you won't be dropped. Term insurance makes the most sense if you don't expect to need life insurance into your sixties and seventies, when it becomes really expensive. Term insurance helps you protect those people who depend on you, but by that age most folks have retirement savings and their children are grown and independent.

SECRET: *Term insurance is often the best deal for self-employed people because entrepreneurs have other means of building up tax-deferred savings. Instead of putting extra money in a cash value life insurance policy just to qualify for its heralded tax-deferral with extra fees, you can buy a cheap term policy and put any extra money in your own Keogh or IRA retirement account.*

If you anticipate needing life insurance no matter how old you are—you will be supporting a handicapped child through adulthood, or your business is worth more than $600,000 in nonliquid assets and your heirs will face a substantial tax burden when it passes to them—compare term rates with those of a cash value, or permanent, policy. These policies couple the insurance part of a term plan with a tax-deferred investment capability. If you expect to need insurance for more than twenty years, a cash value policy might be cheaper than term.

*S*ECRET: *If you have college-age children, be aware that many college financial aid formulas ignore the build up of insurance assets in determining whether your child qualifies for financial aid, and how much. You may improve their chances by saving within an insurance policy, instead of in a separate college fund savings account. But make sure you really need the life insurance, and that it's worthwhile after all the fees are considered.*

Cash value insurance Approach cash value insurance very carefully, however. Commissions that run as high as seventy percent of your first year's premiums can make the policies too expensive to be worthwhile. And some companies build unrealistic interest rate projections into their policies, to make them look far more lucrative than they really are. If the projections fail to come true, you can end up paying higher and higher premiums as the policies mature, instead of seeing those premiums drop.

*S*ECRET: *Life insurance policies can be very complicated. If you think you'll need a substantial long-term policy, pay a fee-only insurance consultant to crunch the numbers and find the best plan for you. You can find one by calling the Life Insurance Advisors Association at 800-521-4578. Or look to one of the new no-commission policies sold directly to consumers or through fee-only financial planners. The two companies currently leading the fee-only life insurance industry are USAA Life, San Antonio, Texas 800-531-8000; and Ameritas Life Insurance Corp., Lincoln, Nebraska 800-552-3553.*

There are four kinds of cash value insurance. Pick one depending on your willingness to actively manage your policy and to take investment risks.

❏ **Whole Life.** Whole life is the old-fashioned kind of life insurance. The premiums, cash buildup, and death benefits are guaranteed. The insurance company invests the cash value where it sees the best mix of growth and safety, and uses dividends earned to reduce future premiums. USAA Insurance, for example, recently offered a $250,000 death benefit in a whole life policy for a forty-year-old at a fixed $3,657 annual or $310 monthly premium (which includes a service charge). At the company's current dividend projections, premiums may disappear altogether by the time the policyholder has paid in for about ten years; the cash value also should be $237,342 by the time the insured person is sixty-five years old. But the cash value actually guaranteed is only $101,930 when the insured is sixty-five—that's less than a five percent annual return on the principal, though the policyholder would be getting a death benefit, too.

❏ **Universal Life.** Universal life insurance lets the policyholder raise or lower the death benefit and vary the amount or timing of the premiums that feed into the cash value part of the policy. This helps you invest more through your insurance policy when you are flush and spread payments out when you aren't. The same $250,000 coverage on the same forty-year-old nonsmoker in the previous example could be bought for only $151.60 a month, though that would stretch payments out until the policyholder is sixty-five, under conservative initial projections. (In real life, interest earned on the policy's cash value would likely end payments before then.) And as time goes on, the policyholder could speed up payments into the policy.

Universal life insurance is better able to take advantage of high interest rates and policy earnings than whole life, but it's also more susceptible to disappointing returns, that could extend or raise the premiums.

❏ **Variable Life.** Variable life insurance gives the policyholder a selection from four or more mutual funds for the investment portion of the policy's cash value. Many insurance companies use captive mutual funds run by their own subsidiaries or related companies, but others arrange investments in well-known funds.

❏ **Variable Universal.** These policies are hybrids that combine the best of two worlds. They became popular in the late 1980s. Policyholders can manage their own insurance investments and use their earnings to adjust their premiums. While these policies provide tax-deferred benefits for your investments, don't mistake them for retirement accounts. They carry mortality charges and insurance-related service fees that make them less valuable than the typical Keogh or SEP for the nest-egg builder.

SECRET: *Don't even bother with a variable or variable universal pol-icy unless you are willing to take the risks that come with the stock market. You usually can't justify the expenses of these plans if all of your premium money is invested in guaranteed investments. If you don't have the stomach for picking stock funds yourself, go with a whole or univer-sal policy, where the insurance company will do it for you.*

Disability Insurance

This is a tricky area. There are a slew of mostly misleading statistics designed to demonstrate just how likely you are to become disabled during your self-employed career. Most are scary, but not particularly helpful or realistic. In truth, permanent, total disability is a possibility but not a likelihood. And there may be cheaper ways to plan for it than by buying disability insurance.

You're unlikely to find an insurance agent who will tell you that you don't need disability coverage. But a surprising number of businesspeople—including experts, such as Alfred Miller, a New York attorney who specializes in insurance matters—admit they don't buy disability coverage for themselves and see its value as limited. Miller says, "I think that one should think ten times before buying disability income insurance." Home-based businesspeople often can maintain their livelihood with injuries or illnesses that would keep a commuting laborer off the job.

Peter Katt, a fee-only insurance consultant from West Bloomfield, Michigan, asserts that the people who buy disability insurance the most—doctors, lawyers, accountants, physicians and dentists—have less than a one in twenty chance of ever being disabled for even sixty days during their careers. Nevertheless, disability policies are promoted with much more alarming statistics. One company brochure that Katt reviewed warns of a fifty-fifty chance of long-term disability. And those people most likely to become disabled, notes Katt, such as farmers or construction workers, seldom can find disability insurance at any price.

But even (or especially) a home-based computer jock can be disabled by a hand injury or other unexpected (and otherwise minor) problem. And though it may be more unlikely than the policy-peddlers admit, a serious, career-ending disability is a possibility. There are five main dis-ability insurers in America; call all of them to see what they offer. They are: Chubb, Northwestern Mutual Life, Paul Revere, Provident Life &

Accident, UNUM, and USAA, which offers discount policies direct without agents. You can find all of them listed in your phone book. If you find one willing to sell you a policy, look for these features:

❏ **Benefit Period:** This is the period of time the insurance must pay. Typical are five years, to age sixty-five, or lifetime. The idea behind the five-year plans is this: They are far cheaper, and will carry you through the time needed to convince the Social Security Administration that you are deserving of federal disability benefits. But that can take some tough arguing or a profound disability, and even then the benefits may not be enough, say the pros. Go instead for up to sixty-five if you think retirement benefits will pick up when your disability benefits leave off.

SECRET: *If you are fifty or younger, be careful of the gap that will develop as the Social Security retirement age is gradually raised. What if your disability benefits end at sixty-five and your Social Security doesn't kick in until you are seventy?*

❏ **Waiting Period:** This is the time between the onset of the disability and when payments start. Like any other deductible, the more you cover or the longer the waiting period, the lower the premiums. Usually, ninety days is a good compromise between quick access to benefits and lower premiums.

❏ **Residual Benefit:** This pays a partial benefit when the insured is not totally disabled. This is absolutely critical, according to Katt. Workers who become partially disabled and can work part-time or in some other limited capacity call upon residual benefits to make up the difference between what they make now and what they made working full-time.

❏ **Own Occupation:** With an own-occupation clause, you can't be forced to take a job in another field when illness or injury prevent you from participating in your own. This is a luxury that may not be worth the price. Katt suggests you place a value of about ten percent of your premium on it; if it's going to cost much more than that, don't bother with this.

❏ **Noncancelable:** This word protects your policy and your benefit forever into the future. It's better than "guaranteed renewable," which allows the company to raise prices.

❏ **Cost of Living:** This rider ensures that your disability benefits will rise with the inflation rate.

❏ **The Numbers:** How much should you get and how much should you pay? Invest in a policy that will reimburse between fifty and eighty percent of your monthly earnings, with sixty percent being a common, and usually adequate and affordable number. If you are over forty, expect to pay $1,500 a year, or more, for your coverage.

*S*ECRET: *Tax laws are complicated when it comes to disability insurance. If your employer pays for it, and deducts the premiums as an employee benefit, all of the benefits are taxable. If you pay for it yourself with after tax dollars, none of the benefits is taxable. If you are your own employer, pay for it yourself, out of after-tax dollars. Forget the few bucks break you might get if you put this on your corporate return.*

Key Person Insurance

If you died or became disabled, would your business die with you? Should it? If you are a one-person business, then the answer to both questions is probably yes, and that's all right. But if you run a family business that also employs your kids and your cousins, you may want the business to stay afloat without you. The business may not be able to afford that, without training and hiring a replacement for you. So buy life and disability insurance for yourself, and make the business the beneficiary. That's key person insurance.

Business Interruption Insurance

How much income and time would you lose if a fire destroyed your hard drive and your inventory? Business interruption insurance keeps the money flowing while you rebuild your company and your livelihood. Business interruption insurance is usually sold as part of the total business owner's package, and usually stops after twelve months. If you can't pull your business together in a year, perhaps you haven't done enough disaster planning beyond insurance buying.

*S*ECRET: *Just because you have a policy doesn't mean you ever want to need it. If your life is on your hard drive, set up a regular back-up schedule that includes off-site backups, and stick to it. Make sure you never have to replace irreplaceable customer records or creative work. Keep adequate copies in different places.*

Protecting Your Health

Health care and insurance are in crisis in America, and nobody knows it better than the self-employed. Most proposed federal "fixes" focus on employer-provided insurance, and ignore entrepreneurs. As our own employers, we don't even get the same tax deductions for paying for our own health insurance as we would if we were corporations providing insurance for our workers. Further, as individuals, we don't qualify for the cheaper, better policies available to groups.

SECRET: *If you are married, you can write off your health care costs by putting your spouse on the payroll, if he or she does legitimate work in your business. See Chapter 10 for details on how to do this.*

The question is, how to obtain adequate for coverage in this market? Briefly, don't stint on coverage, but use some of these money-saving tricks to buy the best policy you can possibly afford. And remember you can buy yourself time while you look for health insurance, if you are just leaving a company; usually, you are eligible for eighteen months or more of continued coverage under your former employer's plan, though you will have to pay higher premiums. This is called COBRA coverage after the federal law that mandates it: The Consolidated Omnibus Budget Reconciliation Act. You can alternatively buy a short-term policy that will cover you for the six months or so it takes you to find a really good plan. But be careful! If you develop a serious illness while you are under one of these temporary plans, you can find yourself without insurance and without eligibility to buy insurance just when you need it the most.

Here's how to find health insurance that works for you.

SECRET: *Expect to repeat the insurance hunt annually. The health insurance marketplace is getting more competitive, and many states are enacting their own laws to limit pricing and mandate coverage. The policy you bought two years ago may not be the best one available now.*

❏ **Join a group:** Still the best advice for the self-employed. You can often find a good policy by affiliating with your professional association or even a local consumer group. One organization, Co-Op America, in Washington, D.C., offers a highly regarded plan through Consumers United Insurance Company. Be careful, though, of some of the new small business associations that seem to exist mainly to sell insurance. Some offer better policies than others. At their worst, they might be a single insurance company with a bad plan masquerading as a small business organization just to sell insurance.

❏ **Call your state insurance regulator:** Many have long files of complaints against particular providers. *Before* you sign up, find out that the company you are considering is only good about collecting premiums, not paying benefits.

❏ **Expect to go HMO:** Most of the country is now under health maintenance organization care. The challenge now is to accept that model, and try to find an HMO with a solid reputation and the conveniences you need.

❏ **Pick a big company with a high insurance rating:** You can get ratings from A.M. Best Co., of Oldwick, New Jersey, or the National Association of Insurance Commissioners in Kansas City, Missouri. Why choose a big company? Deeper pockets, for one; but there's another: Companies are not usually allowed to cancel policies on individuals unless they cancel all of the policies in a particular state. A big company with numerous policyholders in your state is less likely to give up all that business.

 *S*ECRET: *Trust no one where health care is concerned. One Seattle man was insured through a small business association that had sold only a handful of policies in the entire state. When he became seriously ill, the company pulled out of the state, rather than renew his policy.*

❏ **Make sure a company pays its claims:** Ask the company what its claims payout ratio is. It should be at least 60 to 75 percent, according to experts. If a company pays only half of its claims, it may be severely limiting its coverage or hassling doctors to death.

❏ **Ask around:** Ask your doctor, and call the billing department of your local hospital. Say, "I'm considering the insurance offered by company XXX. Do you have problems dealing with them, or are they usually responsible and reliable? Some companies make a habit of sitting on claims for weeks and then kicking them back for tiny errors or missing signatures, and then sitting on them again. Or they repeatedly question necessary treatments. Doctors are not shy about complaining about these companies.

❏ **If you have a preexisting condition, compromise:** Most Blue Cross/Blue Shield plans and HMOs have an "open season," when they must accept all comers. Find out when it is, and sign up if you have the kind of preexisting problem that might make you uninsurable elsewhere.

❑ **If you don't want an HMO, buy a policy that pays prevailing charges:** It's not unusual to find policies that promise to pay whatever the hospital charges and then include, in the tiniest of print "up to $100 a day." Pass on these.

❑ **Look for high ceilings:** Some companies claim to have $1 million or $2 million policies, but bury very low limits per illness in their policies. A serious accident or disease could easily bump you out of coverage when you need it most.

❑ **Get a stop loss:** This is a limit on the out-of-pocket expenses you will have to pay before your insurance company picks up everything. Once you've exceeded your deductible, most policies will pay eighty percent of additional costs and require you to pay twenty percent until you've reached the stop loss, which is also called the out-of-pocket limit. Don't go too low, though; a stop loss of $5,000 will keep your premiums lower but protect your purse in the event of a serious illness or medical emergency.

❑ **Keep your deductible high:** The point of health insurance is not to protect you from ever having to spend a penny on health care; it's to protect your home, family, and bank account from being ruined in the event of a catastrophic illness, and to make sure that you can afford the care such a catastrophe might require. So get very high deductibles, keep your premiums lower, and self-insure against the bumps, scrapes, and steps that everyone faces.

Last year, Congress made it easier for self-employed people to save money and also provide for unexpected health problems, doctor visits, and treatments that fall below the deductibles of their insurance by authorizing legislation that allows for Medical Savings Accounts, a tax-free account that let's you set aside money to pay for medical-related expenses.

Here's how it works: using pre-tax dollars, you open an account with an amount that equals up to 65 percent of your health insurance deductible for a maximum of $1,463 each year. The money in this account can be used to pay for health care expenses including meeting your deductible or paying premiums for long-term care or special health coverage after you leave a job.

Medical Savings Accounts are a good deal. First, they lower your taxable income. Second, if you have a particularly healthy year and the money deposited in the account is not used, you can carry over any amount to the next calendar year. There are restrictions, though, if you withdraw the money for reasons other than its intended purpose you will be required to pay tax on that amount, plus a 15 percent penalty. But, if you wait until you are age sixty-five or older, you can withdraw what's left in your account without the penalty. It's like an extra IRA!

Act quickly! This is a pilot program, although existing accounts will not be affected, the IRS has been authorized to limit the availability of new accounts in 1997. Only the early birds will get their MSAs.

SECRET: If you want to open a Medical Savings Account, but you don't want to tie up extra money every year, the legislation gives you a loophole. You have until your tax return is due to deposit your account for a given year. So you could set up an account in January 1997, and wait until April 15, 1998 to fully fund it. Once 1997 is over, you can add up the amount you've spent on medical care in that year and put exactly that amount in your MSA. Tax deductible health care!

SECRET: Don't buy a health insurance policy that offers "limited coverage"; that is, excludes AIDS, organ transplants, pregnancies, and the like. If you are paying for a comprehensive policy, you should get one. Similarly, avoid policies that pay for only one type of disaster—like cancer or auto accidents. Avoid, too, policies that limit how much they will spend per illness or injury.

SECRET: Many young self-employed people try to get inexpensive health insurance policy by buying a hospitalization plan. The theory behind these plans is that at least you are covered if you have a really serious problem that requires hospitalization. But there are many serious problems that don't require hospitalization, and some hospital plans are better than others. If you go this route, make sure your policy covers the costs associated with hospital-related therapies. For example, if you need surgery, will the insurance pay the surgeon, as well as the cost of the hospital room? If you get cancer, will the policy pay for the out-patient chemotherapy? If all you can afford is a severely limited bad policy, you may not even want to bother. One insurance expert commented, "If you have no option for good insurance and someone is trying to sell you $100-a-day-in-the-hospital plans, I would pass on that. If you are going to owe a million dollars, you might as well owe a million and five thousand dollars."

And finally, my last words on insurance: May you be so healthy, happy, and lucky that you never have to collect on your coverage. I hope you "waste" the money that you spend every year protecting your life, health, income, and professions.

YOU MUST REMEMBER THIS: LESSONS FROM CHAPTER 10

- As a business owner, you not only have to insure against problems that will affect your business but also your personal life as well.

- Insurance is a tool of risk management; it's typically not an investment.

- There are new, better insurance products on the market all the time for small business owners.

11

© Suzette Barbier 1997

"The big problem for many
self-employed people
is the constant tug between their
business and personal budgets."

Midyear and Long-Term Planning

Read This Chapter in June

Summer is a good time for daydreaming, and for turning those dreams into solid plans that can come true for you. The lazy, hazy days are made for reflection. And once you figure out where you want to go, you've got six working months left to make it happen.

To do a proper midyear review, you should plan on five levels:

❏ Cash flow projections

❏ Tax estimating

❏ The business/personal balance

❏ Equipment and spending budget

❏ Long-term goal setting and business planning

Cash Flow Projections

Before you can properly make any plans for your money, you need to figure out about how much money you'll have. Use the spreadsheet that appears in the computer solution later in this chapter to give yourself a

COMPUTER SOLUTION:
PREDICTING CASH FLOW

How much cash will you have next month? And at Christmas? What about next summer? This spreadsheet, developed by Little Rock financial planner Rick Adkins, will help you analyze and predict the rhythm of your financial life.

This is virtually impossible to do your first year in business, and not so easy your second. But every year you have more history to determine your money flows. Use that history to predict your lean and fat periods.

1. Create a line on the spreadsheet for every year of data that you have, and use column A to label the years: 1993, 1994, 1995, and so on.

2. Create 12 columns—B through M—for the 12 months of the year, and fill in the income your business has generated every month.

3. Total your income for each year in column N.

4. Now start creating more revealing formulas, such as the one that figures your business's average annual growth rate. Move one column to the right (column O) and start figuring as follows: In cell O5, subtract the total 1993 income from the 1994 income, and divide the remainder by 1993's total income. Format the cell to express this as a percentage. Your formula should look like this: (N5 – N4)/N4. If you brought in $20,000 in 1993 and $24,000 the next year, you had a 20 percent growth rate for 1994. Good for you!

5. Continue with each successive year, until you have growth rates in column O for every year of business (except the first.) Then, to get a quick-and-dirty average annual growth rate that projects your future earnings, average the four or more figures in column O. Do that in cell O7.

 SECRET: *"Here's the part where you have to inject some common sense," reports Adkins. Simply averaging growth rates, particularly in a fast startup, may overestimate your realistic growth rate for the next few years. Temper this mathematically derived growth rate by what you know about your business and the market.*

PREDICTING CASH FLOW (*continued*)

6. Use that average growth rate to predict your future cash flow. Multiply your most recent annual earnings by the average growth percentages. The number you get is a *rough* approximation of what you'll make this year.

7. Now go back to the monthly data and add a few more lines to the bottom of your spreadsheet. Use the first year's monthly figures to calculate what percentage of your annual income is earned in that month. Do the same thing, on a separate line, for each of the years you are analyzing.

8. Average those percentages on another line, so that you get an average figure for each month. What will you learn? That February is always a strong month, for instance, or that March is always weak. That April is a killer. And that if your business runs as usual, you'll start really picking up in about six weeks with fall orders.

9. Add one more level of detail. Use cell P7 to estimate next year's earnings by applying the growth rate you found in O8 to this year's earnings, posted in N7. That's roughly what you can expect to make next year, if your company keeps growing at its current pace.

10. Once you've found that number, use line 18 to apply each month's average percentage to that figure, and you can get a rough approximation of your monthly income for the year.

What good is this spreadsheet? Well, you can't spend it, but you can take it to the bank to improve your chances for a business line of credit. Even more immediately, you can use it to stop worrying every February, and to schedule your spending patterns for the rest of the year. If it shows you that June is usually slow anyway, why not take a vacation, right about now?

PREDICTING CASH FLOW: Formula View *(continued)*

	A	B	C	D	E	F	G	H
1								
2								
3		Jan	Feb	Mar	Apr	May	Jun	Jul
4	1993	1200	800	2500	3000	3500	1800	2100
5	1994	1400	950	2000	3800	3800	1800	2500
6	1995	1250	700	3100	3500	4000	2000	2300
7	1996	950	1200	3500	3200	4200	2200	3000
8								
9								
10	%1993	=B4/N4	=C4/$N4	=D4/$N4	=E4/$N4	=F4/$N4	=G4/$N4	=H4/$N4
11	%1994	=B5/$N5	=C5/$N5	=D5/$N5	=E5/$N5	=F5/$N5	=G5/$N5	=H5/$N5
12	%1995	=B6/$N6	=C6/$N6	=D6/$N6	=E6/$N6	=F6/$N6	=G6/$N6	=H6/$N6
13	%1996	=B7/$N7	=C7/$N7	=D7/$N7	=E7/$N7	=F7/$N7	=G7/$N7	=H7/$N7
14								
15								
16	Average %	=Average(B10:B13)	=Average(C10:C13)	=Average(D10:D13)	=Average(E10:E13)	=Average(F10:F13)	=Average(G10:G13)	=Average(H10:H13)
17								
18	Proj.	=$P7*B16	=$P7*C16	=$P7*D16	=$P7*E16	=$P7*F16	=$P7*G16	=$P7*H16
19	1997 Inc.							

I	J	K	L	M	N	O	P
					Total	Annual	Next Year's
					Annual	Growth	Projected
ug	Sep	Oct	Nov	Dec	Income	Rate	Income
750	3000	1500	1100	3500	=Sum(B4:M4)		
900	3100	2500	1500	4000	=Sum(B5:M5)	=(N5−N4)/N4	
2000	4000	2800	1500	3750	=Sum(B6:M6)	=(N6−N5)/N5	
3500	4500	3300	2500	4000	=Sum(B7:M7)	=(N7−N6)/N6	=N7+(O7*N7)
					Average Growth Rate	=Average(O5,O6,O7)	
=I4/$N4	=J4/$N4	=K4/$N4	=L4/$N4	=M4/$N4			
=I5/$N5	=J5/$N5	=K5/$N5	=L5/$N5	=M5/$N5			
=I6/$N6	=J6/$N6	=K6/$N6	=L6/$N6	=M6/$N6			
=I7/$N7	=J7/$N7	=K7/$N7	=L7/$N7	=M7/$N7			
=ge(I10:I13)	=Average(J10:J13)	=Average(K10:K13)	=Average(L:10:L13)	=Average(M10:M13)			
=$P7*I16	=$P7*J16	=$P7*K16	=$P7*L16	=$P7*M16			

PREDICTING CASH FLOW: Data View (*continued*)

	A	B	C	D	E	F	G	H
1								
2								
3		Jan	Feb	Mar	Apr	May	Jun	Jul
4	1993	1,200	800	2,500	3,000	3,500	1,800	2,100
5	1994	1,400	950	2,000	3,800	3,800	1,800	2,500
6	1995	1,250	700	3,100	3,500	4,000	2,000	2,300
7	1996	950	1,200	3,500	3,200	4,200	2,200	3,000
8								
9								
10	%1993	4.85%	3.23%	10.10%	12.12%	14.14%	7.27%	8.48%
11	%1994	4.96%	3.36%	7.08%	13.45%	13.45%	6.37%	8.85%
12	%1995	4.05%	2.27%	10.03%	11.33%	12.94%	6.47%	7.44%
13	%1996	2.64%	3.33%	9.71%	8.88%	11.65%	6.10%	8.32%
14								
15								
16	Average %	4.12%	3.05%	9.23%	11.44%	13.05%	6.55%	8.27%
17								
18	Proj.	1,733	1,282	3,882	4,813	5,487	2,757	3,480
19	1997 Inc.							

I	J	K	L	M	N	O	P
					Total	Annual	Next Year's
					Annual	Growth	Projected
Aug	Sep	Oct	Nov	Dec	Income	Rate	Income
750	3,000	1,500	1,100	3,500	24,750		
900	3,100	2,500	1,500	4,000	28,250	14.14%	
2,000	4,000	2,800	1,500	3,750	30,900	9.38%	
3,500	4,500	3,300	2,500	4,000	36,050	<u>16.67%</u>	42,058
					Average Growth Rate	13.40%	
3.03%	12.12%	6.06%	4.44%	14.14%			
3.19%	10.97%	8.85%	5.31%	14.16%			
6.47%	12.94%	9.06%	4.85%	12.14%			
9.71%	12.48%	9.15%	6.93%	11.10%			
5.60%	12.13%	8.28%	5.39%	12.88%			
2,355	5,102	3,483	2,265	5,418			

rough idea of what your business will bring in over the next several months. It is set up to give you a projection of your monthly income based your past monthly earnings.

You can bolster that projection with what you already know about the money coming in. Refer to your accounting program to check your accounts receivable list; it should show you which checks you are expecting in the mail soon. Add in any big assignments you know you are working on or projects about to be completed.

Similarly, think about any anticipated expenses. Do you pay quarterly health insurance premiums? Is your copying machine on its last faded legs? Is your daughter getting married? Do you need a vacation? Determine whether you will have enough to cover these major expenditures through the end of the year. Then budget for them.

SECRET: *It may seem unprofessional to evaluate your business expenses together with your personal expenses when you are doing your midyear planning, but it's more realistic to do so. After all, with most closely held businesses, you can pull more money out of the business when you need it at home, and send more to the business when your professional budget calls for it.*

Mid-Year Tax Planning

By now, you already know how to crunch the numbers that tell you what to pay in estimated taxes. (See Chapter 4.) But this is the session in which you may be able to cut those numbers. Review your estimated tax worksheet and the list of deductions. Then start thinking about what you could do between now and December 31 to cut your taxes. Sometimes, this can involve a major shift in focus.

For example, David was a computer consultant when his brother approached him with a business prospect that sounded appealing, but to take advantage of it, he'd have to cut back on his consulting hours, losing income there, and invest about $5,000 in specialized phone equipment to work with his brother. Could he afford to take the plunge? He didn't think he had that kind of money in his checking account.

So David fed what-if numbers into his estimated tax worksheet. What if he earned $10,000 less this year? He'd cut his taxes by $4,700, so he'd really only be giving up $5,300. And that $5,000 extra he'd be spending? After taxes, it would only be $2,650. So it would cost him $7,350 to join his brother's business, not $15,000. And that, he determined, he could swing.

To do an appropriate midyear tax plan, consider all of the tax-favored spending you could do between now and December 31. You could feed your retirement account. You could buy up to $18,000 in equipment and write it off this year, as long as you had at least that much business income.

Start to schedule these expenses before year end. Put them on your calendar. If, for example, your projections show you'll probably earn $30,000 this year, aim to put 10 percent, or $3,000 in your retirement fund. (That's lower than the max, but leaves you wiggle room in case your earnings are lower than you expect.) Figure out how much you can afford to spend on charitable deductions, consulting help, equipment, and the like. Then plug all of those numbers into your tax estimating worksheet. And pay the smallest amount possible when you make your estimated tax payment.

SECRET: *Pay the minimum amount of estimated taxes that are required to avoid a penalty. That's either 90 percent of your federal tax liability for this year, or 100 percent of the federal taxes you paid last year. (If you earned over $150,000 last year, married filing joint or $75,000 filing single, then this figure is 110 percent of last year's income.) Pay this minimal amount even if you know you're having a really good year and will owe more in taxes. Put the extra money that you expect to owe Uncle Sam in a money market mutual fund. Or, if you've already got it in hand now, buy a six-month CD with it—you'll earn money on your money instead of giving the government that free loan.*

The Business/Personal Budget Balance

The big problem for many self-employed people is the constant tug between their business and personal budgets. Most paycheck-earners have to decide such things as: should they invest in an IRA, buy a swimming pool membership, or trade in the car. You have an added level of decision making. The IRA, the pool, the car, or the new clerical assistant that can really bump up your earning power.

To properly decide where your money should go, evaluate your expenses by their after-tax costs. The spreadsheet in the computer solution later in this chapter shows you how. Basically, legitimate business expenses cost only about half of the price you pay; the other half disappears in tax savings. That is not to say that you should spend money only on items that are tax-deductible, or that you should put all of your money into the business. But you can stretch it further when you spend on an after-tax basis.

To keep a proper business/personal budget balance, consider these questions:

- ❏ Do you feel your life has a proper balance now?
- ❏ Have you taken a vacation in the last year?
- ❏ Are you saving for the personal goals you have (such as retirement)?
- ❏ Are you feeding your business enough money so that it can grow, or at least stay healthy at its current level?
- ❏ Do you see extraordinary expenses on the horizon, in your business, or personal life?
- ❏ Do you twist your personal life so that it fits into the category of "business?"

An Aside about Voluntary Simplicity

There's a new trend on the block called "voluntary simplicity." Adherents purposely spend less so they can earn less and, therefore, work less. For many self-employed people, this is not possible: They live to work. But just as many others are self-employed because they don't want to run their lives by someone else's clock. They keep their own businesses running so they can take time off for afternoon exercise, or time with the kids, or to pursue a favorite hobby.

If you are self-employed by choice so that your life has balance, you can achieve that balance through midyear tax planning. Say you are on course to make $50,000 this year. But what if you only made $35,000? You'd see from your estimated tax spreadsheet that the cut in income would reduce your taxes almost $8,000. You could make up the difference by keeping your car another year, giving up your most expensive business subscriptions, and eat out less, for example. This kind of planning gives you a chance to decide your priorities and then plan for them.

If you are offered a major assignment, just when you were planning to take that long-needed vacation, you can consult your midyear calculations and decide whether you can afford to turn it down.

Budgeting to Grow

On the other hand, perhaps you've already been wallowing in simplicity, voluntary or otherwise, and you've been yearning to boost your business. Use your midyear analysis to see what you can stint on personally to push money into your business. Come up with a budget for the equipment, employees, and supplies you would need to make your business grow. You may find that since all of those investments are tax-deductible business expenses you have to cut less from your personal budget to afford all of them than you thought.

Do an Equipment Budget

You may find yourself needing to buy more than the $18,000 of immediately deductible equipment, especially if the business you run is a manufacturing one. If that's the case, it's best to look at your equipment needs even earlier than midyear to decide how to apportion your expenses throughout the year. Depreciable equipment put in service during the first half of the year nets a bigger write-off than equipment bought in the third or fourth quarter.

SECRET: *If you need to buy so much equipment this year that you'll be depreciating some of it over time (because you'll exceed the $17,500 immediate write-off limit), plan to do so before the end of June. Your deduction will be larger.*

You can also decide to wait to buy some equipment next year. You could, for example, rent a copier this year with the option to buy it next year. Or schedule $18,000 of the most urgent purchases and let the rest slip into January or February.

Having an equipment budget will allow you to do the following:

❏ Line up the cash before you buy the product, so you're not forced into high-interest rate store credit.

❏ Keep your eyes open for good deals on the equipment you know you'll need, so you can buy it when you find it.

❏ Maximize the tax breaks on the money you spend for equipment.

❏ Budget time to do consumer research, so you know which scanner, phone system, or forklift most suits your needs and your budget.

❏ Take the time to scout out used equipment.

❏ Schedule for an orderly equipment transition. For example, plan to switch to a new computer in August, when most of your clients are on vacation.

❏ Take the time to find a good home for your old equipment.

Planning for the Long Term

It makes sense, even if you keep it informal at this point, to spend some time thinking about how your business and personal life will change over time. You can either design a formal business plan or just start making tentative plans for how your personal life and your business will intersect in the future.

Prepare a Formal Business Plan

If you think you may need to apply for a business loan from a bank, you will need a bona fide business plan to convince your banker of your creditworthiness. But even if you never need to borrow money or capitalize your inventory, you may find that a business plan is a useful tool. It can help you focus your future business goals and make strategic decisions now. A good business plan should be a part word and part number profile of where you are, where you want to go, and how you plan to get there.

The words should describe the company—its products and services, competitors, customers, management, operations and marketing structure, industrial outlook, and long-term goals. The numbers should estimate your cash flow, income and expenses, balance sheet (what you have and what you owe), and a break-even analysis.

Most people are intimidated either by the numbers or the words, but once you break down the plan to these essential components, you'll find you can work through your inhibition.

To prepare your own business plan, include the following five easy pieces:

1. **Write a mission statement for your business.** You can't write a business plan until you know what you want to achieve in general terms, so the mission statement is the foundation block of the plan. The statement can be high-minded and mercenary: "To make a lot of money while providing quality marketing help to promising startup companies," for example. While it sounds vague it isn't: A mission statement like this helps you to weed out schlock projects, low-paying clients and businesses. And on bad days, you can refer to it to refocus your eyes on the prize.

2. **Describe your business.** Include what you do, what you *don't* do, (you may discover you are leaving too much money on the table), and how you do it. Ask yourself questions while you are doing this: What do you really need to know to make this business work? Is it realistic to expect that you will be able to do every-

252

COMPUTER SOLUTION:
CREATING A BUSINESS PLAN

There are many fine software programs on the market that will walk you through a business plan. The new generation of software is full of prompts that can direct you when you aren't sure what to do next. Business Plan Pro and Business Plan Toolkit (Palo Alto Software, 800-229-7526) includes a section-by-section outline, along with questions such as: "Why do people buy your product instead of others? Do you offer better features, better price, better quality, better service, or some other factor?" PlanMaker (PowerSolutions for Business, 800-423-1228) has a manual you can use as a guide even if you never load the software. Each section comes with its own questionnaire that can similarly push you through the process. "Do you know of any trade publications that have cited the growth potential of your industry, product, or service?" it asks, for example. Get one of these programs and use it, even if you don't do a complete business plan. It will help you focus.

Business Plan Pro provides detailed instructions for recording expenses and automatically charts your balances.

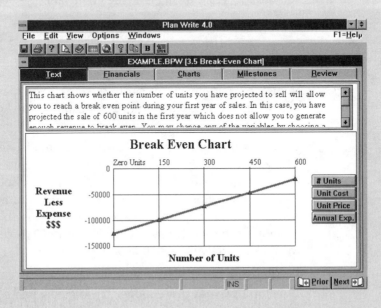

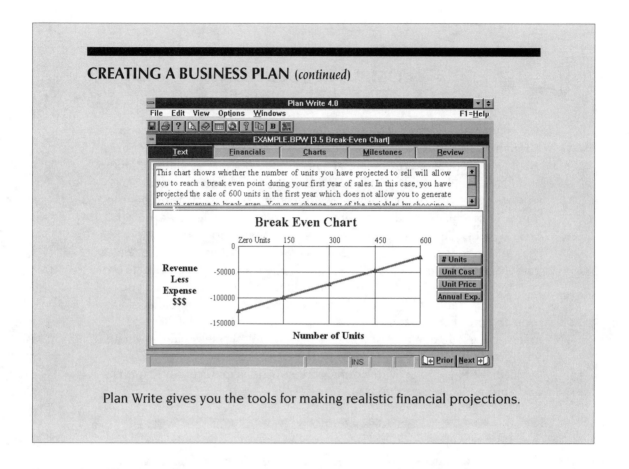

Plan Write gives you the tools for making realistic financial projections.

thing the company needs? Your business plan may point out areas—marketing or accounting, for example—where you'll want to hire help.

3. **Include a marketing plan.** Figure out, as realistically as possible, who your customers are and how you are going to reach them. Calculate the costs of reaching them, through direct mail, advertising, commissioned salespeople and other methods. When you write your plan, outline it as specifically as possible; which letters will you write to which lists in which months? Once the plan is written, you only have to follow directions.

4. **Predict your cash flow** as described earlier.

5. **Develop five-year projections.** Try to guesstimate your sales, expenses, and profits for five years, using spreadsheets or the calculators built into business plan software. This is really an

HOW TO HAVE
AN ANNUAL PLANNING MEETING BY YOURSELF

It's a good idea, during summer or any other day-dreamy time of year, to schedule a one-day plan-making, goal-setting retreat by yourself. Visit a pretty place far from the phone, and ponder where your business is headed, how it fits with your personal life, and where you want both to move in the future.

Tim, a management consultant, has become a master at conducting his own annual meetings. He starts with a six-week countdown prior to the actual meeting. Each week he lists an accomplishment he would like to achieve from the business in the coming year. This can range anywhere from a vacation in Paris during spring, or publicity in a magazine, or a 15 percent increase in income, to adding new clients and expanding the market for his business. Tim isn't actually setting goals, he's giving himself a six-week countdown to the big event, figuring out what he really cares about.

On the day of his solo meeting, he shuts the door, sets up a giant notepad on an easel (the kind you'd use for a meeting presentation) and starts to narrow down the list. Once he decides to establish one of his "wants" as a goal, he begins to plan for it, by formulating questions such as: What do I have do to achieve this goal? What are the specific actions I need to take? How can I plan and schedule those actions?

For example, if Tim's goal is to add to new clients by expanding into new markets, he might first define what kind of client he wants. Then, he might decide he needs to adjust his marketing strategy, perhaps to a more professional level to attract the type of client he wants. By the end of the day, he would have a specific action plan for when, where, and how he would change his marketing plans to win the clients he wants.

At the very end of the day, Tim rewards himself with a cafe latté at a local coffee house. He looks over his action plan and feels pretty good about his accomplishments during the year past and his plans for the year to come.

Here's how you can hold a successful annual meeting of your own:

1. **Write the date on your calendar.** Schedule the meeting at least two months into the future and stick to it.

2. **Percolate before you plan.** Before you go away, let your subconscious go where it will. Think about what you want to be when you grow up, and daydream about how you'd really like to spend your time.

HOW TO HAVE AN ANNUAL PLANNING MEETING (*continued*)

3. **Bring toys and tools.** This includes anything that will spur you on: resource directories, highlighters, one of those carry-around organizers, pretty file folders.

4. **Review and crunch numbers.** Assess your past performance. Are your sales growing properly? Are you developing the right client mix? Are all of your activities profitable? Use the annual checkup in Chapter 16 to guide you.

5. **Figure out why you didn't meet past goals.** Be brutally honest. What didn't you do that you should have? What don't you know that you haven't admitted to yourself?

6. **Define specific goals in a very specific way.** Establish goals that are concrete: I want to earn $50,000 this year; I want a book contract; I want to take the month of July off; I want to pick up one multinational client; I want to sell an ad campaign that I love. Create some goals that make you stretch. Put each goal on top of its own page of paper, so that you'll have plenty of room to fill in a strategy plan.

7. **Identify the roadblocks to those goals.** Chances are, they are the same roadblocks that held you back last year. Say, for example, that you've set "earn 20 percent more" as a goal for the coming year, but you already feel you are working as hard as you can. That's a roadblock.

8. **Select strategies that will knock down those blocks.** In the preceding example, you could hire someone to take over routine tasks that would free you up for more client work, or you could raise your rates.

9. **Create an action plan.** This is the nitty gritty. In each stage, you ought to be refining your plans and getting more and more specific. An action plan should be as detailed as any recipe: Buy QuarkXpress and spent two hours a week on it until you've learned it well. Send a letter to everyone in the neighborhood announcing the business. Make twelve marketing calls every morning. This is the kind of checklist to post next to your desk.

10. **Celebrate!** After your day (or days?) of deliberation, reward yourself. Take yourself out to dinner, get a massage, and don't collect your messages until tomorrow.

COMPUTER SOLUTIONS:
THE COMPUTER, THE KEOGH, THE COUCH, AND THE COCKTAIL PARTY

This is a spreadsheet that can help you see the after-tax cost of your planned expenses. Every expense in this sample has a different after-tax cost, even if the pretax cost is the same.

Say, for example, that you unexpectedly come into $2,000, and you're aren't sure what to do with it. You could buy a new computer, or you could put the $2,000 into your Keogh retirement plan. Maybe you should just blow it all on a networking cocktail party for your favorite and potential clients. On the other hand, this is found money. And your living room sofa has been looking kind of ratty lately.

And while taxes shouldn't be the only factor in your decision, if you plan to spend money in a tax-smart way, you might be able to afford more than $2,000 worth of spending.

Here are the different expenses, and their tax consequences:

- The computer, assuming you only use it in business, is fully deductible as a business expense, and thus reduces your self-employment taxes as well as your income taxes.
- The Keogh is deductible, but only as an item on your personal 1040.
- The cocktail party is a legitimate expense, but as a meal, it is only 50 percent deductible.
- Sorry, you have to buy the couch with after-tax money.

This a simple spreadsheet that will help you calculate your real expenses: For the tax rate used in columns B and C, assume a personal tax bracket of 28 percent and a state income tax of 5 percent. The 45 percent rate is derived by adding the state and local income tax rates to a self-employment tax rate of 14.1, and then by subtracting that portion of the self-employment tax that would be deducted from your 1040. (This self-employment tax gets tricky. It's really 15.3 percent of 92.35 percent of your income. Half of that is 7.1 percent, times .33 equals 2.3 percent of a tax reduction. Put it all together: Your effective self-employment rate is [0.153 * 0.9235] −.23 or .11.8. Add that to your state and local tax, and you get an effective business tax rate of .45.)

THE COMPUTER, THE KEOGH . . .: Formula View *(continued)*

	A	B	C	D	E
1	The Expense	Basic 1040 Deduction (Keogh)	Simple Business Deduction (Computer)	Entertainment Business Deduction (Cocktails)	Sorry, No Deduction (Couch)
2					
3	2000	=A3*.33	=A3*.45	=(A3*.5)*.45	=A3*0
4					
5	900	=A5*.33	=A5*.45	=(A5*.5)*.45	=A5*0
6					
7	304	=A7*.33	=A7*.45	=(A7*.5)*.45	=A7*0
8					

Data View

	A	B	C	D	E
1	The Expense	Basic 1040 Deduction (Keogh)	Simple Business Deduction (Computer)	Entertainment Business Deduction (Cocktails)	Sorry, No Deduction (Couch)
2					
3	$2,000.00	$660.00	$900.00	$450.00	$0.00
4					
5	$900.00	$297.00	$405.00	$203.00	$0.00
6					
7	$304.00	$100.00	$137.00	$68.00	$0.00
8					

THE COMPUTER, THE KEOGH . . . (*continued*)

   This spreadsheet demonstrates that if you spent the entire $2,000 on the computer, you'd get a tax break of $900, which you could then invest in a Keogh (line 15). That will give you a tax break of $304. You could give a smaller cocktail party for that amount of money, or perhaps a dinner party for your favorite clients. And save $68 on your taxes. Okay, even a foam sofa costs more than $68. But you could buy a couple of cool throw pillows or a spread, too.

   The moral of the story: Use spreadsheets to plan your spending on an after-tax basis. It's the only way to spend the same money more than once!

inexact science, but it will give you some idea of where you are headed and how to get there.

SECRET: *Don't worry about being wrong. "If people had an infallible way of doing this, there would be no business failures," observes Thomas Carroll, the entrepreneur who wrote PlanMaker software. But err on the side of caution. It's better to overshoot projections than to fail to meet them.*

Long-Term Personal and Business Budgeting

While you are spending time figuring out how to stretch your business money and your time over the rest of this year, it's not a bad idea to do the same for your personal life as well. Here are some long-term personal issues that you might want to include with your personal/business budgeting session.

❑ **College Planning:** Do you have children you intend to send to college? Use your self-employment status as an advantage for this. Try to time your income. Loan officers look most intently at your annual earnings for the year that starts in January of your child's junior year in high school. Consider earning more until then, and reduce your earnings during that year.

❑ **Vacations:** Perhaps you want to travel more. You can budget for it. Plan a five-year "trip budget" and try to make the places and times overlap with business purposes, so you can deduct a greater percentage of your trips. (But don't get so obsessed about making every trip so business-related that you defeat its purpose as recreational.)

❑ **Office Crunch:** Is yours a home office? Is it roomy enough for your business, or do you see yourself needing more room or a different office within five years? It's best to start planning early. You may need to decide whether to move your business out of the house, or pay for an addition.

❑ **Will You Need to Borrow Money?** The earlier you know this, the more leeway you have. You can jump at a refinanced mortgage while rates are low and put the money in the bank until you need it. You can spend a couple of years romancing your banker and building your business, until it is creditworthy on its own. You can stretch out the loans you already have—say on cars and houses— to give you more cash to pay off the business loan you expect to need. You can plan to borrow against the business, and use cash from the business to pay off your debts. (That's a savings strategy because business interest is deductible, but personal consumer interest is not.)

❑ **Will Your Spouse's Working Situation Change?** If you have a spouse who will return to work full-time, or stop working in the next five years, try to plan for the change. A spouse who returns to work may save money on health insurance, but you will probably end up paying more in taxes, clothes, and commuting. A spouse who retires or resigns from his or her job can cut total cost-of-living expenses, reduce tax burden, but also reduce cash flow.

❑ **Where Else Do You Want to Go?** Now is the time to plan how to make both your business and your personal life. Dream your dreams, assign them priorities, convert them to plans, and figure out how to pay for them.

The more planning you do, the more likely you are to reach the goals important to you. But there's one big aspect of planning we haven't talked about yet—though just about everyone else in America is—and that is retirement planning, which for self-employed people, can be more complicated, more expensive, and more lucrative than for anyone else. Read on!

YOU MUST REMEMBER THIS: LESSONS FROM CHAPTER 11

- Decide where you want to go and how you want to get there.
- Make future plans that consider taxes, cash flow, lifestyle, and equipment purchases, for the long haul.
- Use computer tools to make your plans easy and meaningful.

© Gary Hovland 1997

"All I *need* is one big client,
one new job, one more assignment,
and I can retire before I'm eighty."

Do You Want to Do This Forever?

Retirement Planning for the Self-Employed

Picture this: It's thirty years into the future, and you are seventy. All of your friends and colleagues have retired to places like Cozumel and Key West, where they golf, fish, sun (by then it will be safe again), read, relax, and congratulate themselves on the size of their corporate pensions.

But not you! You're still living the dream you started in your thirties—sitting at a computer, wheedling business from people who are now the age of your grandchildren, living from check to check, and whining about the inadequacy of Social Security.

Sure, your friends invite you down to visit, but you can't afford to take the time off. If you don't work in February, you don't eat in March. You repeat to yourself, "All I need is one big client, one new job, one more assignment, and I can retire before I'm eighty."

Pension Realities

Of course, that scary little story is based on a few faulty assumptions. For starters, that those with traditional jobs will be well taken care of by their corporate pensions. Self-funded retirement plans and successive rounds

chapter

12

Do You Want to Do This Forever? Retirement Planning for the Self-Employed

of layoffs belie that theory. In fact, corporate employees may be at a bit of a disadvantage to those of us who work for ourselves. At least we know we have to take care of our own future. Nine-to-five employees may mistakenly think that someone else is going to do it for them.

There's a second advantage we have over our employed colleagues. The future for today's workers includes sequential careers, working longer, and supplementing retirement income with part-time and on-the-side jobs. If you are self-employed, you already know how to scramble for clients, squeeze in a little work on the side, and find new ways to make money when the old ones don't work.

All this is not to say that you may want to slow down on some unspecified day in the future, you may want to take off in February, visit your leisure-class friends or—gasp!—actually retire. To be able to do that, though, you'll have to develop and feed your own retirement plan. Which is okay, because who is going to take care of you better than you will?

Learn to Roll Over

If you are leaving a job to devote yourself to your business, you may be confronted by a large sum of money in the form of proceeds from your 401(k) or other savings mechanisms you've been participating in. What do you plan to do with that money?

Hmm, good question. And you'd better come up with the right answer because if you make the wrong choices, you can suffer serious consequences: unexpected tax bills, loss of retirement income, or the inability to access your money when you need it.

Whatever you do, don't touch the funds! Right now they are in a protected, tax-deferred account. If you take possession of the funds, even briefly with the intent of rolling them into another investment, your employer is required to withhold 20 percent of it against the income taxes you would owe if you didn't roll it over. This is a mess you want to avoid. Say, for example, you have $40,000 in your 401(k). You cash in the account with the idea of rolling it over into a tax-deferred retirement account in a mutual fund company. But the check you receive is only for $32,000. That other $8,000—or 20 percent—was withheld as federal income taxes.

What happens if you invest the remaining $32,000 in the rollover account? Next year, when you file your tax return for the previous year, you'll also owe taxes on that $8,000 that you didn't roll over—about $2,240 in federal taxes alone. That's because you have to pay taxes (and a 10 percent penalty, if you're under age 59 1/2) on any money you take out of your tax-deferred retirement account.

If you want to avoid paying taxes on that $8,000, you'll have to make it up when you roll the money over into a new retirement account. In other words: Even though your company only sends you a check for $32,000, you'll have sixty days to reinvest a full $40,000 somewhere else. Once you do, you'll get the full $8,000 refunded when you file your tax return in the following year. But finding an extra $8,000 isn't easy, and you can avoid the whole mess if you arrange to have the funds transferred directly into a new rollover account.

Do it this way: Pick the broker, mutual fund company, or bank where you want the money to be deposited. Set up the plan, and direct your company to have your company pension assets transferred directly into that account, which is called a Rollover IRA. No fuss, no muss, and no 20 percent withholding.

Once you've rolled that money over, you can watch it grow and move it from one investment into another. But don't mix it up with other money. It's different from the IRAs you may have had from the early eighties, and it's different from the pension plan you will set up for yourself now that you are self-employed. As long as you keep that rollover separate, you are free to mix it later with another company plan should you reenter the workforce. Keeping it separate also prevents you from complicating your tax situation by mixing an after-tax IRA with a tax-deferred IRA.

Leave It Alone

Some companies let you keep your money in their retirement fund when you leave. This isn't a bad idea. New York tax attorney Stuart Kessler warns that you lose some advantages when you move money out of a company pension plan into a personal rollover account. Income averaging, a technique that allows workers to take lump sums when they retire and then spread the tax burden over five years, is only available to retirement funds kept with an employer. And often, employer-held plans afford a higher level of professional management for a lower fee than an individual IRA, says Kessler. Note that the most recent tax law disallows income averaging except for people who will take their retirement distributions between now and the end of 1999.

Move It

You have three basic places to put your rollover money. You can direct it to a bank, which will put the money in certificates of deposit or other bank accounts, and know that your money will be insured by the Federal Deposit Insurance Corporation (FDIC). You can choose a mutual fund investment firm (such as Vanguard or Fidelity) that will help you to pick and choose among the plans they offer. Or you can choose a brokerage

chapter

12

Do You Want to Do This Forever? Retirement Planning for the Self-Employed

firm like Merrill Lynch or Charles Schwab that can place your funds in a broad variety of investments, including stocks, bonds, and mutual funds.

If you decide you want the full investment menu that's only available through a broker, consider that there are two types of brokers. Full-service brokers, like Merrill Lynch, do research, offer advice, and charge full commissions for every decision you make and investment product you buy. Discount brokers, like Charles Schwab, charge reduced commissions and offer no load mutual funds, but no advice or research, leaving the decision making to you.

SECRET: *Note that there are now brokers that conduct business out of bank branches. Don't get confused: They are not bankers! These brokers are employees of a brokerage firm that is related to the company that owns your bank. When you invest in stocks, bonds, or mutual funds at a bank, you're using a brokerage firm. It's no different than going to an independent broker. Your investments are not insured or guaranteed by the FDIC.*

What are the pros and cons of the different venues? Check out the "Where to Take Your Retirement Rollover" table.

Where to Take Your Retirement Rollover			
Where	**Investment Options**	**Pros**	**Cons**
Bank	Certificates of Deposit	FDIC insured, simple	Earnings too low for long-term investing
Mutual Funds	Mutual funds that invest in stocks and bonds	Low fees, investment guidance	Limited to the funds offered by one family
Full-Service Broker	CDs, stocks, bonds, mutual funds, options, futures	A broad investment menu, professional advice	Fees and commissions are high; the broker may not have your best interests at heart
Discount Broker	Same as full service broker	Lower fees with same broad choices; you make your own investment decisions	You make your own investment decisions, no advice from the pros!

All of these entities have a lot of experience creating rollovers. Once you choose the account you want, they will walk you through the forms you need to transfer your money simply.

Choose your parking place carefully. Once you've decided where you want your money, you can't move it again in the same year.

Retirement Planning for Yourself

That takes care of the money you already have. What about the money you want and need? It comes down to a simple rule: Save as much as you can, as early as you can.

*S*ECRET: *When you are self-employed, there are always many choices about where to put your money. With the tax deferral built into most retirement plans for the self-employed, there's no better place to put your money. If your combined federal/state tax bracket is 35 percent, the government will pay you $350 for every $1,000 you sock away in your own retirement fund! Studies by financial planners demonstrate that even if you eventually have to take the money out, paying taxes and an early distribution penalty of 10 percent, you would still be ahead if your money had stayed tax deferred at least seven years.*

Start Early

Many retirement planning companies use this illustration, or a similar one, to demonstrate that nothing is as good as an early start. Fidelity Investments, which is one of the key players in retirement investing, points out that a person who starts saving for retirement at age thirty needs to save only half as much as the person who waits until forty to start.

If you start at age thirty-five and save $5,000 a year until you are forty-five (a total of $50,000) and then never save another penny, you will have $655,049 when you reach seventy (assuming a 9 percent annual return, which is reasonable given typical long-term investment returns.)

Wait until you are forty-five to start, and you'll have to salt away $7,733.79 every year for twenty-five years—a total investment of $193,345—to hatch the same nest egg when you are seventy. If you start when you are twenty-five, you can save a little more than $2,000 a year for ten years, then stop and still have $655,049 when you are seventy.

chapter

12

Do You Want to Do This Forever? Retirement Planning for the Self-Employed

How Retirement Dollars Grow

The "Retirement Dollars Growth" table on page 269 clearly illustrates the three basic rules of retirement investing:

- ❏ The earlier you start, the more money you'll end up with.
- ❏ The more you invest, the more you'll end up with.
- ❏ Return matters. The higher your returns, the more money you'll have.

Choosing the Right Retirement Savings Vehicle

By now you should be hot to save, save, save. But first, you have to pick the right type of retirement savings account for your situation. Consider your age, your financial situation, your retirement goals, and whether you have or plan to have employees. You have many choices:

- ❏ Individual Retirement Account (IRA)
- ❏ Sep IRA
- ❏ SAR-Sep
- ❏ Profit-Sharing Keogh
- ❏ Money Purchase Keogh
- ❏ Paired Keoghs
- ❏ 401(k) Plan
- ❏ SIMPLE
- ❏ Defined Benefit Plan

Each one has very specific advantages, disadvantages and limits.

Individual Retirement Account

The plain vanilla IRA holds no magic for the self-employed. Anyone can have one. You can invest up to $2,000 a year (as long as you earn up to $2,000 a year), and the income will build tax-deferred, until you take it out at retirement. You may be able to deduct the annual $2,000 contribution, too, if you meet either of these requirements:

- ❏ Neither you nor your spouse if you are married is covered by another pension plan.
- ❏ Your earnings are below a certain level; currently $40,000 for a married couple and $25,000 for a single individual.

IRAs are not the best choices for self-employed savers; there are others that are so much better.

Retirement Dollars Growth				
Age You Start Saving	Invest monthly tax-deferred until age 65	For a total investment of	With a 5 percent annualized return, at 65	With a 10 percent annualized return, at 65
30	$250	$105,000	$284,023	$929,160
	$500	$210,000	$568,346	$1,898,319
	$1,000	$420,000	$1,136,092	$3,796,638
35	$250	$90,000	$208,065	$565,122
	$500	$180,000	$416,129	$1,130,244
	$1,000	$360,000	$832,259	$2,260,488
40	$250	$75,000	$148,877	$331,708
	$500	$150,000	$297,755	$663,417
	$1,000	$300,000	$595,510	$1,323,530
45	$250	$60,000	$102,758	$189,842
	$500	$120,000	$205,517	$379,684
	$1,000	$240,000	$411,034	$759,369
50	$250	$45,000	$66,822	$103,618
	$500	$90,000	$133,644	$207,235
	$1,000	$180,000	$267,259	$414,470
55	$250	$30,000	$38,821	$51,211
	$500	$60,000	$77,641	$102,422
	$1,000	$120,000	$155,282	$204,845
60	$250	$15,000	$17,002	$19,359
	$500	$30,000	$34,003	$38,719
	$1,000	$60,000	$68,007	$77,437

SEP-IRA

The simplified employee pension-IRA is almost as easy as the standard IRA and far more worthwhile. You have a lot of leeway to set one up: You can open a SEP account up until your taxes are due for that year. So if you file extensions on your 1997 tax returns and they aren't due until let's say, October 15, 1998, you have up to that date to open and/or feed your SEP for the prior year. Tax-deferred contributions to a SEP are limited to 13.04 percent of the net income from your business (your Schedule C bottom line.) Each year you can change how much you contribute to your SEP (as

chapter

12

Do You Want to Do This Forever? Retirement Planning for the Self-Employed

long as you don't go over the limit). There's no minimum contribution. A SEP, however, becomes more complicated if you hire employees. If they are twenty years old and have worked with you for three of the last five years, you have to create a SEP for them too—even if they are part-timers. You also must pay in at least as high a percentage for them as you do for yourself. That can be costly, and more than you want to pay, especially if your employees are young and would rather have the cash than the retirement benefit.

Profit-Sharing Keogh

A Keogh is considered a "qualified" plan. Which means you have some tax leeway when you take the money out after retirement. Income averaging rules that allow you to spread out the tax burden are available for Keoghs but not for SEPs. And Keoghs are more often off limits to bankruptcy courts and college financial aid officers than are SEPs.

But you pick up a little more complexity with Keoghs. You must establish them before December 31 of the year for which you first want to make tax-deferred contributions, though you can still make those contributions. And once your Keogh reaches $100,000 in assets, there are additional reporting requirements for the IRS.

Your Keogh also must cover employees, but the rules are different. Part-timers who don't work 1,000 hours per year (about twenty hours a week) may be excluded, as may employees who are under age twenty-one. Full-time employees over the age of twenty-one who have been with your company for at least a year usually must be covered.

With a profit-sharing Keogh, you can decide every year how much money you want to contribute, as long as it is no more than 13.04 percent of your Schedule C net, or $22,500. That's the same limit as with a SEP.

Money Purchase Keogh

The same deadlines, tax reporting, and participation rules apply to this kind of Keogh, but the contribution rules are different. When you establish a money purchase Keogh, you must commit to a fixed percentage of income that you will contribute every year. That percentage may be as high as 20 percent of your Schedule C net (or 25 percent of your Schedule C net, minus half of your self-employment tax) up to $30,000. So you pick up the ability to write off higher contributions, but you lose some flexibility. If you set up a money purchase Keogh at the max, and establish a 20 percent contribution, you can find yourself cash squeezed.

$\mathcal{S}$ECRET: *Set up paired Keoghs! You can get maximum flexibility and deductibility by pairing two Keoghs—a money purchase and a profit-sharing plan. Set the money purchase limit at 10 percent (6.96 percent of your Schedule C net) and aim for the profit-sharing goal of 15 percent (13.04 percent of your Schedule C net.) In good years, you can contribute to the max to both and shelter 20 percent of your earnings. In bad years, you only have to put away 10 percent. Your upper limit for the paired plans is $30,000.*

401(k) Plan

These plans are nifty and give you lots of options. But there really isn't any point to setting up a 401(k) plan unless you have many employees. There are complicated rules requiring that participation not be "top heavy." So even if you want to contribute the max, you may not be able to if your employees at the bottom don't do the same. The limits are more restrictive, too. You can contribute up to 25 percent of your earnings, but not more than $9,500 in 1996.

The good news is if you have enough employees to make a 401(k) worthwhile, it is getting easier to set one up, though you should still expect to spend at least $1,000 up front and $500 a year to get it going and keep it going. Among the providers who will set up and administer plans for small businesses are:

- ❏ Fidelity Investments, 800-544-8888.
- ❏ The 401(k) Association, 215-579-8830.
- ❏ Scudder Investments, 800-323-6105.

SIMPLE

Update: Last year's Congress authorized a new small business retirement account, the Savings Incentive Match Plan for Employees (SIMPLE.) These plans are aimed at small business owners who have fewer than 100 employees. They allow you, as the employer, to fund your workers retirement plans directly into IRAs or simplified 401(k) plans. They let you out of some of the more complicated reporting rules that govern 401(k) plans, but they have stiffer penalties for employees who pull their money out early. They don't offer particular advantages for sole proprietors.

The Defined Benefit Plan

All of the plans discussed so far are "defined contribution" plans. The combined amount established by law and by your own targets is the amount you put into the plan. The last type of plan to consider works

chapter

12

Do You Want to Do This Forever? Retirement Planning for the Self-Employed

backwards: You define the amount you ultimately want to take out of the plan to determine how much to put in.

A defined benefit plan can be very beneficial for an older, self-employed worker. If you are in your fifties and your cost of living is low, you can shelter almost everything you make in a retirement savings account.

How does a defined benefit plan work? You need an actuary to set it up, and you should expect to pay at least $500 for the service. Initially, you establish a retirement age and income goal, based on your three highest earning years. So, if you aim to retire at sixty-five with 75 percent of your highest three-year average salary, the actuary would write the plan document and crunch the numbers to tell you what you have to contribute annually to the plan to meet that goal.

You aren't limited to $30,000, or 15 percent, or any other number in a defined benefit plan. Instead there's a limit on how high your benefits goal can be. For 1996, for example, the dollar limit at retirement age 65 for a participant born before 1939 is $10,000 a month. If you set up a plan when you have less than ten years before retirement, there are penalties that reduce the dollar limit. If you were already sixty, your dollar limit would be $5,000.

Block Consulting provided these sample figures: You earned $100,000 a year in the last three years and are aiming for a retirement income of $75,000 a year. If you are fifty, you should contribute $37,000 a year to the plan. But If you are already fifty-five, your tax-deferred contribution would be $66,000!

You can see how a defined benefit plan can be a really great deal for an older worker of more or less independent means. You can shelter vast amounts of earnings while building a retirement nest egg fast. It's far less valuable if you are younger. Even if you are in your forties, you are probably better off with a Keogh plan.

One caution regarding defined benefit plans. Even if you have a bad year, you still have to make the contribution, even if you have to take out a loan to do it. You can adjust your plan downward before year's end, but that requires another big actuarial bill, and it isn't something you want to make a habit of.

Choosing a Plan for You?

The "Retirement Plans" table on the facing page summarizes the key points of your retirement options. Use it to choose the best plan for you. But remember, if your situation changes, it isn't difficult to cancel most of these programs and start over with a new plan.

| | | | | Max. contribu- |
| | | | Contribution | tion on $100,000 |
Plan	Pros	Cons	limits	income
IRA	Easy to set up	Too limiting	$2,000; no higher than total income	$2,000
SEP-IRA	Can establish after Dec. 31; easy to set up	Can't make contributions past age 70½, even if you're still working; must cover most part-timers	13.04% of your income, up to $22,500	$13,040
Profit-Sharing Keogh	Total flexibility; some protection in bankruptcy	May not let you contribute as much as you want; Dec. 31 setup deadline	13.04% of your income, up to $22,500	$13,040
Money-Purchase Keogh	Bankruptcy protection, bigger contributions possible	Rigid; Dec. 31 setup deadline	20% of your income, up to $30,000	$20,000
Paired Keoghs	Flexible; bigger contributions possible	Dec. 31 deadline	20% of your income, up to $30,000	$20,000
401(k)	Best plan for covering many employees	Lower contributions; top-heavy rules	$9,500	$9,500
SIMPLE	Easy, few reporting requirements, if you want to cover a few employees	Tough withdrawal limits within first two years, smaller contributions than 401(k)s	$6,000	$6,000
Defined Benefit Plan	Good shelter for older entrepreneurs	Need an actuary; Dec. 31 deadline; complicated	High limit, based on retirement objective	$66,000

Retirement Plans

chapter

12
====

Do You Want to Do This Forever? Retirement Planning for the Self-Employed

Who Ya Gonna Call?

Don't confuse, as many people do, the type of retirement plan you have with the institution charged with monitoring it. Once you've decided on a retirement plan, you must decide where to keep it. Your main choices are:

❑ A bank

❑ A brokerage

❑ A mutual fund company

Each has distinct advantages. In a bank, your deposits are insured by the FDIC up to a specific level, but your investment choices are limited to certificates of deposits. (Although you can buy stocks, bonds, and mutual funds at the local branch of your bank these days, don't confuse the issue: this is really a brokerage owned by or affiliated with the company that owns your bank.)

A mutual fund company offers convenience, expertise, and the cheapest alternative. Some, such as Fidelity Investments, T. Rowe Price, and Vanguard, specialize in helping individuals set up their own retirement plans. You can choose among their many funds and pay only a minimal annual fee (in some cases, no fee at all) to keep the plan going. If you choose a mutual fund company, pick one that has many highly-rated funds and that offers a "no load" option, funds that don't levy sales or marketing charges on their investors.

Where can you find good mutual funds? Many magazines, including U.S. News and World Report, Kiplinger's, Money, Forbes, and Fortune, regularly run articles rating the funds. You can also check the performance of a mutual fund in a reference directory. In fact, there are almost as many directories as there are funds! A few good reference tools are:

❑ **Investors Guide to Low-Cost Mutual Funds:** from the Mutual Fund Education Alliance, Department 0148, P.O. Box 419263, Kansas City, MO 64193-0148.

❑ **The Mutual Fund Encyclopedia:** by Gerald Perritt, Dearborn Financial Publishing, Inc., 520 North Dearborn Street, Chicago, IL 60610-4354.

❑ **The Handbook for No-Load Fund Investors:** by Sheldon Jacobs, The No-Load Fund Investor, Inc., P.O. Box 318, Irvington-on-Hudson, NY 10533.

You can also request information from the major no-load fund families directly. They are known for their low-cost funds, broad fund choices and solid investor services:

American Century Mutual Funds, 800-345-2021

Dreyfus Corporation, 800-227-1341

Fidelity Investments, 800-544-8888

INVESCO Funds, 800-525-8085

Janus Funds, 800-525-8983

Scudder Funds, 800-225-2470

Stein Roe Mutual Funds, 800-338-2550

T. Rowe Price, 800-638-5660

Setting your retirement fund up as a brokerage account may cost a little more, but it's likely the best alternative for the long term. Why? As you get older and your plan acquires more assets, you won't want to be limited by the investment choices of a particular mutual fund company. You might want to mix stocks, bonds, and funds from different companies in your retirement portfolio.

When choosing a broker, you have still another level of choice to make. Do you want a broker who will charge high commissions to give you advice, like Merrill Lynch, or that person sitting at a desk in the lobby of your bank? Or do you want to pay a discount broker a smaller fee and make all of your investment choices yourself?

Many discount brokers offer no-load funds for your retirement account, although you still must pay annual fees approaching $50 to keep the account running. The leaders are

Charles Schwab & Company, 800-435-4000.

Fidelity Investments Discount Brokerage, 800-544-9697.

Jack White, 800-323-3263.

You can open more than one account, though by doing so your life might get more complicated. You could have a Keogh at one fund company and another Keogh at a brokerage. But your annual contribution limits stay the same, even if you are parceling your 13.04 percent annual contribution among three or more Keoghs.

Where Should You Invest Your Money

There are shelves of books available on the subject of modern portfolio theory, but this isn't one of them. All I'll say here is that the keys to successful long-term investing are:

❑ Diversification protects return and minimizes risk.

❑ You won't get top returns unless you keep a substantial portion of your portfolio in stocks.

chapter

12

Do You Want to Do This Forever? Retirement Planning for the Self-Employed

COMPUTER SOLUTION:
SOFTWARE FOR RETIREMENT PLANNING

To crunch the numbers that retirement projections require, pop in the disk from one of these programs, such as Prosper (shown opposite), punch in your age, annual earnings, and current savings, and, like magic, they show exactly how much you should be stashing away if you want to be able to afford the golf course lifestyle of your dreams.

Remember, though, that predicting the financial future is an inexact science—or else the chairman of the Federal Reserve Board would be a multimillionaire instead of a government official. So before you put your life's work online, consider these caveats:

- The economic assumptions that underlay any software program may be faulty. Experts generally assume the long-term inflation rate will be around 4 or 4.5 percent; you should too.

- The projected returns may be faulty. Steer clear of programs that make you look good by assuming you'll earn an average of 14 percent a year on your money. You're unlikely, over the long term, to beat 10 percent, and even that's only if you have everything invested in stocks.

- Don't forget retention of principal. Do you want to draw on your nest egg in your retirement years or save it for your children? Some programs let you calculate retirement needs both ways; others don't.

- A spouse in the house? Will you be retiring with someone? A good program lets you link two retirements.

- Don't give up on Social Security. Your program shouldn't either. Find a program that guesstimates your Social Security earnings and includes them in the mix.

- Don't forget taxes. If you are saving in a tax-deferred plan (of course you are!) your savings will build much more quickly than if you are saving after taxes. But those savings will be taxed upon withdrawal. Make sure your program considers the tax effects on your projections, both in the build-up and the draw-down years.

SOFTWARE FOR RETIREMENT PLANNING *(continued)*

- Game playing. The point of retirement planning is to keep up with your changing fortunes. A program that won't let you change numbers easily and play what-if games isn't worthwhile. One that allows easy adjustments will help you learn about the impact of your financial decisions before you make them.

- Beware computer-projection depression. You may plug in all the numbers only to find out that you'll be eating cat food if you don't put away $12,000 a month, starting last year. Don't despair, regardless of what you see on the screen. Start planning now, put away what you can, and realize that, somehow, you'll muddle through.

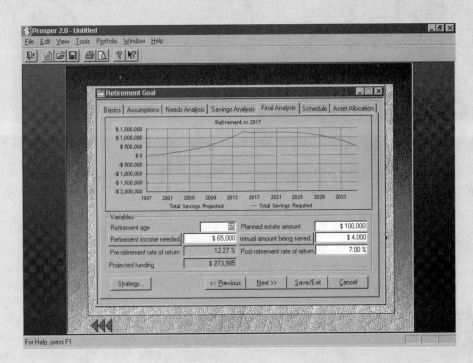

chapter
12

Do You Want to Do This Forever? Retirement Planning for the Self-Employed

SOFTWARE FOR RETIREMENT PLANNING *(continued)*

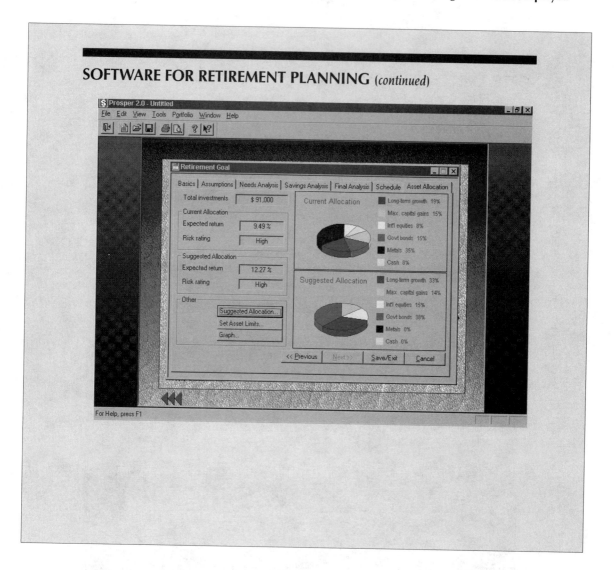

SECRET: *If you are self-employed, don't forget to consider how your investment choices mesh with your business. It's probably smart to balance your investments. For example, if you earn your living as a software consultant, don't just purchase software company stocks. Then if the industry tanks, your company might suffer, but you won't lose your nest egg at the same time. And if you have a fair amount of money tied up in your business, and it's a risky business, invest your retirement portfolio more conservatively.*

To amass a retirement portfolio, take this advice:

❏ **Invest in stocks.** You probably won't find a financial professional these days who hasn't steered the bulk of his or her own retirement fund into the stock market. The pros agree that over time, stocks offer superior returns over every other kind of investment. Ibbotson Associates, the Chicago research firm that has long studied this question, reports that in the 69 years between 1926 and 1995, stocks have averaged 10.5 percent a year; long-term bonds have paid 5.17 percent, and Treasury bills have paid 3.72 percent. What's the difference? If you put $5,000 a year into the stock market, you'd have $904,407 after 30 years; in bonds, you would have $342,057; and in T bills, $267,662. There has never been a five-year period in which stocks posted a negative return, reminds Ibbotson's Carl Gargula.

❏ **Invest through mutual funds.** Some hobbyists like to pick stocks, and some companies are going out of their way to welcome retirement account shareholders directly. But for the bulk of your money, tap the diversification that mutual funds offer.

S ECRET: *Many financial professionals are embracing a new strategy of using index funds in their retirement portfolios. Index funds mangers don't pick and choose stocks to beat the market—they aim to match it by buying and holding a large selection of stocks that replicate the market. For example, you could buy an index fund that aims to match the Standard & Poor's index of top 500 stocks. The fund would hold all of the stocks in the S&P 500, and offer returns that, except for very low management costs, followed the index. What are the advantages of this? Most mutual fund managers don't beat the stock market indexes over time. When you invest in an index fund, you are getting most of the stock market's performance at the lowest possible fees. Vanguard Investments (800-643-9998), is the market leader in indexes and in low-fee funds.*

❏ **Diversify.** When you mix the type of investments in your portfolio, you reduce the risks and pick up most of the return. Consider keeping most of your portfolio in stocks, but add some bonds. As you amass more money, you'll want to diversify the stock part of your portfolio by seeking out funds that buy large, small, and foreign stocks.

chapter

12

Do You Want to Do This Forever? Retirement Planning for the Self-Employed

❏ **Consider the fees.** If you're going to do your own research, select no-load mutual funds. The loads, or sales charges, are commissions paid to brokers who recommend funds, and have no correlation with return whatsoever. Particularly on the bond side of any portfolio, a sales fee can turn a good bond-fund return into a mediocre one, a mediocre return into a poor one.

*S*ECRET: *Even no-load funds sometimes have hidden charges: So-called 12(b)1 fees are annual marketing charges levied by some funds. At 1 percent a year, they can often outstrip old-fashioned up front sales charges. And even no-fee funds have necessary expenses, but keep them to a minimum too. There are plenty of good funds with expense ratios under 1 percent a year; anything over 1.5 percent can be very hard to justify.*

❏ **Learn about investment styles.** There are at least two basic stock investing styles, and they do not correlate with each other. Growth investors will pay a premium for a fast-growing company stock on the theory that the company's strong engine will pull the price up. Value investors hunt for bargains. They tend to buy stock from companies that are out of favor and have cheap prices relative to their assets and expected earnings. As your pension portfolio grows, make sure both styles are represented in your holdings (unless you've opted for the "passive" strategy of using index funds).

❏ **Do your own research.** With about a dozen magazines on the market publishing special mutual fund issues, and the libraries and newspapers crammed full of investing sources, there's no excuse for not learning at least a little about where to put your money. A couple of mutual fund companies stand out for distributing excellent educational material, free, in the hopes that you will become a shareholder. They are: Scudder, 800-323-6105 and T. Rowe Price, 800-638-5660.

❏ **Invest regularly and gradually.** Instead of sending in your $6,000 contribution on one day, cultivate the habit of sending in regular installments, of say $500 a month. This allows it to compound faster and protects you from a market that drops dead the day after your $6,000 bought in at the top. If you send in your $500 every month, you'll buy more shares at low prices when the market is down, and fewer shares at market tops. This is called "dollar cost averaging" and is a tried and true way of beating the market. You can also try "seat of the pants averaging." When the market is down, send in more than your usual $500. When it's pricey, send in less. If the market is up and up and up, like it's been as this book is being written, you pretty much have to ignore the seat of your pants and just send in your $500 anyway. If it helps, just stop reading the paper.

Even if you want to work in your own dream business forever, it's a mistake to ignore the task of retirement planning and saving, especially when there are special breaks available to self-employed workers.

Read on, to discover some other major mistakes that entrepreneurs often make.

YOU MUST REMEMBER THIS: LESSONS FROM CHAPTER 12

- You have to be responsible for your own retirement; no one else will be.

- There are many special tax breaks and retirement accounts available only to self-employed entrepreneurs, and you may have to switch plans as you grow older.

- Start early, diversify, and invest in stocks, bonds, and mutual funds for long-term growth.

13

© Michael Moran 1997

"Self-employed people may actually need more vacations than the average wage earners, because of the stress that doing your own thing can cause."

Unlucky Chapter 13: How *Not* to Run Your Business

You can't do everything right, especially when you are juggling a business and a personal life. Even those entrepreneurs who seek out advice can end up reinventing their own wheels; simply put, you can't build a business from scratch without making a few mistakes. But there are some doozies that too many entrepreneurs make and that you can avoid. Self-employed people have a tendency to dig their own graves when they overspend, undercharge, and ignore their personal finances to build the business.

This, then, is unlucky Chapter 13. The good news is, you don't have to do anything. In fact, the point is not to do—just avoid these major blunders, and it will be like taking an insurance policy on your future.

Ten Deadly Sins That Can Kill Your Business

1. **Overuse those rose-colored glasses:** When you are starting your own business, it's tempting to daydream about how wonderful

283

the future will be when you've made it big. But keep those day-dreams in their place by relying instead on serious market research about your business and its prospects. You say you're going to start a high-priced lawn mowing business in a neighbor-hood full of teenagers? I don't think so. Or charge $4.50 for coffee in your deli, which is right next door to a Starbucks? Probably not. In creating your business plan and pricing structure, be honest with yourself. And ask others who will be honest with you.

2. **Overspend on overhead:** Mark and Susan almost killed their consulting practice the day they signed the lease on their new 2,500-square foot offices. They didn't realize their mistake for more than a year.

At first, the multi-year lease seemed like a good deal. Times were flush, and the couple filled every office with an employee serving all that billable time and earning them money on every square foot. But times changed and their business slowed down. They were forced to lay off employees and the extra offices sat empty, the rent eating up all of the extra cash that Mark and Susan could have been taking in as profit.

"Never spend one dime until you absolutely have to and can't do it any other way," offers entrepreneurial expert Bernard Tenenbaum, who founded the George Rothman Institute of Entrepreneurial Studies at Fairleigh Dickenson University in Madison, New Jersey. The moral: Keep your office small, hire temporary or contract help until you really need an employee, think three times before you spend anything on "image," and justify every expense.

3. **Buy your equipment without planning:** It's especially unsettling these days to buy computer equipment. With new models coming out monthly and prices falling even faster, it seems like a better deal is always a week or two away. So you defer buying until you have to, and then run out and pick up whatever's on sale that day. Or you pick up something on sale that you're not even sure you need, because it seems like such a good deal.

Take time to project what you want your computer and other office equipment to do for you this year, and in three years. Figure out who else might be using it, where you'll get it serviced, and where you'll put it. Develop a long-term equipment plan, and stick to it, allowing for new developments in the field and in your business.

4. **Dance with the wrong kind of client:** Who hasn't wasted time doing the mating dance with a client who refused to kiss us in the end? Or worse, took advantage of our services and goods, but then didn't pay? To some extent it's a cost of doing business. But when it stems from your reluctance to say no, you're in trouble. Experience will help in this regard. Until then, prequalify all clients by checking references and talking early in the relationship about your fees. Don't lay out money for new clients; make them lay out money for you.

5. **Charge too little:** This is the fill up your dance card at any cost approach. Consider what you are going to do when you're booked with low-paying work and the big fish calls.

   This happens all of the time to my friend Terry, a bookkeeper who fears her last client will be, well, her last client. She knows what she's supposed to charge: after all, she's a bookkeeper and she did a lot of the number-crunching called for in Chapter 5. But when Terry was faced with the rent and electric bills, she's was afraid to say no to any work. Especially when a client sweet talks or strong arms her into doing more for less. Plus she often does work "pro bono" for friends.

   One February, she went to a party at a cousin's house, where her name got passed around as a good tax preparer. Guests crowded around, asking her to take them on. Worried that she might not have a big enough clientele (January had been slow), Terry agreed to prepare twenty different tax returns at $50 each. You might guess what happened. None of these clients brought their forms to her until April, her busiest time of year; before she realized it Terry had filled her dance card and had to turn down potentially big clients who would have paid her hundreds of dollars to do their returns.

   Instead of pricing by the minimum-you-need method, build in all of your overhead and consider what the market will bear. If all that's available now is cheap work, consider passing on some of it to spend your valuable time marketing for better work.

6. **Fail to be firm on collections:** Some entrepreneurs are actually afraid to ask for their money. It's like the junior high school babysitter syndrome: "Umm, whatever you think I'm worth." Others invoice once, but carry their clients for months because they don't want to seem offensive or desperate. Stop it! Professional business people pick up the phone after thirty days and say,

"Your bill is past due; when will I be paid?" Develop that skill to keep cash flowing smoothly, or you will starve. And a quick collections policy will nip problems in the bud, before deadbeat clients have time to disappear. If your client is having legitimate cash problems and you don't want to lose him or her, work out a pay-out plan satisfactory to both of you.

7. **Give one client too much power over your business:** Chances are you are self-employed so you can achieve a level of independence. But how independent are you if one client is a 500-pound gorilla? This is difficult to control in the early days of a business, but it is crucial. Doing most of your work for one client can throw both of you into tax trouble: the IRS might interpret that you are an employee of your client.

This is exactly what happened to Dave, a computer programmer who did most of his work onsite for a manufacturing company outside of Los Angeles, where he lives. Several other programmers worked there all day, too. But when the IRS began to investigate why the company had such high contract expenses and so few employees, it decided that Dave was really an employee and not an independent contractor. The company gave him a choice: Come on staff at a lower rate of pay (now they had to pay benefits, after all!) or leave. He left, but found he didn't have enough other clients to meet his overhead, and he had to rebuild his business all over again.

This mother-of-all-clients problem can zap you even when the IRS doesn't get involved. Pete is a freelance photographer who usually works on short-term assignments that run from two or three hours to two or three days. Recently he was asked to photograph an entire guidebook for *National Geographic*. It would take four months, and allow him to travel throughout the west. How could he say no? It still means something for a photographer to have a *National Geographic* book in his portfolio. Pete took the assignment, but was forced to turn down all over work during that four month period. Now the book is in editing, and Pete is finding that many of his standby clients have found other photographers. He's back to the drawing board, albeit with a better resume than before.

The one-client syndrome will distort your workflow, limit your experiences, and bring you to your knees if anything bad happens to that client.

8. **Live for today:** Jay Conrad Levinson, in his series of Guerrilla Marketing books, argues that you have to put your name in front of a prospect twenty-seven times before he or she is ready to buy your wares. That may seem extreme, but the general premise— that every positive contact is an investment for the future—is value. Living for tomorrow means maintaining relationships with colleagues who haven't produced a client for years, but may eventually. It means not hiring the cheapest computer repair person, but cultivating a relationship with a consultant who will do house calls and leave a home number. It means burning bridges only when all else has failed.

9. **Confuse gross and net:** It's inevitable—you get your first check or two and are amazed at how easy it is. Like rolling off a log, you tell yourself, and for more money than you were making in your last job! Then you start to subtract income taxes, Social Security taxes, health insurance, life insurance, a retirement plan, sick days, a vacation. And you aren't left with a much. This happened to Jerry, a Pennsylvania consultant who had a rude awakening the first time he filed a business tax return. He had become accustomed to tax refunds in the $2,000 range and was already thinking about the vacation his refund would buy him. When he filled out a Schedule C form (for self-employed income), he had netted about $5,000 in his first year of part-time freelancing.

   Suddenly Jerry had to face the hidden tax of self-employment: The Social Security and Medicare tax that takes 15.3 percent off the top of income. "It was devastating," he remembers. Instead of that fat refund, he owed the government $824, and had to take a cash advance against his credit card to pay the tax bill. "It took me a year to recover."

   You need to remember all of the hidden costs of self-employment not only when you are saving to pay your taxes, but when you are setting your fees in the first place. Entrepreneurs who forget to budget all of those expenses into their prices won't make it. It's that simple.

10. **Keep your own counsel:** It's good to be true to yourself, listen to your gut and all those other clichés. But not exclusively. A common cause of business failure is the know-everything and do-everything-yourself syndromes. Financial professionals, attorneys, computer consultants, and marketing pros are worth

paying for when you're in over your head. To succeed in business, you need to know when to pay for outside advice and when to take it. And spend money to keep in touch with what your colleagues are doing, through professional associations, conferences, informal get-togethers, and trade magazines.

Ten Personal Traps to Avoid

The preceding are the sins that can kill your business. But the newly self-employed can fall into a personal financial abyss as well. Here are the behaviors to avoid as you establish your company.

1. **Start with inadequate cash:** Build a personal emergency fund of at least six month's necessary income before you start your business. Otherwise you'll panic too early. It takes time to bring in enough money to pay for personal expenses.

2. **Ignore the need for a safety net:** You need health insurance, disability insurance, and some cash or credit to use in case of medical, automotive, or career crises. Make sure that this net is in place, either through benefits of a working spouse, a cache of cleared credit cards, or a raft of insurance policies.

3. **Skip vacations:** Rest and recreation restores emotional health and reclaims your brain for business. Many an entrepreneur has awakened too late to ask: "Why did I work all those hours?" Self-employed people may actually need more vacations than the average wage earners, because of the stress and isolation that doing your own thing can cause.

4. **Fail to account for illness:** What happens if you get sick? Do your prices have enough leeway built into them to keep groceries on the table if you're down and out with the flu for a week or two? Is there a backup phone- and mail-answering plan? More important, what will you do for cash if you suffer a permanent disability? If you are married, will your family incur extra company liability while you are on your back?

Unfortunately, there are no easy answers to these questions. Most disability policies for the self-employed are too expensive to afford. And with much of today's business taking place in front of a home office computer monitor, it's more difficult to prove you are disabled enough to collect on one of these policies anyway.

Go through the motions, though, by interviewing insurance agents about what they think you need and can afford in the way of disability insurance. And come up with some back-up plans that will at least keep the business from being an added liability.

5. **Force your family to work in your business:** Elsewhere in this book, a strong case is made for entrepreneurs to hire their spouses, children, and friends to save taxes, bring the family into the fold, and so on. But this only works if it's done professionally. If your family and friends are not interested, don't care, or hate the work, don't hire them just to save on taxes. You'll inspire antagonisms and it's not good for business if they aren't qualified or can't do the work for which you're paying them.

6. **Plan your retirement without considering your company:** Are you building a business you expect to sell when you retire? Maybe you don't need to be putting as much in your IRA, then. On the other hand, if your business is a one-person, folds-when-you-do kind of company, you should be putting above-average amounts in a retirement plan.

   Finally, don't forget, too, entrepreneurs have the added responsibility of investing their retirement assets to balance the money in their business: If your business is in the construction trade, for example, you want a retirement portfolio light on construction investments. Otherwise, a catatonic condo market could ruin your livelihood and your nest egg.

7. **Share equipment and supplies:** This is an easy mistake to avoid. Don't run your business from a desk that is also the personal tax- and bill-paying or homework headquarters. Not only will this cost your business money and time, it will eliminate your home office tax deduction. When starting a business, keep your personal and business work areas separate. You'll find it may be more productive. If you have children, take them shopping and buy them their own stapler, tape dispenser, pens, pencils, rulers, hole punchers, etc. If you keep your children well-stocked they will be less tempted to dip into your supply closet.

8. **Ignore the word "liability insurance":** If you are a sole proprietor or a one-person corporation, you have quite a quite deal of personal liability if something goes wrong with your company. If a UPS man comes to deliver a business package, trips on your porch steps, and breaks a leg, your homeowner's insurance may not cover it. Similarly, your home can be on the line if a client

sues you for malfeasance, or malpractice. As soon as you decide to go into business, talk to the issuer of your homeowner's or renter's policy to find out what additional coverage you need to buy to protect yourself from business liabilities.

9. **Try to make every expense a business deduction:** Many of us have met the entrepreneur who takes vacations, orders HBO, and buys the kids' shoes, and so on all on "company expense." This is not only illegal, it is poor personal and business financial management. When you use your company as a shell to cover personal expenses, you lose the ability to get quality information about your business, so you don't know what you are really making, or how. It takes away legitimacy from those aspects of your life that are not business-related. If you can't go on a vacation unless it has a business purpose, you never really rest. And sooner or later, you'll probably get caught.

10. **Make no plans for transition:** Probably the thought of leaving your business hasn't crossed your mind yet. But small business owners are notorious for leaving their finances in a shambles if they die suddenly or haven't considered who will take over after them—if there's anything left to take over. If your business will be transferred to family or colleagues after you, you might have to buy enough life insurance to make sure your heirs can afford to pay the taxes on the business. If you plan to retire from the business and turn it over to partners, children, or new owners, transition plans become just as important for the smooth operation of the business, and the continued good relationships between present and future managers.

Without a succession plan, you can turn your kids against each other, and you can turn everyone against you. Talk to everyone in your family about what they do and don't want to do with your business should you no longer be able or inclined to run it.

Just Don't Do It

It may not be possible to make all the right decisions in your business, or in trying to achieve a balance between your business and personal lives, but you're likely to come out ahead if you manage defensively. Avoid the big blunders laid-out in this chapter and there is a very good chance you'll succeed. To find out just how well you are doing, and to highlight those areas that need improvement, take the self-evaluation test in the next chapter.

YOU MUST REMEMBER THIS: LESSONS FROM CHAPTER 13

- It's no secret what causes businesses to go under: Entrepreneurs who fail always report the same or similar mistakes.
- Learn key errors and avoid making them; that will put you ahead of the pack.
- Many of the worst mistakes are characterized by a lack of honesty or disclosure: If you're honest with your clients, your colleagues, your family, the IRS, and especially yourself, you probably won't make many mistakes.

© Michael Moran 1997

"It's a sign of health
if your cash flow keeps strengthening,
your sales keep growing,
and you keep getting more clients."

The Annual Checkup

In your gut, you probably already know how your business is doing and how well it is supporting you. But at least once a year, you should go beyond a basic gut check. Analyze your strengths and weaknesses, so that you can continually improve your situation.

How do you take your business temperature? Compare your business to those of your competitors, by using standard ratios. Measure yourself against the rules of thumb common among financial professionals. Make sure that your business practices are those that optimize your finances. This chapter explains how to do all that, and more.

*S*ECRET: *You may find that you are consistently weak in certain areas of financial management. Maybe you are very aggressive about bringing in new business and charging enough, but you forget to keep good records. Or maybe you are a meticulous recordkeeper, but constantly overspend on supplies and the other basics you need to keep your business running. Hire to your weakness. If it's recordkeeping that defeats you, hire a bookkeeper. If it is overspending, consider using a financial advisor or accountant to help you plan a budget and "coach" you to stick with it. Nobody does everything right, especially the first time through.*

Ratios That Tell You How You're Doing

How would your business look to a banker? Forget, for the moment, the inspirational stories, and look to these key numerical guidelines to see if you are measuring up to independent standards of success.

Your Business Pays More for Your Money Than Your Bank Does

If you had $10,000, you could put it in the bank and earn an easy $500 on it in a year. Or you could invest it in the phone system, fax modem, and business cards you need to launch a major marketing effort. Your business ought to be able to cover that $500 on top of your salary. To figure out whether it does, add up the capital you invested to set up your business and the money you put in to keep it running. Every year, figure out what percent of that figure your business earns, after you subtract a reasonable salary for yourself.

You may be taking this extra $500 out of the business as part of your salary. Figure your salary on the basis of what you would earn for your job if you weren't the owner of the business.

How does this look on a spreadsheet? here's the formula:

$$\frac{\text{Business net income - your salary}}{\text{total investment}} = \text{percent earnings}$$

So, if you put $10,000 into your start up, and came out this year with a salary of $25,000 and a remaining net profit of $750, your earnings on your investment would be 7.5 percent. That's not bad.

$$\frac{\$25,750 - \$25,000}{\$10,000} = .075$$

In your second year, say you invest another $2,500 in your business, taking money out of your personal checking account to buy a scanner, for example. You still earn a $25,000 salary, but the net is $30,000. Set it up:

$$\frac{\$30,000 - \$25,000}{\$12,500} = .4$$

Forty percent on your money! That's more like it!

Your Business Is Earning Enough to Cover Your Next Major Purchase

In another three years, you'll probably need another computer. How will you pay for it? The successful businessperson is already setting aside money for future purchases. In most sole proprietorships, this often doesn't happen. Instead, you take all the money out of the business and, when the business needs a big investment, you put it back in. Ideally, though, the business ought to be generating enough, and you ought to be setting aside enough to cover those costs.

Your Sales Are Rising and So Are Your Earnings

If you were a potential investor consider buying stock in your company, you'd like to see revenues (sales) moving up at an average annual rate of 15 percent, and you'd like to see earnings (revenues minus expenses) track that same growth.

For a quick review, you can set this up on a spreadsheet that tracks quarterly. Simply create four columns for quarterly sales and four columns for net earnings. Every line represents a year; and every quarter, post your numbers to the right cell. By the second year, you can perform the subtraction-division that gets you an annual growth rate:

```
This year - Last year      =      growth rate
     last year
```

You Own Twice as Much as You Owe

Add up your current assets—everything your business owns or is owed in a year. Divide that figure by the liabilities due over the same period. This is called the "current ratio," and it ought to be at least 2:1, writes Michael Tyran in the *Vest-Pocket Guide to Business Ratios* (Prentice-Hall, 1992). The current ratio is one of the key guidelines that banks and investors use to evaluate the health of businesses.

You Have at Least as Much on Hand as You Owe

Similar to the "current ratio," this test is called the "quick ratio" or, better, the acid test. Add up your liquid assets, including money owed you over the next year, but not including hard-to-sell equipment or property. Divide by liabilities and hope that you end up in positive territory. That means that if the bottom fell out, you could pay your bills out of what's already liquid. Bankruptcy is not a threat.

You Have a Healthy Cash Flow

This can be a pretty spongy measure. You don't want to be so pressed that you can't pay yourself or your creditors. But if you are awash in cash because you're not investing in future equipment, advertising, or growth, that can be trouble. Chart your company's liquidity (financial assets minus liabilities) against your company's investment in growth-producing assets, including inventory and equipment. Every company's chart will look different, but over time you'll be able to figure out where the best balance lies for you.

You Compare Favorably with the Competition

In addition to looking at debt ratios and cash flow, consider how well you do compared to others in your field. Some trade groups publish membership surveys you can review. For example, the American Institute of Professional Bookkeepers publishes financial surveys of its members, as does the National Writers Union. You could also cultivate a friendly banker and ask his or her opinion. Robert Morris Associates in Philadelphia publishes industry-specific guides for bankers that explain how different kinds of businesses should look on spreadsheets. You can find them at some business libraries, and most banks.

You Earn More Working for Yourself Than You Would in a Job

Don't fall into the trap of paying for the privilege of working for yourself. You should earn more working on your own than you would in a salaried job. If a company is willing to pay you $35,000 a year, plus health insurance, plus retirement benefits, to do what you do, you should be able to better that on your own. Conduct occasional spot-checks with others in your field to find out what you're worth on the open market.

You Have Insurance and a Retirement Plan

These are all legitimate and necessary costs of doing business, and unless yours is able to provide these benefits, it's not really making it. That's the simple if brutal truth.

You Have at Least Three Clients

Any fewer than this and you run the risk of being classified an employee and not a bona fide business. More important, if you earn all of your income from one or two clients, you're too vulnerable to their mishaps, bad judgments, or budget problems. Aim to diversify in the future.

Your Trend Lines Are Up

Follow all of the statistics and measures noted here over time. You might plot your quarterly sales, earnings, debt-to-equity ratios, and other formulas on a spreadsheet. Over time, these numbers should be moving in the first direction. It's a sign of health if your cash flow increases, your sales grow, and you add more clients. All companies, but especially fledgling ones, are more likely to have credit extended to them when moving in the right direction, even if the numbers aren't as strong as you'd like them to be.

Success Is Cultivating Good Habits: Walk the Walk, Talk the Talk

Life isn't all numbers. A major element to becoming successful is acting successful. That doesn't mean buying a flashy car and expensive jewelry: It means doing the things that healthy businesses do. How many of the following are part of your professional demeanor?

Clarity of Vision and Purpose

When people ask you what you do, you have it down to an enthusiastic twenty-five words or less. You never say, "Well, it's hard to explain; it's sort of like…" Kathleen Hagan, executive director of the MIT Enterprise Forum, isolates this characteristic as the leading indicator of success. You should have a very clear idea of what is unique about your business and how you position that selling point. Every business decision you make should be in keeping with that central vision.

You Are Wired

Small businesses, especially, must make up with technology what they lack in time, staff, and money. You acquire and develop the tools—good database records, voice mail, tape backup systems, computer-based faxing—that enable you to be as productive as possible. If you are the last Luddite in town, you aren't going to make it in the nineties and beyond.

You Give Good Phone

You always answer your phone and in a professional manner or a user-friendly machine does it for you. Customers don't get busy signals, or young children who are untrained in the art of message-taking. Calls are always returned. Your clients all are made to feel their business is important to you.

Your Business Info Is Current and Accurate

You know who and where your potential customers are what and when they buy. You know which parts of your business are most profitable and just what your profits are. You can't make good decisions on the basis of bad information.

You Limit the Expenses You Pay for Clients

In most cases, you lose opportunities and take unnecessary risks when you lay out money for clients. You could keep growing to cover the float, but why not use that earning power yourself? Ask for up-front fees to cover expenses; bill late payers as early as you can.

You Get and Take Professional Advice

Many sole proprietors fall prey to the chief-cook-and-bottle-washer syndrome, but remember: you don't have to know everything about everything. Successful businesspeople use other successful businesspeople: accountants, lawyers, and consultants to help them frame strategies, make decisions, and plot direction.

You Hire to Your Weaknesses

Maybe you are a brilliant copywriter, but you hate handling the money. You may think you can't afford it, but in the long run, you could make your business more successful by hiring a business manager or accountant, or "renting" one for a few hours a month. That's a successful business strategy.

You Believe That Failure Is Not an Option

All business owners have problems, failures and disasters. The successful ones bounce back, learn from their experiences, and move on. You recognize a brick wall when you hit one, too. You have to recognize when something isn't working, when you have to give up on a beloved project or client or goal, and find another way. Giving up on a project, a client, or even part of your business doesn't mean that you or your business are failures. It means you're isolating what works and what doesn't, and taking a new tack.

You Market and Plan

Even when you're busy, you are constantly working to keep your name out there, to develop new clients, and to define your niche. The best way to measure success is your own goals and then weigh how well your business meets them. Successful entrepreneurs plan on many different levels. They may aim at overarching mission statements, but schedule their marketing efforts for the next six months, too.

You Are Resourceful

You are resourceful in the colloquial sense: If you can't afford to go first-class all the time, you find alternatives. And in the literal sense: You know about and use all of the resources around you, like high-school kids who can stuff envelopes, public libraries that do free research, government databases you can search for pennies. You are disciplined about managing your time and your money, you accept important interruptions, but protective nevertheless of your need to allocate these two precious resources.

You Build Teams

Even if you work alone, you form alliances. Successful entrepreneurs travel to trade shows because it gives them a chance to meet others in their field. They network with other professionals in their community. They form long-term relationships with vendors and customers.

You're Getting Better All the Time

Businesses in the eighties pushed productivity; in the nineties the focus has been on quality management. You care about both: Your service is better and faster; you've added more frills to your basic package. Both by nature and habit, what was good enough for last year isn't good enough for this year.

Your Personal Finance Test

Let's assume your business is booming, but your personal life isn't. Whether you are self-employed or a wage earner, you should be able to meet these personal financial objectives:

You Have an Emergency Fund

You have three to six months of living expenses readily available. The best places for such a fund are a bank savings account or money market mutual fund. You also have a secondary source of emergency cash. Maybe it's a business or home equity line of credit. Maybe it's your uncle's bank account, a couple of credit cards, or a combination thereof.

Your Credit Cards All Have Zero Balances

With interest rates on credit card debt in the high teens, don't keep paying and paying. Consolidate all your card debt on the lowest-rate card you can find and pay it off in big chunks, even if you have to skimp on other expenses.

You Have an Eye on Your Mortgage

You're not spending more than 25 percent of your gross monthly earnings on your mortgage. That's the recommendation of the Mortgage Bankers Association of America, and they like to loan you as much as they possibly can. Since rates over the past two years have been very low, you should have refinanced by now. If you haven't and you're rate is over 9 percent, consider doing it now, unless you are planning to move in less than two years, or rates have moved up substantially while this book was in production.

You're Not Drowning in Debt

Monthly payments on all of your debt together doesn't exceed 36 percent of your monthly gross income (net of business expenses). If they do, you won't have money for savings, emergencies, or fun, and you'll feel increasingly squeezed.

You Are Fair, But Tough, with Uncle Sam

You don't pay one cent more in taxes than you have to. That means you know enough about what you can deduct, and keep good records to capture it all. And you know your marginal tax bracket, so you can make financial decisions on an after-tax basis. If you're in the 36 percent tax bracket or higher, you've considered tax-free money funds and other investments.

You Never Get Big Tax Refunds

Stop that free loan to Uncle Sam! Tighten up on your withholding and estimated tax payments, so you're paying the minimum required to avoid penalty. Then bank the extra, and earn interest until April 15.

You Think About the Future

You're taking maximum advantage of any tax-deferred retirement plan you can get. That includes Keoghs, 401(k)s, SEP-IRAs, IRAs, and anything else you qualify for. Saving pretax money is like earning an extra 28 percent or better in your first year, and the compounding keeps making it better.

You Save Money
At an absolute minimum, you're saving 5 percent of your income. That's better than the average American, 10 percent is better. There isn't any hard and fast rule about how much to save, but the bigger your savings, the more freedom you buy yourself in the future.

You Invest
At least some of that long term savings is in stocks, either directly or through mutual funds.

Your Money Flows to Your Priorities
You have figured out what you care about, and that's the future you are funding. This is strictly personal. Some of us drive very old cars and spend all of our spare cash on theater tickets; others live with car payments so they can drive in style and comfort.

Your Personal Income Isn't Seasonal
Many professionals—for example, roofers, retailers, and tax attorneys—have months during which they earn the bulk of their annual income. Successful business owners find a way to spread that around, so that their personal income is stable.

You Take Vacations
This reveals two things about your business success: You're earning enough to afford vacations, and you are recharging your batteries so that you continue to do so.

You Have a Personal Life
Nobody in America has all the time they would like to spend with their family, friends, and golf clubs. But if your work makes you miss too much, your business isn't meeting all of your goals.

You Take Advantage of That Flexible Time
What the self-employed always brag about: you sneak out during the day to go to the grocery store, to the bank, or to the movies. And every once in a while, you can (and do) hang-out the "Gone Fishin'" sign. Now that's success!

Index